Biofeedback and Related Therapies in Clinical Practice

DONALD MARCER

CROOM HELM
London & Sydney

Croom Helm Ltd, Provident House, Burrell Row,
Beckenham, Kent BR3 1AT
Croom Helm Australia Pty Ltd, Suite 4, 6th Floor,
64–76 Kippax Street, Surry Hills, NSW 2010, Australia

British Library Cataloguing in Publication Data

Marcer, Donald
Biofeedback and related therapies in
clinical practice.
1. Biofeedback training
I. Title
615.8′51 RC489.B53

ISBN 0-7099-3527-7
0-7099-3528-5 (pbk)

Filmset by Mayhew Typesetting, Bristol, England

Printed and bound in Great Britain by
Biddles Ltd, Guildford and King's Lynn

CONTENTS

To Catherine, Hilary and David

PREFACE

During the latter part of this century many behavioural scientists have come to accept that a wide range of illnesses can be treated by methods based upon psychological principles. Such methods include various forms of behaviour therapy, meditation, relaxation training and that which is the subject of this book, biofeedback. (In fact, it will become clear virtually from the outset that it is only possible to describe and evaluate the effectiveness of many forms of biofeedback by also discussing the effects of various forms of relaxation training.) Despite the interest that these procedures have aroused amongst psychologists, few medical students or medical practitioners have more than a vague idea of what they involve. It would be easy to attribute this state of ignorance to the almost legendary conservatism of the medical profession. Yet my own experience, gained while working in the pain relief clinic at a large general hospital, indicates that this is not the case. While some doctors do undoubtedly assert that such procedures have no place in clinical practice, many more express at least a measure of interest in them. However, their interest is not unquestioning and they demand that the scientific basis of the treatment be stated and its efficacy demonstrated in controlled clinical trials. Regrettably, scientific rigour has not been the distinguishing feature of some of the more vociferous advocates of biofeedback. Indeed, some claims made on its behalf are enough to make even the most enthusiastic drug representative blush! For example, it has been described as follows: 'An extraordinary technique which allows you to control the state of your health, happiness and well-being solely through the power of your mind.' Or 'A revolutionary method of getting quickly in touch with the inner self.' (Quoted by Birk, 1973.) Not to be outdone, even the most simple meditative techniques have been attributed with the power to 'Bring perfect health and longevity to the individual and the nation . . . including reversal of the ageing process' or 'Eliminate emotional problems from life. Conquer bad habits and overcome pain. Ignite enthusiasm. Radiate super health.'

Faced with such inflated claims even the most open-minded members of the medical profession can be forgiven for shaking their heads in amused disbelief before returning to the more familiar methods of orthodox medicine. Yet, understandable as this reaction might be, it is unfortunate. For alongside the extravagant claims described above there has emerged a growing body of scientific research into biofeedback; in the period 1980 to 1984, *Index Medicus* alone cited over 400 publications dealing with this method of treatment. It is to an evaluation of this research that this book is devoted.

It would be easy to describe the present status of biofeedback by adopting the format of a typical review article in which literally hundreds of studies are each accorded a brief mention. Without doubt such articles can offer a convenient starting point for the full-time researcher who plans to spend several years investigating a particular subject. However, the audience to which this book is directed is unlikely to have either the time or the inclination to investigate biofeedback in such depth. Consequently I have chosen to discuss in detail a limited number of key studies. This allows not only the authors' interpretations of their findings to be presented (often in their own words), but also the description of the data in sufficient detail to enable the reader to judge for himself the efficacy of the specific application under review. Not that this will be an easy task. The results of clinical trials have rarely proved straightforward, the outcome of one study frequently appearing directly to contradict that of another. In order to steer the reader through the complexities of underlying theory and clinical efficacy, I have dealt with them separately by dividing this book into two parts.

Part One begins by tracing the development of biofeedback and various forms of relaxation training to the point where they began to be regarded as viable clinical procedures. It ends by outlining (in more detail than is usual in a book of this kind) important methodological issues that are encountered when efficacy is assessed. The question of efficacy is taken up in Part Two, which begins with the treatment of three cardiovascular disorders (essential hypertension, Raynaud's disease and cardiac arrhythmias). My reasons for dealing in depth with hypertension are threefold. First, it is one of the most frequently encountered of the so-called stress-related illnesses. Second, the extent to which it responds to biofeedback and relaxation training has been extensively investigated. Third, this wide-ranging body of research has led to the identification of a number of underlying mechanisms that almost certainly operate when other stress-related conditions are subjected to these forms of treatment. These conditions include tension headache and migraine, to which the majority of Chapter 6 is devoted.

Although Chapters 4–6 are largely concerned with illnesses in which stress is believed to play at least a part, it would be a mistake to assume that biofeedback has no relevance outside the treatment of these conditions. Indeed some of the most interesting applications are to be found in the areas of neuromuscular and sphincter disorders, as well as rehabilitation following stroke or physical injury. Chapters 7–9 are devoted to an appraisal of these applications.

In order to give clinical substance to some of the theoretical issues raised in Part Two, I have made use of a category of information that rarely finds its way into the typical review article. I refer to individual case reports. Although case reports are usually regarded as scientifically suspect, with little part to play in the formulation or testing of hypotheses, they can often clarify an argument in a way that cannot be achieved by any other means. Consequently, throughout Part Two, as well as describing hard empirical data, I have drawn on my own clinical experience with individual patients.

Reference has already been made to the ambiguity that surrounds a great deal of the data described in the following chapters. Undoubtedly much of this is attributable to the diverse aetiology of almost all the conditions discussed. For example, although headache is a common and unremarkable complaint, it is frequently the outward manifestation of a complex interaction of anatomical, neurological, biochemical and psychosocial factors. This immediately poses a problem. Although this book is written primarily for the medical and paramedical professions, many readers (such as first- or second-year medical students) will not yet have undergone training in clinical medicine. Others (such as undergraduates in the behavioural sciences) never will. Consequently, in a number of instances I have begun the discussion with an outline of the clinical condition under review. While I believe these outlines to be factually correct, inevitably they oversimplify some exceedingly complex disease states. The reader is reminded, therefore, that they are included in order to give meaning to a particular method of treatment. Certainly no overworked medical student should fall into the trap of believing that he has found a shorter alternative to any standard textbook of medicine!

Finally, given the psychological orientation of this book, the reader may be surprised to find that there is no chapter devoted to the treatment of psychiatric conditions. I have adopted this approach for two reasons. First, there is already a vast literature available on the behavioural control of anxiety, depression and related conditions. Moreover, for reasons that will become clear in Chapters 4–9, I am not convinced that biofeedback offers the best psychological method of treating such conditions. Second, by not dwelling in depth on this specific application, I have been able to devote more space to the less widely recognised (but equally important) applications of biofeedback described in Part Two.

ACKNOWLEDGEMENTS

A number of individuals have read all or part of this text and I am grateful to all of them for their assistance. In particular I am indebted to Professor Donald Mayor, Professor Estlin Waters, Dr Margaret Orr and Dr Kate Harding for their comments and suggestions. Similarly I acknowledge the help of all those students (especially Karen Blackwell and Michelle Kaniuk) who never hesitated to draw my attention to those parts of the manuscript that required clarification. Special thanks are due to my wife Elizabeth who, as well as typing and correcting the manuscript, also provided endless encouragement when my motivation began to flag. In the interests of aesthetics, all the figures reproduced here were redrawn to a common format by the Department of Teaching Media at the University of Southampton. They deserve special thanks for meeting some wholly unreasonable deadlines, as does my senior editor Tim Hardwick for his patience when I failed to meet mine.

Finally I gratefully acknowledge the many authors cited in the text who have allowed me to draw upon their sources, as well as the editors and publishers of the following journals:
Acta Physiologica Scandinavica; American Journal of Ophthalmology; Archives of General Psychiatry; Archives of Physical Medicine and Rehabilitation; Behavior Therapy; Behaviour Research and Therapy; Biofeedback and Self-Regulation; Brain; British Journal of Orthodontics; British Journal of Psychiatry; British Journal of Urology; British Medical Journal; Circulation; Clinical Science; Gastroenterology; Headache; Journal of Abnormal Psychology; Journal of the American Medical Association; Journal of Applied Behavior Analysis; Journal of Consulting and Clinical Psychology; Journal of Psychosomatic Research; Neurology; Perceptual and Motor Skills; Physical Therapy; Physiotherapy; Postgraduate Medical Journal; Psychophysiology; Psychosomatic Medicine; Scandinavian Journal of Psychology; Seminars in Neurology; Journal of Pediatrics; The Lancet; New England Journal of Medicine.

PSYCHOLOGY AND MEDICINE SERIES: FOREWORD

Series Editor Donald Marcer

It is no exaggeration to say that throughout the first half of the twentieth century psychologists and doctors were seen as quite independent professionals, which if not openly hostile, had little to say to each other. Happily, the last two decades have seen a breaking down of these barriers as the two professions have come to recognise that they have much to learn from each other. This change in attitude is nowhere better illustrated than in the increasing part that the behavioural sciences have come to play in the training of doctors and health professionals. Not surprisingly this shift of emphasis in medical education has been accompanied by a minor deluge of text-books, all concerned with the relationship of psychology to medicine. Though many of these are excellent, the very depth of the subject matter that they seek to encompass necessarily implies that many complex issues cannot be covered at other than a superficial level. Consequently, when I was asked by Croom Helm to produce such a text, I proposed instead a series under the general heading 'Psychology and Medicine'. This volume on biofeedback is the first in the series.

The series consists of individual texts, each dealing in some depth with a particular issue in which the two disciplines have a shared interest. Though written by psychologists with an established academic record, they are aimed primarily at practising professionals. Consequently the contributing authors have all had experience in teaching students or members of the medical and other health professions, and with very few exceptions have worked in a clinical setting. Thus they are well suited to fulfil the brief that is common to all the books in this series. That is, while the theoretical basis of the issue under discussion must be spelled out, it must be done so in such a way that it enables readers (be they doctor, nurse, physiotherapist, or student) to practise their professions more effectively.

PART ONE:

GENERAL BACKGROUND

1 STRESS AND ILLNESS

Few informed observers would deny that during the past 100–150 years the Western industrialised countries have witnessed some remarkable advances in the control of infectious diseases. Due largely to improvements in public health services and the introduction of a wide range of powerful drugs, many serious infectious diseases have been eradicated. Thus smallpox, cholera and poliomyelitis, which once ravaged whole communities, are now so rare that even isolated cases make headline news. Unfortunately, the story does not end there, for during the same period there has not been a corresponding decrease in non-infectious diseases. For example, Seer (1979) has described hypertension as reaching epidemic proportions, thus echoing Benson (1975), who pointed out the following:

> We are in the midst of an epidemic, one that is all too prevalent in the United States and other industrial nations. The name of this epidemic is hypertension, . . . Hypertension predisposes one to the diseases of atherosclerosis (hardening of the arteries), heart attacks, and strokes. These diseases of the heart and brain account for more than 50 percent of the deaths each year in the United States. Therefore, it is not surprising that various degrees of hypertension are present in 15 to 33 percent of the adult population. Although this epidemic is not infectious in nature, it may be even more insidious, simply because its manifestations do not affect large numbers at the same time and because we are not generally aware that the disease is slowly developing within us. Throughout its course there are few, if any, symptoms. Yet each day we see it strike without warning, cutting short by decades the lives of our friends and loved ones. According to carefully compiled Government vital statistics, the diseases resulting from this epidemic account for an average of two deaths every minute in the United States alone. Put another way, that is nearly one million out of two million deaths a year.

Somewhat less dramatically, disorders such as gastrointestinal lesions, migraine and chronic anxiety states continue to place an ever-increasing burden on our health care resources. Although these various conditions may present in quite different ways, they have one property in common;

they are not transmitted through the medium of a virus or bacterium. Rather, as Benson observed, they develop slowly within us. It is this fact which has led a number of authors to suggest that the aetiology of these conditions is to be found in the stresses that go with living in a competitive, industrialised society.

Stress and Chronic Disease

It is not uncommon for a patient to suggest to his doctor that his symptoms might be due to stress. This suggestion is usually meant to imply that he has been under so much pressure, either at home or work, that his physical or mental well-being has been adversely affected. Unlike some self-diagnoses made by patients, this one is usually taken seriously. Indeed, quite frequently a patient will be told by his doctor that his condition will only begin to show lasting improvement when he learns to 'take things more easily'. So often are the effects of stress invoked in this manner that it comes as something of a surprise to learn that several writers have questioned its validity as an explanatory concept. Yet Steptoe (1981) has gone so far as to deliberately avoid using the term in his text book *Psychological Factors in Cardiovascular Disorders*.

On closer inspection it is not difficult to see why Steptoe resorted to such extreme action. Despite the frequency with which it is employed to explain a whole range of clinical phenomena, stress remains an extremely ill-defined concept. For example, it is often used to describe aspects of the environment that may have adverse effects on the individual (Weinman, 1981). We shall encounter examples of this usage in Chapter 4 when discussing studies designed to relate the effects of working in a stressful environment to the onset of essential hypertension. Looking ahead to this discussion, the weakness of conceptualising stress in this manner should be obvious. Except perhaps at a physical level, environments in themselves are not stressful. Rather they are perceived as such by individuals who seek to function within them. The recognition that perceptual processes are central to any evaluation of stress led Lazarus (1976) to argue that it is best regarded as a perceived threat. According to this view, stress is not to be understood in terms of either stimulus or response alone. Instead, it arises when an individual assesses the demands of a situation as being beyond his capacity to cope with them. As Weinman (1981) has observed, the value of this approach is that it accommodates the wide range of reactions that different individuals exhibit to a given external stressor (or the different responses exhibited by the same individual on different occasions). Thus he argues as follows:

> This can explain the individual variation in response to stressors since the individual's evaluation of the situation now becomes the key factor. Thus the intensity of any threat will depend on how well the individual feels he or she can deal with the situation. Situations which are perceived as threatening will give rise to emotional arousal, behavioural attempts to 'cope' and a range of underlying physiological changes.

Undoubtedly this view of stress deals with many of the difficulties of definition referred to earlier, and it is the one which will be assumed in the following discussion.

The Autonomic Nervous System (ANS)

The nervous system is divided into two parts, variously described as central and peripheral, central and autonomic, voluntary and involuntary, or (using the convention adopted here) somatic and autonomic. The somatic nervous system controls the activity of striated muscles, while the ANS innervates the internal organs, glands, heart, lungs and smooth muscles. It was long assumed that, unlike responses mediated by the somatic nervous system, those controlled by the ANS were automatic, though, as we shall see in the following chapter, research carried out in the 1960s appeared to challenge this view. As well as being distinguished from its somatic counterpart, the ANS is divided into two branches, the sympathetic (SNS) and parasympathetic (PNS) nervous systems. Although behaviours mediated by the SNS and PNS are said to be incompatible, neither system is ever totally inactive. Consequently, the contribution of either to ongoing autonomic activity should be regarded as relative rather than all-or-none; thus, the PNS is dominant when the organism is relaxed or asleep. Conversely, SNS activity predominates in behaviours that are preparatory to action, including action to cope with a perceived threat or stress.

It is widely accepted that the initial response to stress results from increased SNS output, which gives rise to changes in a wide range of bodily processes. These include an increase in heart-rate and dilation of blood vessels supplying the skeletal muscles. At the same time dilation of the bronchi allows for an increase in oxygen supply, and extra energy is made available as the liver converts more glycogen to glucose. Other changes arising from sympathetic stimulation include a slowing of the digestive process, increased sweat gland activity and dilation of the pupils. The totality of these changes was summed up by Ross and Wilson (1972) as follows:

> Sympathetic stimulation as a whole can be closely associated with the action of adrenaline, which is secreted from the medulla of the supra-renal glands. It prepares the body to withstand extenuating circumstances, strengthening its defences in excitement, danger and the hazards of extremes of temperature. In other words the body is mobilised for 'fight or flight'.

The Fight or Flight Response

While it is clear that changes arising from increased SNS activity in response to stress prepare the organism for action, it is equally clear that it is action of a primitive, physical nature. Within an evolutionary framework this no doubt made very good sense. However, a number of authors have pointed out that violent physical action is rarely an appropriate method of coping with the complex demands of contemporary society (Charvat, Dell and Folkow, 1964; Benson, 1975). As I have observed elsewhere (Marcer, 1985):

> Faced with a predator, early man would have little choice but to fight or take flight. However, such behaviour is rarely appropriate to the stresses encountered in modern society. We are no longer faced with the sabre-tooth tiger or the woolly mammoth. Instead we are called upon to deal with their modern counterparts, the uncommunicative garage mechanic, or the receptionist who has dedicated her life to preventing us from seeing the doctor.

Given that the fight-or-flight response may have largely outlived its usefulness, attempts to link organic disease with psycho-social stress take on a certain plausibility. Faced with psychological pressure rather than physical danger, the effects of increased SNS output will not be dissipated through physical action. As Charvat *et al.* (1964) pointed out:

> There are, however, good reasons to assume that the visceromotor and hormonal changes, induced in connection with emotional stress and the defense-alarm reaction, will remain essentially the same. This implies that the mobilization of the cardiovascular and metabolic

> resources intended to support a violent physical exertion will not be utilized in the natural way. For such reasons the hormonally produced changes of the blood and the chemical environment of the heart and blood-vessels can be expected to be more long-lasting than when a violent muscular exertion ensues.

Intuitively this is an appealing hypothesis. Nevertheless, it does raise a number of questions. Notably, what evidence is there that the temporary physiological changes associated with the fight-or-flight response can lead to chronic disease? This issue will be dealt with in some detail in the following chapters. However, it is appropriate to refer here to a study by Folkow and Rubinstein (1966), which indicated that raised levels of SNS activity may indeed have long-lasting, adverse effects — at least in rats.

It is generally recognised that the hypothalamus plays a crucial part in controlling the various physiological changes outlined above. To quote Benson (1975), 'stimulate a specific area of the hypothalamus and there will be an outpouring of adrenalin . . . and related hormones controlled by the SNS with the associated physiologic changes'. Folkow and Rubinstein took advantage of this fact to observe the effects of prolonged SNS output resulting from electrical stimulation of the hypothalamic defence area of the rat. The outcome of the 17-week study is shown in Table 1.1.

Folkow and Rubinstein summarised their findings as follows:

> This small series of pilot experiments on chronic rats is promising insofar as the results suggest that a gradual shift of the resting blood pressure level really takes place in the stimulated animals. This, despite the fact that the topical hypothalamic stimulations in the present experiments were throughout very mild and did not involve any drastic, acute disturbances of either behaviour or the cardiovascular equilibrium.

It would, of course, be foolhardy to suggest that a laboratory investigation involving twelve rats tells us much about the long-term effects of psychological stress on humans. Equally, however, it does nothing to weaken the hypothesis linking prolonged stress with raised SNS activity and hence with the slow onset of non-infectious chronic diseases.

Table 1.1: Mean Blood Pressure Levels ± Standard Error (S.E.) in the Stimulated Rats and the Non-Stimulated Control Rats during the Entire Period of Experiment

Weeks	Stimulated group (mean ± S.E., 6 rats)	Non-stimulated group (mean ± S.E., 6 rats)	Significance (*P* less than)
1	107 ± 1.8	110 ± 1.6	N.S.
2	105 ± 1.9	110 ± 2.0	N.S.
Stimulation on			
3	106 ± 2.3	108 ± 2.5	N.S.
4	111 ± 2.2	109 ± 1.9	N.S.
5	111 ± 2.4	110 ± 2.2	N.S.
6	116 ± 2.3	111 ± 2.2	N.S.
7	118 ± 2.5	114 ± 2.4	N.S.
8	119 ± 2.4	112 ± 2.3	N.S.
9	122 ± 2.2	114 ± 2.3	0.05
10	126 ± 2.5	113 ± 2.3	0.01
11	128 ± 2.6	115 ± 2.0	0.01
Stimulation interrupted			
12	120 ± 2.1	116 ± 2.2	N.S.
13	120 ± 2.0	117 ± 2.3	N.S.
Stimulation restarted			
14	131 ± 2.4	118 ± 2.0	0.01
15	136 ± 2.3	116 ± 2.1	0.01
16	128 ± 2.2	118 ± 2.2	0.02
17	128 ± 2.1	117 ± 1.9	0.02

Note: N.S., not significant.
Source: 'Cardiovascular Effects of Acute and Chronic Stimulations of the Hypothalamic Defence Area in the Rat', B. Folkow and E.H. Rubinstein, *Acta Physiologica Scandinavica* (1966), *68*, 48–57, Table 1.

Pharmacological Control of Stress: the Benzodiazepines

Because pharmacological methods proved so successful in controlling acute infectious diseases, it is hardly surprising that attempts have been made to deal with stress in a similar manner. However, not only have these attempts proved to be largely ineffective, in many instances they created a larger problem than the one they set out to cure. Nowhere is this better illustrated than in the case of the benzodiazepines, usually referred to as the minor tranquillisers.

Although not introduced until 1961, by the late 1970s over 4 per cent of *all* prescriptions written in the UK were for one form of benzodiazepine alone (diazepam), while in 1981 Petursson and Lader reported that on any day or night some 2 per cent of the adult population were taking tranquillisers. When first introduced, the benzodiazepines were seen as a major breakthrough in the treatment of a wide range of anxiety states. Unlike the barbiturates, they did not pose a significant suicide threat, they carried none of the risks of non-prescribed alternatives such as tobacco and alcohol, and, crucially, it was believed that dependence was not a problem at any but the highest doses. Indeed, as recently as 1980, the Committee on the Review of Medicines reported (British Medical Journal, 1980, pp. 910–12) as follows:

> However, following an extensive review of all available data the committee concluded that, on the present available evidence, the true addiction potential of benzodiazepines was low. *The number dependent on the benzodiazepines in the UK from 1960 to 1977 has been estimated to be 28 persons*. [my italics] . . . Such cases of addiction were observed to occur most frequently in drug misusers, particularly in patients with a history of psychological or social inadequacy. Although some reports were available which described dependence occurring during medically supervised treatment, such cases were comparatively rare and occurred usually in susceptible patients only when high doses (often exceeding the therapeutic dose range) were used for extended periods.

Even in 1980 there must have been many a general practitioner who wryly reflected on why it should be that on a 'bad day' all 28 persons referred to above seemed to find their way to his surgery! However, it was Barbara Gordon's harrowing account (Gordon, 1981) of her own attempt to give up taking diazepam that really brought the problem of benzodiazepine dependence into the open. Perhaps for the very reason that it was not a scientific report this autobiographical account quickly attracted the interest of the mass media. Thereafter it soon became apparent that whatever the niceties of defining the term 'addiction', literally thousands of individuals found it virtually impossible to discontinue using these drugs. For example, in June 1983, the BBC television programme *Thats Life!* reported the experiences of three individuals who had become dependent on benzodiazepines. The result of this single broadcast was that over 3000 people wrote to the BBC describing similar experiences. For example, to cite Lacey and Woodward (1985):

> When I tried to cut down my pills I felt as if the floor was moving. Walls seemed to give beneath my touch. I had a feeling that my skull was being crushed. I could not cope without taking tranquillisers. But until I read a newspaper article about addiction, I didn't realise these

were side-effects. I simply thought my original illness was getting worse. Just knowing I was an addict gave me the incentive and will-power to go through the withdrawal period, because I knew that eventually it would get better. And it did. My husband brought me food, and drinks in bed, and gave me moral support. I realised I would never stop taking tranquillisers if I didn't put up with the symptoms and go through the withdrawal.

Accounts such as this gave added substance to reports that had begun to appear in the medical literature. These showed that withdrawal effects are wide-ranging and can occur following the discontinuation of even the most conservative doses (Table 1.2).

Table 1.2: Symptoms Following Withdrawal of Diazepam, Lorazepam, or Clobazam (mean daily dose, 16.6 mg, 5.25 mg, and 30 mg, respectively)

Symptom	No. of cases *N* = 16	Symptom	No. of cases
Anxiety, tension	16	Loss of appetite	9
Agitation, restlessness	16	Nausea, dry retching	9
Bodily symptoms of anxiety	16	Depression	8
Irritability	9	Perspiration	7
Lack of energy	6	Metallic taste, hyperosmia	12
Impaired memory & concentration	4	Blurred vision, sore eyes, photophobia	9
Depersonalisation, derealisation	4	Incoordination, vertigo	9
Sleep disturbance	16	Hyperacusis	6
Tremor, shakiness	13	Paraesthesia	5
Headache	12	Hypersensitivity to touch, pain	4
Muscle pains, aches, twitchings	10	Paranoid reaction	2

Source: 'Withdrawal from Long-Term Benzodiazepine Treatment', H. Petursson and M.H. Lader, *British Medical Journal* (1981), *283*, 643–5, Table 1.

Since Petursson and Lader published their findings, a number of replication studies have been reported. For example, Power, Jerrom, Simpson and Mitchell (1985) reported significant withdrawal symptoms in a group of patients receiving 5 mg of diazepam three times daily for six weeks. At the same time, leading articles in the medical literature continue to draw attention to the extent of the problem (Catalan and Gath, 1985).

It may appear odd to begin an evaluation of biofeedback and other self-control techniques with a discussion of the benzodiazepines, however, its inclusion can be justified on two grounds. First, it provides yet one more illustration of the extent to which the effects of stress have come to permeate our society. Second, and more importantly, I believe this episode to have been a crucial factor in leading doctors and patients alike to re-examine their attitudes to non-pharmacological remedies such as biofeedback and relaxation training. The value of these techniques in controlling conditions such as essential hypertension and migraine is assessed in Part Two of this book. First, however, we need to examine what such techniques involve and outline some of the methodological problems encountered when we come to assess their efficacy.

2 BIOFEEDBACK, MEDITATION AND RELAXATION TRAINING

Biofeedback

Recently I asked a group of 40 first-year medical students what they knew about biofeedback. The reply given by 35 of them can be summed up in three words: 'nothing at all'. Bearing in mind that a more scientific survey elicited a similar response from members of the medical profession (Weinman, Mathew and Claghorn, 1982) it seems prudent to start at the very beginning and ask you to imagine that you are visiting a clinic at which biofeedback training is practised. The first patient that you see is lying on a flat bed and is breathing slowly and rhythmically with her eyes lightly closed. Attached to her forehead are three electrodes that lead to a small box, rather like the amplifier from a modern hi-fi system, which intermittently emits a 'clicking' sound (Figure 2.1).

Figure 2.1: A Patient Undergoing Frontalis Electromyographic (EMG) Feedback Training

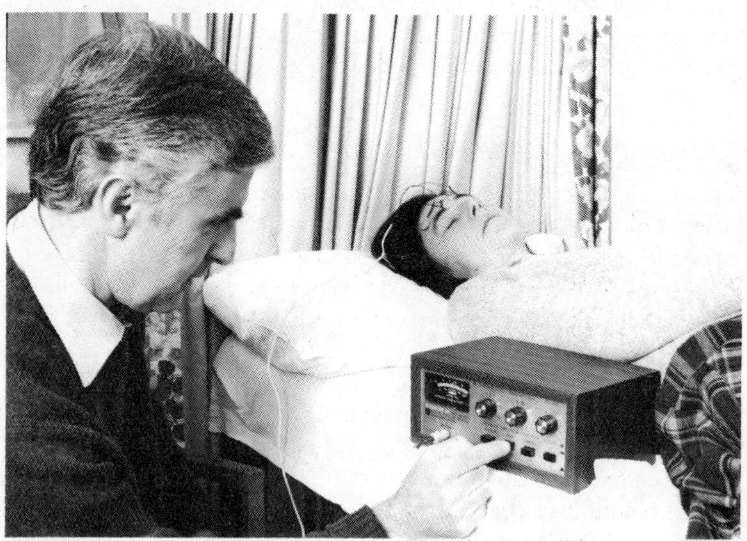

The second patient is sitting at a table. Lightly taped to one of his fingers is a single electrode that is connected to a meter scaled in degrees centigrade. The patient is concentrating on the meter needle, which is slowly swinging across the scale.

As the visit continues, you observe several more patients, all engaged in biofeedback training. Although the procedures may look different, they all share a common feature; the patient is linked to some form of monitoring device that from time to time produces a visual or auditory signal. Furthermore, despite procedural differences, all the variants of biofeedback being practised are based upon four shared assumptions. These are:

(1) If we are to enjoy good health then a number of bodily processes (often, but by no means always, those controlled by the ANS) must be maintained at an optimum level of performance.
(2) Usually we are unaware of the level at which these processes are operating but,
(3) by the use of various monitoring devices this information can be made available so that,
(4) with practice, we may learn to control their activity.

Virtually any physiological activity that can be monitored may be fed back to the individual undergoing training. However, in this section the discussion will be dominated by four types of biofeedback. These involve blood pressure, sweat gland activity, muscle tension and finger temperature.

(1) Blood Pressure Feedback

Routine monitoring of blood pressure in the clinic usually employs a simple mercury sphygmomanometer. An inflatable cuff is wrapped round the patient's upper arm and inflated to a pressure higher than systolic blood pressure (SBP) so that blood is unable to pass through the arteries beneath the cuff. As pressure in the cuff is gradually released, a point is reached at which it is less than SBP, whereupon arterial blood flow is resumed. By listening through a stethoscope placed on the brachial artery below the cuff the resumption of blood flow can be detected as a distinct sound (referred to as the Korotkov or K sound). As pressure in the cuff nears diastolic pressure (DBP) the K sound takes on a muffled tone, before disappearing completely as cuff pressure reaches DBP. Although this method meets most clinical needs, it does not provide the accurate continuous monitoring that feedback training requires.

Consequently, a number of more sophisticated techniques have been developed. Most of these are based upon the automated constant cuff pressure system devised by Tursky, Shapiro and Schwartz (1972). Briefly this involves inflating the cuff to a pressure at which the first K sound is heard on 50 per cent of the heartbeats within a predetermined cycle. This value defines median SBP. Likewise median DBP is defined as the pressure at which the final K sound is present on 50 per cent of heart-beats within the cycle. It is then possible to add a tracking device that monitors blood pressure beat by beat and automatically adjusts pressure within the cuff every three to four beats. Feedback takes the form of a tone, the pitch of which varies with blood pressure (Elder, Longacre, Welsh and McAfee, 1977).

(2) Feedback of Sweat Gland Activity (the Galvanic Skin Response [*GSR*]*)*

The assumption underlying this form of biofeedback is that sweat gland activity and autonomic arousal are positively correlated. Given this assumption it is an easy matter to monitor very small changes in arousal through a simple galvanometer attached to the subject's fingers by two electrodes. There are, however, several problems associated with this form of feedback. First, the assumption that the GSR and ANS activity necessarily co-vary is almost certainly an oversimplification. Second, the GSR is affected by changes in ambient temperature, humidity, the condition of the subject's skin and placement of electrodes. In a clinical setting it is rarely feasible to hold these factors constant for any length of time, thus making it virtually impossible to interpret differences in GSR measured on different occasions.

(3) Muscle Tension (EMG) Feedback

This method, illustrated in Figure 2.1, relies on the fact that electrical activity of muscles can be detected by electrodes placed on the surface of the skin. It is then a simple matter to amplify this activity and convert it to a visual or auditory signal. It must be emphasised that changes in EMG activity only reflect changes in muscle contraction. They do not provide an index of anxiety, peace of mind or mental state. It should also be noted that electrical activity monitored by surface electrodes represents the summed output of more than one muscle or group of muscles. Thus as Rugh (1979) has pointed out, many dramatic reductions in EMG activity monitored at the forehead may in fact be due to nothing more than the subject learning not to swallow during trial periods.

(4) Temperature Feedback

As its name implies, this form of feedback provides the subject with information about changes in body temperature. Most feedback devices employ a highly sensitive thermistor, the resistance of which changes with temperature. We shall see later that it has been argued that changes in finger temperature reflect altered ANS activity. For now it should be noted that the extreme sensitivity of modern thermistors makes this form of feedback very susceptible to the effects of changes in ambient temperature and inadequate habituation periods. Therefore, like GSR feedback, this technique rarely allows reliable inter-trial comparisons to be made.

By the 1970s, biofeedback had taken on many of the characteristics of a boom industry. The public was subjected to a barrage of advertisements for electronic devices, the prices of which were frequently matched only by the inflated claims made for what could be achieved by using them. It is almost inevitable that any scientific innovation which is described in the manner illustrated on page vii will sooner or later be subjected to a detailed reappraisal. Biofeedback was no exception, and soon a number of critical articles began to appear in the medical and psychological literature (e.g. Turk, Meichenbaum and Berman, 1979). Yet despite this sceptical reappraisal, biofeedback has continued to command the attention of scientists engaged in basic research as well as practising clinicians. Among the applications described in the 1983 edition of *Index Medicus* are the treatment of bruxism, dysmenorrhea, hypertension, insomnia, irritable bowel syndrome, migraine, nystagmus, Raynaud's disease, spastic dysphonia and tension headache. While in some of these conditions the use of biofeedback has been confined to a handful of cases, in others its application is much more widely accepted. For example, Schuman (1982) reported that by 1981, 37.5 per cent of all pain relief clinics in the USA were using some form of biofeedback.

The Historical Background

Most advances in science and medicine do not appear out of thin air, but are based upon extensions of established theoretical models. It makes sense, therefore, to begin the evaluation of the current status of biofeedback by examining its scientific pedigree.

Feedback first emerged as an important scientific concept in the mid-1940s. It arose out of the work of a number of scientists, amongst whom probably the most influential were Arturo Rosenblueth, of the Harvard Medical School, and Norbert Wiener, Professor of Mathematics at the Massachusetts Institute of Technology. In what is now regarded as a classic piece of work Wiener (1948) defined feedback as: 'A method of controlling the system by reinserting into it the results of its past performance.' Of course, even 40 years ago there was nothing especially new or revolutionary in emphasising the importance of control systems of this kind. As Wiener readily acknowledged, many long-established forms of marine steering devices rely upon feedback mechanisms. More commonly, we are all familiar with central heating systems that rely upon feedback through a thermostat in order to keep the temperature of a room constant. Thus the importance of Wiener's work was not that he 'discovered' feedback, but that he saw that it was crucial to the operation of biological as well as mechanical systems. This will be apparent to anyone who has learned to drive a car. By receiving continuous feedback from a number of sources, we gradually learn the effects of turning the steering wheel and applying various degrees of pressure to the accelerator and foot-brake. Interestingly, during the early stages of learning the novice driver often ignores the most appropriate source of feedback. For example, he will insist on trying to learn to change gear by closely watching the series of movements involved, frequently taking his eyes off the road in the process! Only gradually does he learn to ignore visual feedback and begin to rely on kinaesthetic information arising from the appropriate muscles and joints. Clearly, without feedback we could never master the complex set of skills involved in driving. Similarly, without the aid of visual proprioceptive feedback a baby would never learn hand-eye coordination. It is only after a process of trial and error that the infant finally learns to control the intricate series of movements that go to make up the act of reaching out and gently taking hold of a small, delicate object.

Although the preceding discussion shows that feedback is crucial to learning, it says nothing about the extent to which it continues to be necessary if a newly acquired skill is to be preserved. This question was the subject of an enormous volume of research that followed from the work of Wiener and his associates. Most of it was of a technical nature and need not concern us here, although there is one aspect that is directly relevant to the present discussion. If, as Wiener argued, feedback is crucial in maintaining stable behaviour in a changing environment, then disrupting it should have profound consequences on behaviour. Such disruption may be temporary and result from various experimental techniques, or be permanent, usually as the result of accident or disease.

Loss of Feedback in Humans

One of the most easily demonstrated effects of temporary disruption is brought about by the method known as *delayed auditory feedback*. This requires a subject to tape-record a spoken message while wearing heavily padded earphones that serve two purposes. First, they attenuate the sound of the subject's voice as he speaks. Second, they allow the recorded message to be relayed back to him while he continues to read aloud. By using a tape recorder in which the recording and play-back heads are spatially separated it becomes possible to introduce a time lag between the subject speaking a word and subsequently hearing it. The delay time varies as a function of the tape speed but typically it is of the order of one-half to one second. The effect of delaying feedback by even this small amount is often little short of catastrophic. Speech becomes laboured and in some cases the subject finds it impossible to utter more than five or six words without a complete breakdown in vocalisation. A very similar effect is frequently observed in individuals who become profoundly deaf in adult life. Denied feedback of their own voice there is a gradual change in vocalisation, especially in voice pitch and speech rhythms. Both of the above examples illustrate the disruptive effects of either delaying or eliminating feedback. Similar effects have been observed when feedback is distorted. Perhaps the most familiar example is the distortion of visual feedback by the use of spectacles that invert or displace the visual field. Only after a long period of active practice is the wearer able to adapt to this new visual environment and move about with relative ease.

So far, apart from a passing reference to deafness, the discussion has concentrated on the effects of temporarily disrupting feedback in a laboratory setting. However, it is in organic diseases such as the ataxias that some of the most profound effects of loss of feedback are to be observed. Ataxia is the term used to refer to a loss of coordination of muscular activity, usually without a corresponding loss of muscle power. Typical of such conditions is *tabes dorsalis*, a disease which appears at a late stage of syphilitic infection and involves sclerosis of the dorsal column. Stated simply, the patient suffers a loss of proprioceptive feedback from his limbs, thus rendering him dependent on visual feedback in order to know their position. As a consequence he adopts an unusual gait, walking with legs apart, peering intently at the ground and lifting his legs excessively, before slapping his feet down. When blindfolded or in the dark he is unable to point in a given direction, not because he lacks the muscular power to lift his arm, but simply because he is no longer able to judge its position. It would be easy to describe and analyse many more examples of how loss of feedback affects behaviour; however, for the purpose of the present discussion it is sufficient to have demonstrated that disrupting feedback does in fact produce the catastrophic consequences that Wiener predicted. Indeed, it is difficult to envisage how, without continuous feedback, we could ever learn the adaptive behaviours that are essential for our survival in a constantly changing environment. Once we recognise this fact, it is easy to agree with the comment made by Birk (1973) that what should surprise us is not that biofeedback should work, but that it was not 'discovered' earlier than it was. In order to understand why this should be so, it is necessary to resume a historical perspective and examine the views about the nature of learning that prevailed during the early part of this century.

Classical Conditioning

The study of the conditioned reflex or, as it subsequently became known, the conditioned response, derives from the work of the Russian physiologist and Nobel Prize winner, Ivan Pavlov. The principles that he expounded can be summarised as follows. Certain stimuli lead regularly and reliably to the production of reflex responses. For example, the knee jerks when the patella tendon is tapped, the pupil constricts when a light is shone in the eye, and salivation occurs in response to a range of gustatory stimuli. Reflexes of this kind are referred to as *unconditioned reflexes* (UCR), while the stimulus that produces them is termed the *unconditioned stimulus* (UCS). What Pavlov demonstrated was that if a second stimulus (which does not normally elicit the UCR) accompanies the UCS, then eventually it too will evoke a response that closely resembles the UCR. The second stimulus is referred to as the *conditioned stimulus* (CS) and the response that it evokes, the *conditioned response* (CR).

This paradigm is best illustrated in Pavlov's own experiments into the salivation response. Briefly, he demonstrated that not only did dogs salivate (UCR) when meat powder (UCS) was placed in their mouths, they soon began doing so (CR) in the presence of any stimulus (CS) that originally accompanied the UCS. Apparently Pavlov first became interested in the phenomenon when he observed that the dogs began to salivate at the sound of his footsteps as he approached the laboratory! However, most of his experiments employed a more conventional CS, usually a visual or auditory signal.

Instrumental (Operant) Conditioning

Just as classical conditioning is synonymous with the name of Pavlov, so the instrumental (or operant) conditioning paradigm has become associated with one man, the Harvard psychologist, B.F. Skinner. Typical of Skinner's work is the procedure whereby an animal is placed in a cage and fed each time that it makes a particular response, such as pressing a lever. At first the response occurs only sporadically, but after it has been rewarded a number of times it becomes an established part of the animal's behavioural repertoire. While much of the early research into conditioning was carried out on animals, many of the principles that emerged have since been applied to a wide range of complex human behaviour. For example, these early experiments form the basis of many behavioural therapies that now play an important part in contemporary psychiatry; these therapies are routinely used to treat conditions such as chronic anxiety, obsessional states, phobias and depression. Given the success of behavioural therapy it seems paradoxical that the view of learning on which so much of it is based should at the same time have inhibited the development of biofeedback. In fact the reason for this paradox is to be found in the assumptions that were made about the nature of the learning that resulted from classical and instrumental conditioning. At the cost of oversimplification these can be summarised as follows:

(1) There are two classes of human responses, voluntary and involuntary,
(2) Voluntary responses are controlled by the somatic nervous system, and apply to those behaviours that depend upon skeletal muscle for their execution.
(3) Involuntary responses are controlled by the autonomic nervous system (ANS), which (as was stated in Chapter 1) controls the activity of the internal organs, glands, smooth muscles, heart and lungs. The responses are acquired and modified by classical conditioning, and, critically, *they cannot be brought under voluntary control by the use of instrumental conditioning*.

This theoretical position has been elegantly summarised by Gatchel and Price (1979) as follows:

> It was assumed that internal physiological events could not be operantly conditioned. After all, it was argued, how can this type of conditioning occur if the organism cannot voluntarily control and emit an

> internal response in order to receive reinforcement? If you tell a hungry man that he will receive food (reinforcement) if he decreases his blood pressure to a certain level, chances are he will remain hungry. Most people cannot voluntarily control this internal response when requested, and therefore operant conditioning of the response does not have a chance to occur. In contrast, if you tell that same hungry man that he must perform a skeletal muscular response such as jumping up and down three times in order to receive food, he will eat to his heart's content. The man has voluntary control over this somatic response, and it would be a safe bet to assume he would continue to perform the response as long as you continue to supply the food reinforcer.

The implications of this view for the emergence of biofeedback as a method of treating stress related illnesses are obvious. As was indicated in Chapter 1, inappropriate autonomic activity is assumed to underlie many such conditions. If it really is the case that autonomic responses cannot be brought under voluntary control, then it is arguable that there is nothing to be gained from making the patient aware of them by the use of biofeedback. Presumably this view would have continued to the present day had not a number of workers begun to challenge the prevailing orthodoxy.

Operant Control of Involuntary Responses

In 1970, Lang described one of the methods that the Great Houdini used to perform his escape routines. Having been thoroughly searched, he would be handcuffed and bound in chains that were secured by a padlock. Shortly afterwards he would reappear from behind the curtain, having performed yet another 'miraculous' escape. There was of course, no miracle. Once Houdini was out of view of his audience he simply unlocked the padlock with a key that he had learned to hold suspended in his throat. Lang went on to point out that normally if we get an object stuck in our throat we start to gag. We can't help doing so, as it is an unlearned, automatic reflex. But Houdini had learned to control his gag reflex by practising for hour after hour with a small piece of potato tied to a string. Even before Houdini had begun his career, cases had been cited which suggested that control of involuntary responses could be achieved. In particular, reports that Eastern mystics were able to exert quite remarkable control over their bodies seized the imagination of the general public, if not the scientific establishment. It is interesting to speculate why such phenomena were largely ignored by those scientists involved in the study of learning. I suspect that in part it was due to the general conservatism that is the hallmark of the committed research worker. He feels more at home working within the confines of well-defined, tightly controlled laboratory experiments. Aberrant phenomena 'out there in the real world' tend to be dismissed as simply that, especially when to take them seriously would involve talking to mystics and magicians. As recent attempts to explain the 'Geller Phenomenon' (the supposed ability of certain individuals to bend metal objects by power of mind alone) remind us, scientists rarely emerge from such encounters without egg on their faces! On the whole then, even if there was little direct evidence to support the established view that involuntary responses were incapable of operant control, few were prepared to doubt it. That was until the late 1960s, when Neal Miller and his associates described a series of experiments which appeared to rewrite the text books.

They reported that it was possible operantly to condition a whole range of autonomic behaviour in rats that had been temporarily immobilised with curare. (This was a necessary control to ensure that any changes in autonomic behaviour were not in fact the indirect results of voluntary musculo-skeletal responses.) The responses described by Miller included changes in heart-rate, blood pressure, and the rate of urine flow in the kidneys. In fact it seemed that there was no autonomic response that could not be modified by operant conditioning, and it was even suggested that a rat could be taught simultaneously to increase the flow of blood to one ear and decrease it to the other.

Thus, the picture was finally complete. The implication of the ANS in a wide range of illness was widely accepted, as was the role of feedback in the learning process. Modern electronics offered the individual the opportunity to be made aware of the activity of his own autonomic responses and the work of Miller and his associates had shown that given this awareness he could learn to control them. Only one further problem was to emerge. Subsequent attempts to replicate Miller's original findings proved unsuccessful, so that by 1978 he stated that we ought not to rely on any of his experiments on curarised animals for evidence of the instrumental learning of visceral responses. So far the failure to replicate Miller's original findings has not been adequately explained, although a number of suggestions have been advanced. One of these is that the effects of mediation by way of the musculo-skeletal system were inadequately controlled in the early experiments. That mediation of this kind can occur has long been recognised, and it is a 'nuisance variable' that needs to be rigorously controlled by the scientist engaged in pure research into the workings of the ANS. In a clinical setting the issues that it raises are somewhat different. Adopting a purely pragmatic approach, if it can be shown that biofeedback training helps a chronic hypertensive to lower his blood pressure, it matters little that this is mediated through changes in the musculo-skeletal system rather than by the acquisition of direct control of the cardiovascular system. At the same time, however, if mediation is the crucial factor then the need to provide feedback is called into question. In theory, at least, we should be able to dispense with the machines yet still obtain the same effects by introducing the patient to some form of relaxation training. The implications of this question are dealt with at some length in the following chapters. First, however, let us examine what is involved in this form of training.

Meditation

Although my 'straw poll' of medical students revealed a near total ignorance of biofeedback, all of them claimed some knowledge of meditation. This is hardly surprising, for since the early 1960s transcendental meditation (TM), or some variant of it, has proved to be virtually irresistible to publishers of up-market magazines, television producers and organisers of evening classes. Introduced to the USA in 1959 by Maharishi Mahesh Yogi, TM soon spread to the UK, largely through its links with the pop culture that grew up around rock music. The technique is simple, involving little more than 'sitting comfortably with eyes closed, for 20 minutes twice a day, and thinking to oneself a Sanskrit sound or mantra' (Bakal, 1979). This brief description quite closely resembles that given by my sample of medical students, most of whom mentioned a calm, relaxed state in their accounts. However, as a number of authors have pointed out, meditation encompasses a far wider range of behaviours than those contained in TM. In a comprehensive review, Shapiro (1982) described how:

> Some involve sitting quietly and produce a state of quiescence and restfulness. Some involve sitting quietly and produce a state of excitement and arousal. Some, such as the Sufi whirling dervish, tai chi, hatha yoga, and Isiguro Zen, involve physical movement to a greater or lesser degree. Sometimes these 'movement meditations' result in a state of excitement, sometimes a state of relaxation.

Given such diversity, it is not easy to arrive at a single definition of meditation. However, by focusing upon attentional mechanisms, Shapiro offered the following: '. . . meditation refers to a family of techniques which have in common a conscious attempt to focus attention in a nonanalytical way and an attempt not to dwell on discursive, ruminating thought.' Obviously the account of TM given by Bakal poses no problem for this definition. Nor do many methods of meditation that have evolved within the Christian tradition. For example, Benson (1975) describes how St Gregory Palamas suggested that the 'Jesus Prayer' should be recited as follows:

> Sit down alone and in silence. Lower your head, shut your eyes, breathe out gently, and imagine yourself looking into your own heart. As you breath out, say 'Lord Jesus Christ, have mercy on me.' Say it moving your lips gently, or simply say it in your mind. Try to put all other thoughts aside. Be calm, be patient and repeat the process very frequently.

As even this brief description makes clear, whatever else they may have in common, biofeedback and meditation are rooted in quite different philosophical traditions. Biofeedback has its origins in experimental psychology and physiology and is firmly based on Western empiricism. Not surprisingly therefore, its application has been almost entirely clinically orientated. This is not the case with meditation. Gregory did not advise his followers to recite the Jesus Prayer in order to wean them off benzodiazepines or to cure their hypertension! He did so in order that they might advance their spiritual development; that they might achieve union with God. Likewise the very fact that the Maharishi adopted the adjective 'transcendental' implies that he placed TM in the spiritual domain. It might appear odd, therefore, that as recently as 1983, the *British Medical Journal* should contain an article by Fenwick entitled 'Can we still recommend meditation?' In fact this was not a sign that this prestigious publication had 'gone religious'. Rather it reflected a view that had emerged over the past two decades that, irrespective of its spiritual value, meditation has the power to combat a wide range of illnesses, especially those believed to be associated with stress. Much of the impetus for exploring the clinical application of meditation came from research into the relaxation response, which was conducted by Herbert Benson and his colleagues at the Harvard Medical School.

The Relaxation Response

In brief, Benson argues that despite some superficial differences, practices such as TM and that described by Gregory share certain key elements. For example, Benson, Kotch, Crassweller and Greenwood (1977) suggested the following: 'Four elements seem to be integral to these varied practices and are necessary to evoke the relaxation response: a quiet environment; decreased muscle tone; a mental device, i.e. a sound, word or phrase repeated silently or audibly; and a passive attitude.' The authors then went on to describe 'a simple noncultic technique', which, though free from any religious connotations, incorporated all four elements.

(1) Sit quietly in a comfortable position and close your eyes.
(2) Deeply relax all your muscles, beginning at your feet and progressing up to your face. Keep them deeply relaxed.
(3) Breathe through your nose. Become aware of your breathing. As you breathe out say the word *one* silently to yourself. For example, breathe in . . . out, *one*, in . . . out, *one*; etc. Continue for 20 minutes. You may open your eyes to check the time, but do not use an alarm. When you finish, sit quietly for several minutes at first with closed eyes and later with opened eyes.
(4) Do not worry about whether you are succesful in achieving a deep level of relaxation. Maintain a passive attitude and permit relaxation to occur at its own pace. Expect other thoughts. When these distracting thoughts occur ignore them by thinking 'Oh well' and continue repeating 'one'. With practice the response should come with little effort. Practice the technique once or twice daily, but not within two hours after any meal, since the digestive processes seem to interfere with the subjective changes.

Most people would agree that practising this simple exercise leads to a pleasant, relaxed feeling. However, when Benson *et al.* speak of the 'relaxation response' they imply much more than merely taking time out for a quiet rest. For them 'the elicitation of the relaxation response results in physiologic changes which are thought to characterize an integrated hypothalamic response.' Moreover, they claim that such changes are 'distinctly different from those observed during quiet sitting or sleep and characterize a wakeful hypometabolic state'. The basis of these claims is to be found in a series of laboratory studies that Benson and his associates conducted during the 1970s.

In 1971, Wallace, Benson and Wilson investigated the physiological changes that occur during TM. Thirty-six individuals who regularly practised TM participated, each acting as his own control. Measurements were made during a 30 minute pre-control period, a 20–30 minute period of meditation and a 20 minute post-control period. The results showed that during meditation there was a decrease in oxygen consumption, carbon dioxide elimination, respiratory rate and minute ventilation, blood lactate and blood pH. Subsequent research by Beary and Benson (1974) revealed that the technique described on page 24 led to very similar physiological changes. Summarising this work, Benson *et al.* (1977) argued that the physiological changes that they had described were consistent with generalised decreased SNS activity and thus represented effects directly opposite to those associated with the fight-or-flight response. They then went on to claim that 'Regular elicitation of the relaxation response may be of preventive and therapeutic value in diseases in which increased sympathetic nervous system activity is implicated.' Undoubtedly this was an important hypothesis. It appeared to offer a simple, non-invasive method of combating a number of intractable illnesses by allowing the individual to control autonomic activity. Moreover, unlike those achieved through biofeedback training, these effects would not be confined to a particular autonomic function and could be achieved without expensive equipment and highly trained personnel. Indeed it was findings such as those described by Benson which fuelled the speculation that the outcome of biofeedback training might in fact be no more than the generalised effects of muscle relaxation. However, like all hypotheses, this one contained certain assumptions that could only be verified by empirical research. Thus, it had first to be shown that the relaxation response leads to physiological changes that differ qualitatively from those accompanying other forms of relaxation training, and second, that changes observed in the laboratory (usually using fit young volunteers) carry over to everyday life and are of long-term therapeutic value.

Whatever problems may confront a researcher wishing to investigate the first assumption, he would find no shortage of relaxation techniques with which to compare meditation. As Rimm and Masters (1979) have pointed out, 'It is likely that humankind has been devising non-pharmacological (as well as pharmacological) ways to relax from the time we dwelled in caves.' Whether or not this is really so, it certainly seems that way. Even a cursory inspection of the literature reveals a plethora of such techniques, each with its band of enthusiastic adherents. However, only two of them (progressive relaxation and autogenic training) will be described here. The reader seeking a more extensive (yet admirably concise) account should consult Yates (1980).

Progressive Relaxation and Autogenic Training

Progressive relaxation is associated with the work of Jacobson (1938, 1970), though clinical reports suggest that most practitioners adapt the basic method that he described. Briefly, an individual undergoing this form of training is made aware of muscle tension by first tensing and then relaxing certain groups of muscles. The following abbreviated account, based upon the work of Rimm and Masters (1979), is typical of the instructions that precede this form of treatment.

> The tension . . . you normally experience . . . comes from tense muscles, though you might not even be aware your muscles are tense . . . I am going to teach you to relax those tense muscles, systematically, so you will be calm instead of anxious. After you've learned the method, you will be able to do it on your own . . . The method requires tensing a particular muscle or set of muscles, then relaxing the same muscles . . . (The therapist might demonstrate what he means by making a fist, relaxing his hand, extending his fingers, and relaxing once again to illustrate what is meant by opposing sets of muscles.) After we have completed relaxing your hands, we will relax your arms, and then your shoulders, and so on until your entire body is relaxed.

The authors go on to describe similar exercises for biceps and triceps, shoulders, neck, mouth, tongue, eyes and forehead, back, midsection, thighs, stomach, calves and feet, and finally toes.

Autogenic training was first described by Schultz in 1932, but as Yates (1980) has pointed out, such was the influence of Freud at that time it was not until 1969 that an English translation became available (Schultz and Luthe, 1969). However, as if to make up for lost time, this ran to several volumes and the interested reader might well find it more rewarding to refer in the first instance to a paper by Luthe (1963). Briefly, autogenic training differs from progressive relaxation in that while both seek to induce a state of muscular relaxation, the former aims to involve vasomotor and cognitive processes as well. This is achieved by teaching the trainee a series of mental exercises involving sensations of heaviness and warmth. For example, Stoyva (1983) describes how he first draws upon progressive relaxation training in order to develop an 'awareness of muscle tension'. Thereafter he introduces the following autogenic exercises:

> . . . the patient silently repeats to himself, 'My right arm is heavy.' The training phrase, which is repeated continuously — and *slowly* — during the exercise, helps one both to maintain passive attention on the arm and to keep out intruding cognitive activity . . . Over several sessions, usually two to three weeks, the patient progresses with warmth training to both hands and feet in the same fashion as with the heaviness exercise. After mastery of this exercise the (permanent) summary phrase becomes, 'My right arm is heavy. My arms and legs are heavy and warm.'

Stoyva then goes on to describe how breathing exercises are added, the emphasis being upon easy, regular breathing, so that 'Respiration should be effortless — as if something else is doing it! Since respiratory irregularities are very common in patients with anxiety and stress-related disorders, this is often a useful exercise. Trainees frequently indicate a marked liking for it.'

Although the accounts of the various techniques described here are brief, they are sufficient to show that meditation, progressive relaxation and autogenic training have much in common. Which brings us back to the first question posed on page 25. Does meditation lead to physiological changes that are qualitatively different from those produced by more simple forms of relaxation? A number of comprehensive reviews of the literature indicate that it does not. For example, Shapiro (1982) concluded that:

> Although it seems clear that meditation can bring about a generalized reduction in many physiological systems, thereby creating a state of relaxation, it is not yet clear from the available data that this state is differentiated from the effects of other relaxation techniques, whether they be hypnosis or deep muscle relaxation. Most studies have found that the constellation of changes is significantly different between meditation groups and placebo control groups but not between meditation and other self-regulation treatments.

Very similar conclusions were reached by West (1979) and Yates (1980), although it needs pointing out that these views are not universally accepted. For example, Jevning and O'Halloran (cited by Shapiro, 1982) have argued that the failure to observe a unique response to meditation arises because most comparative studies have been confined to novice meditators.

The fact that the physiological changes that accompany meditation, progressive relaxation and autogenic training are very similar, does not, of course, necessarily imply that they are of no importance. Any practice that reduces inappropriate SNS activity is worthy of attention, especially if these effects are large, achieved without adverse side effects and robust enough to survive the transition from laboratory to everyday life. And here we return to the second major assumption implicit in the hypothesis advanced by Benson and his associates. In this case most scholarly reviews are guardedly optimistic. For example, Fenwick (1983) concluded that we can indeed continue to recommend meditation, suggesting that it is a useful treatment for a number of conditions, including anxiety, insomnia and mild hypertension. At the same time, however, he pointed out that similar therapeutic gains can be obtained from using simple relaxation techniques and various forms of biofeedback. In the chapters that follow the veracity of this conclusion is evaluated. This will involve examination in detail of numerous studies designed to assess both the absolute and relative efficacy of biofeedback and various forms of relaxation training. However, in any such review it rapidly becomes apparent that this area of research poses major problems of methodology and design that, regrettably, very few researchers have succeeded in overcoming. It is appropriate, therefore, to preface an evaluation of these studies by discussing some of the more important methodological problems common to many of them.

3 METHODOLOGICAL ISSUES

Although every clinical trial requires careful consideration to be given to experimental design and analysis of data if misleading outcomes are to be avoided, this is especially so when we come to deal with illnesses in which psycho-social factors are assumed to play a part. Not only is the pathogenesis of the condition at best only partly understood, symptoms frequently fluctuate for no apparent reason. Add to these difficulties that of measuring subjective symptoms such as pain or depression and it becomes apparent why attempts to establish the efficacy of biofeedback and relaxation training face major methodological problems. These can be classified under four headings: selection of subjects, spontaneous remission, experimental control, and the measurement of change.

Selection of Subjects

However convinced they may be of the efficacy of their methods, few practitioners go so far as to suggest that they are universally applicable. Consequently there is almost always an element of selective sampling of patients entering a clinical trial. In clinical practice it is, of course, desirable that treatment be directed at those patients most likely to derive benefit. However, as the following example shows, when assessing efficacy, this approach can produce misleading data.

A number of authors have argued that the most effective method of dealing with benign chronic pain is to treat it as learned behaviour rather than a disabling sensation. Proponents of this view go on to argue that if the patient is to be rehabilitated we should change his behaviour rather than seek to remove his pain. Thus, in line with the principles of operant conditioning, treatment programmes have been devised in which pain behaviours are ignored while pain-free behaviours are encouraged. Commenting on this approach, Roberts (1983) reported that his own work demonstrated that '77 per cent of those treated were still functioning at normal levels without the use of pain-related medications from 1 to 8 years following treatment'. Bearing in mind that these were patients who had not responded to other forms of treatment and that the criteria by which success was judged were exceedingly stringent, this was an impressive outcome. However, on closer examination, the original data reported by Roberts and Reinhardt (1980) reveal a more modest success rate. Of 112 patients referred for evaluation, 44 were rejected as unsuitable for this form of treatment. Of the remaining 68, 34 declined to take part, while only 26 of those who were treated provided follow-up data. The 77 per cent success rate cited by Roberts is based upon these 26 patients, of whom 20 were judged to be leading normal lives. If, however, success is defined in terms of the total number of cases originally referred (112), the success rate drops to only 18 per cent. A similar analysis by Turk and Genest (1979) of data presented by Anderson, Cole, Gullickson, Hudgens and Roberts (1977) produced a virtually identical outcome, the success rate dropping from 74 per cent to 19 per cent. Fortunately, in both the above examples the authors presented their data in such a way as to make clear how they arrived at their conclusions. Thus there is no question that they were trying to mislead us into believing that more than 70 per cent of *all* chronic pain sufferers benefit from this form of treatment. Regrettably not all authors have proved to be so forthcoming with details of how participants were selected, or how many were rejected, dropped out, or failed to provide follow-up data. In such instances, bare 'success rates' should be treated with extreme caution.

Spontaneous Remission of Symptoms

Although the clinical conditions discussed in the following chapters differ in many ways, they share a number of common features. One of the most important of these, from a methodological standpoint, is that they are often long standing and of varying intensity. For example, I was asked recently if I could help a 60-year-old health service worker who since the age of 16 had been subject to 'blinding headaches'. Fortunately, there had been long periods during the preceding 44 years when he was free from symptoms, although on other occasions he was so incapacitated as to make work impossible. It is this cyclical nature of so many long-standing illnesses that can lead the unwary practitioner or researcher into error. Patients usually seek help when their condition is at its worst and pronounce themselves satisfied and take their discharge when symptoms abate. It would have been all too easy, therefore, to accept Mr X for treatment when his headaches were especially severe and discharge him as 'yet another success' as they followed their cyclical course. Moreover, we cannot rely on such patients letting us know when their symptoms begin to recur. Faced with one more failure to find lasting relief they are likely to write us off and turn elsewhere for help. Consequently, if he is not to be misled, it is up to the researcher to ensure that his trial includes a long-term follow-up evaluation which he initiates. Furthermore, the problem of spontaneous remission emphasises the need for adequate pre-treatment baseline data and, whenever possible, the inclusion of an untreated control group.

The Problem of Control

The Placebo Effect

One of the most all-pervading phenomena to be found in medicine is the placebo effect. According to Shapiro (1976), a placebo is:

> any component of therapy that is deliberately or knowingly used for its nonspecific, psychologic, or psycho-physiologic effect, or that is used unknowingly for its presumed or believed specific effect on a patient, symptom, or illness, but which, unknown to patient and therapist, is without specific activity for the condition being treated.

As this definition makes clear, the placebo effect is often put to clinical use. In such cases, the practitioner is well aware that there is no pharmacological justification for the treatment he is prescribing (often large, attractive-looking vitamin capsules). Rather he is seeking to capitalise on non-specific effects, such as reducing the patient's anxiety, while waiting for nature to carry out the healing process. There are other occasions, however, when the practitioner is even more convinced than the patient that he is prescribing a powerful treatment, only for subsequent research to show it to be of no therapeutic value whatsoever. The history of medicine is littered with examples of 'wonder treatments' that have met this fate. Indeed, Osler is reputed to have advised us to 'Make haste to use a new remedy before it is too late.' (Alderson, 1974). Two classic experiments show how both patients and therapists can be misled in this manner.

The effect of a placebo on patients was demonstrated by Frankenhaeuser, Jaerpe, Svan and Wrangsjoe (1963). A group of female subjects made three visits to the laboratory — a familiarisation session followed by two experimental sessions in which they were given capsules that they were informed contained first a depressant and then a stimulant drug. In fact both capsules contained the same inert substance. Throughout each session various subjective and objective measures were

Figure 3.1: Comparison of the Effects of a 'Depressant' and a 'Stimulant' Placebo on Various Objective and Subjective Reactions. Each vertical bar represents the average per cent increase or decrease in reaction following administration of the two types of capsule

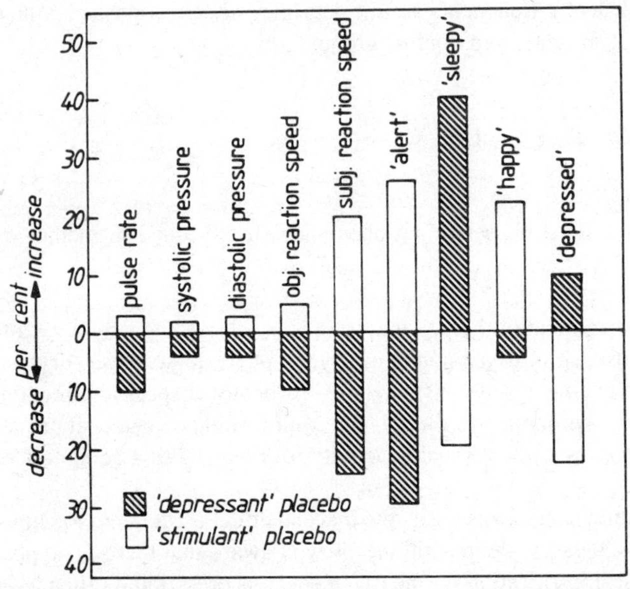

Source: 'Psychophysiological Reactions to Two Different Placebo Treatments', M. Frankenhaeuser, G. Jaerpe, H. Svan and B. Wrangsjoe, *Scandinavian Journal of Psychology* (1963), *4*, 245–50.

recorded. The results are shown in Figure 3.1.

These results are especially relevant to the studies that are reviewed in the next chapter, for not only did they show how placebos produce appropriate changes in subjective feelings, they also demonstrated how suggestion can lead to objective changes in blood pressure and pulse rate, both of which are controlled by the ANS.

That the placebo effect is not limited to patients was elegantly demonstrated by Heaton-Ward (1962). He described a study, the stated aim of which was to investigate the effect of nialamide on the behaviour and IQ of patients with Downs' syndrome. Initially, half the subjects received the active substance, the rest being treated with an inert placebo. It was stated that half way through the study the conditions would be reversed; those receiving nialamide being given the placebo and vice versa. (This is known as a cross-over design and is an established method of testing drugs.) However, unknown to anyone involved in the trial (including those carrying out the assessments) the cross-over did not take place; patients received either nialamide or placebo throughout the trial. The results showed that nialamide was superior to placebo in the first half of the trial, but in the second half the placebo produced the better outcome. Alderson (1974) interpreted this finding as follows:

> Presumably, the drug had been correctly spotted early in the trial because of its side-effects, and the observers' bias in its favour had carried through into the second half of the trial. Such studies provide a salutory warning of the bias that can creep into the recording of observers' assessments of the effect of therapeutic agent and placebo.

Both studies offer a clear demonstration of how the placebo effect can confound all but the most meticulously controlled investigation. In testing the efficacy of a new drug this is achieved by including a group of patients who receive the placebo under double-blind conditions; that is, neither the patients nor those conducting the trial know who is receiving the active compound. Furthermore, the placebo resembles the active substance in every way except its therapeutic properties. Thus the two look and taste alike and prescribing instructions are identical. By adopting such precautions and by subjecting the data to rigorous statistical analysis, it is usually possible to measure the efficacy of a drug independent of the placebo component. However, when we come to evaluate behavioural treatments, the problem of providing an appropriate control is much more complex. For example, consider the method devised by Benson *et al.* to evoke the relaxation response (p. 24). It is extremely difficult to stipulate a control treatment analogous to the 'dummy' pill employed in drug trials. Similar difficulties are encountered in trials of biofeedback. Although in some instances the provision of false feedback meets many of the criteria required of a placebo, in others an individual is perfectly well able to judge whether or not he is being given false information. Regrettably, many researchers appear to have dealt with this problem by ignoring it; most of the early trials were carried out without controls of any kind. This is unfortunate, for the complex equipment associated with biofeedback gives it many of the properties that go to make up a powerful placebo. At a purely clinical level it might be argued that so long as the treatment proves effective it matters little that we are unable to specify the extent to which the favourable outcome is a placebo effect. However, even in this limited case the argument is untenable for outcome is measured by the observer, rather than the patient, and as Heaton-Ward demonstrated, the preconceptions of the observer can lead him to perceive efficacy where none exists. Stated simply, in these cases the patient does not even benefit from the placebo effect, though it may help to convince the therapist that he is doing something of value! We shall return to this issue in the final chapter.

The Effects of Measurement

Even if the methodological problems outlined so far were to be overcome, one difficulty would remain. This is the tendency for certain psychological and physiological states to be affected by the measurement process itself. This phenomenon was demonstrated by Burstyn, O'Donovan and Charlton (1981), who measured the blood pressures (BPs) of a group of normotensive volunteers, the reported values being the mean of five cuff inflations, measured over a period of approximately seven minutes. Eight days later the procedure was repeated. All subjects completed three psychometric scales designed to measure anxiety, extraversion, neuroticism and personal confidence. The results showed that mean pressure fell from an initial mean value of 129.2/85.1 mm to 124.9/82.0 mm after eight days, the reductions in both systolic and diastolic pressures being statistically significant. Additionally, 31 subjects were judged mildly hypertensive on the first visit, but of these 13 were no longer so on the second. Furthermore, as the data shown in Table 3.1 make clear, not all subjects showed the same degree of change across the two visits.

Table 3.1: Mean BPs (± S.E. mean) of 36 Persons whose Systolic Pressures Dropped by 10 mmHg or more Between the First and Second Visits (Labile BP) Compared with the BPs of the Remaining 75 Persons (Stable BP)

	First visit		Second visit	
	Systolic	Diastolic	Systolic	Diastolic
Labile BP	137.7 (2.9)	88.2 (1.5)	123.5 (2.9)	80.2 (2.9)
Stable BP	125.1 (1.7)	83.9 (1.2)	125.1 (1.7)	82.7 (1.1)
	$P < 0.001$	$P < 0.05$	NS	NS

Note: Both the systolic and diastolic pressures of the 'labile' BP group on the 1st and 2nd visit are statistically significantly different from each other with $P < 0.001$ (systolic) and $P < 0.001$ (diastolic).
Source: 'Blood Pressure Variability: The Effects of Repeated Measurement', P. Burstyn, B. O'Donovan, and I. Charlton, *Postgraduate Medical Journal* (1981), *57*, 488–91, Table 3.

It is also of interest that the labile group showed significantly higher anxiety scores than did the stable group, though no such differences appear to have been detected on the other three personality scales. A second study, which compared the effects of repeated measurements on trained and untrained subjects, yielded similar results. In this case, unlike experienced subjects, those who were unused to having their blood pressure measured showed a significant decrease in systolic pressure across three readings (Table 3.2).

Table 3.2: The First and Third BP Measurements (mean ± S.E. mean) of a Group of three taken over 4 min in 36 'Untrained' Individuals and in 36 'Trained' Individuals who had their BPs Measured three times/week for at least 1.5 weeks. Pressure values are compared with each other using either Student's *t* test or the *t* test for pairs of values, where appropriate

	Untrained	Trained	
First cuff inflation			
systolic	128.7 (2.3)	117.8 (1.7)	$P < 0.001$
diastolic	76.6 (1.4)	73.7 (1.3)	NS
Third cuff inflation			
systolic	123.5 (2.2)	117.8 (1.6)	$P < 0.05$
diastolic	76.9 (1.2)	75.0 (1.3)	NS

Note: Paired *t* test comparing first and third systolic measurement for untrained subjects: $P < 0.001$.
Source: 'Blood Pressure Variability: The Effects of Repeated Measurement', P. Burstyn, B. O'Donovan, and I. Charlton, *Postgraduate Medical Journal* (1981), *57*, 488–91, Table 1.

The implications of this study are all too obvious. Had the labile subjects been participants in a clinical trial then the mean decline in pressure of 14.2/8.0 mm (Table 3.1) occurring between the first and second visit might easily have been accorded the status of a specific treatment effect. In fact, the decline was probably due to this anxious group of individuals habituating to the measurement procedures. Burstyn *et al.* concluded as follows:

> Frequent BP measurements are essential in experiments designed to observe changes in BP. If subjects are not thoroughly trained to the measurement procedure during the control period, the effects of subsequent experimental measurements may distort the result.

Given that their subjects were healthy young volunteers who were simply being tested 'in the interests of science', it is quite possible that the outcome reported by Burstyn *et al.* would be even greater with patients. Certainly it is not difficult to imagine the effect on a patient as he sits in a waiting room ruminating over the possibility that he may have a serious illness, before being summoned into the presence of a white-coated figure and requested to 'roll up his sleeve'!

Summary

Clinical trials of biofeedback and relaxation training call for sophisticated experimental designs if spurious results are to be avoided. In evaluating the studies described in the following chapters the reader should bear in mind the following criteria:

(1) The criteria by which patients were admitted to the trial must be clearly stated.
(2) Wherever possible the aetiology, duration and present treatment of the condition should be stated, along with any changes in other forms of treatment that occur during the trial.
(3) The effects of non-specific factors must be estimated by including appropriate control groups.
(4) Changes in symptoms must be measured against a stable baseline.
(5) Observer bias should be controlled by ensuring that readings are made blind, i.e. by an individual who is not aware which patients are receiving active treatment.
(6) In the case of hypertension each individual data point should be based upon the mean of several readings taken *before* the treatment session.
(7) Ideally, readings should be made in a different environment to the one in which the treatment is undertaken.
(8) Provision must be made for long-term follow-up data to be acquired.
(9) Reduction in symptoms should not only be statistically significant, it should also be large enough to be clinically relevant.
(10) The effect must be capable of replication by independent researchers.

PART TWO:

APPLICATIONS

4 HYPERTENSION

In 1981 Coope stated that general practitioners should have a recent record of the blood pressure of every patient over the age of 35. For, he argued, without this information four patients in every hundred may be deprived of life-saving treatment. According to Bannan, Beevers and Jackson (1981) he could have gone on to argue the case even more forcibly for they claimed that in England and Scotland only half the cases of hypertension are diagnosed and of these only half are given treatment. Moreover, of those that are treated, only half achieve a clinically significant outcome. In other words, according to the 'rule of halves' only one hypertensive patient in eight will receive effective treatment. Although the extent to which mild hypertension should be aggressively treated remains controversial, there can be little doubt that the failure to detect so many hypertensives is a cause for genuine concern. Left untreated, high blood pressure can have serious consequences; it is associated with an increased risk of heart failure and stroke, as well as damage to the kidneys and eyes. In statistical terms, the life expectancy of a 35-year-old man with an untreated diastolic pressure of 100 mm Hg is reduced by 16 years. Given that hypertension is a potent coronary risk factor, it seems odd that so many cases go undetected. Perhaps the largest single reason for this failure to diagnose the condition is that in all but the most severe cases it is virtually asymptomatic, the sufferer rarely being aware that anything is amiss. However, the problem is not confined to one of diagnosis. Even when the condition is detected, treatment frequently has to be undertaken on a long-term basis and, unfortunately, most pharmacological treatments are accompanied by adverse side effects. This combination of adverse side effects and an asymptomatic condition poses major problems of compliance and accounts for many of the failures to control diagnosed cases. The problem of compliance will be discussed in more detail at the end of the chapter.

Prevalence of Hypertension

Even were the whole population to be screened, it would still not be possible to state the prevalence of hypertension in other than an arbitrary manner, there being no absolute cut-off point above which blood pressure ceases to be normal. Moreover, a number of screening programmes have shown that pressure increases steadily with age (Figure 4.1). Consequently, hypertension is defined in terms of what is normal for a given age group. For example, in the industrialised Western world a value in excess of 140/90 mm Hg would be regarded as high in a 20-year-old, whereas at 75 years hypertension is defined as a value in excess of 170/105 mm Hg. Using these norms, a number of surveys show some ten per cent of the male population within the UK to be hypertensive.

Figure 4.1: Mean Systolic and Diastolic Pressures in two Welsh Populations by Age, and Sex. The area of each square is inversely proportional to the standard error of the mean

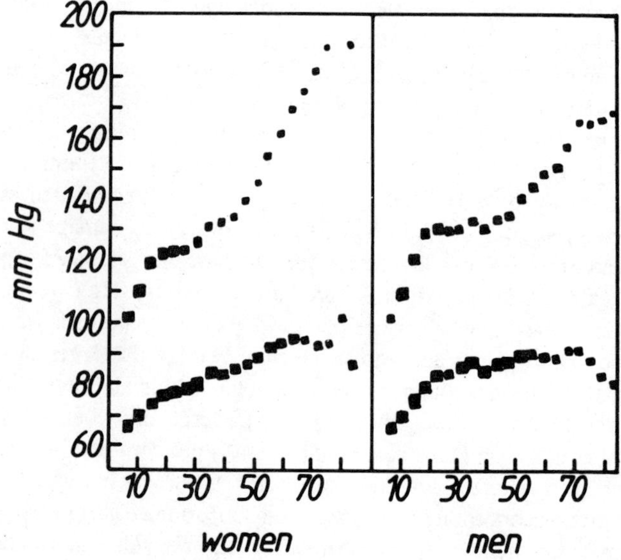

Source: 'The Hereditary Factor in Arterial Blood Pressure', W.E. Miall and P.D. Oldham, *British Medical Journal* (1963), *1*, 75–80.

At a purely intuitive level the data shown in Figure 4.1 come as no surprise. After all, as we get older our eyesight and hearing fade, muscle power decreases and our memory starts to let us down. Why then should blood pressure be spared the ravages of the ageing process? In fact raised blood pressure is not a necessary consequence of ageing, many individuals showing very little change in pressure with age. Moreover, as Figure 4.2 makes clear, cross-cultural studies yield very different outcomes to those shown in Figure 4.1.

Figure 4.2: Distributions of Systolic Blood Pressure Amongst Men in Selected Populations Showing the Stability of Pressure Level Over Age. ▲– – –▲, Highland Chileans (Cruz-Coke *et al.*, 1973); ■–·–·–■, Najafgarh of India (Padmauati *et al.*, 1959); ×——×, US aviators (Oberman *et al.*, 1976); ●– – – –●, Navajo Indians, USA (Fulmer and Roberts, 1973)

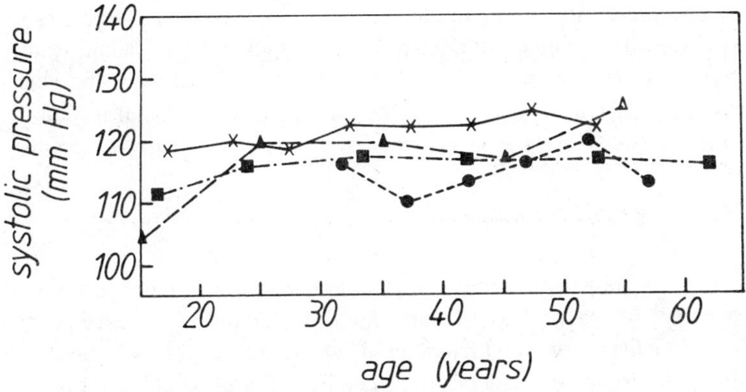

Source: *Psychological Factors in Cardiovascular Disorders*, A. Steptoe (Academic Press, London, 1981), Figure 3.2.

It is of course arguable that all that cross-cultural comparisons reveal are genetic differences between the different populations. However, in the case of blood pressure this seems not to be so. As Steptoe (1981) has pointed out:

> Such groups are not protected genetically from pressure increase, since under different environmental conditions the conventional pattern is followed. Thus the lowland relatives of the Chilean group plotted in Figure (4.2) start at the same modest pressure in youth, but typically exhibit marked rises with age (Cruz-Coke *et al.* 1973).

This is an important observation, for at the very least it points to the role of environmental factors in determining hypertension. Indeed it is not uncommon for such findings to be cited as proof that psychological stress *causes* hypertension. Briefly, the argument goes as follows. Being uprooted from the tranquil ordered life of a rural community with its close family ties and deposited in a noisy, high-powered and largely anonymous modern city represents a severe psychological trauma. This is sufficient to produce increased blood pressure, which is maintained by the stresses of living in this new, alien environment. Although this is an appealing argument it is almost certainly an oversimplification, for changes that follow migration are notoriously difficult to interpret. At the very outset, it is unlikely to be a random sample of the population that moves away to the 'big city'. Moreover, on arrival they are liable to encounter differences in diet, levels of exercise and a whole range of factors that, though unrelated to psychological stress, could lead to hypertension. For, whatever else we still have to learn about the causes of hypertension, it is clear that they are complex and multifarious.

The Causes of Hypertension

Normally, healthy individuals are able to tolerate changes in posture, activity, intake or loss of salt and fluid, ambient temperature and emotional stress without catastrophic changes in blood pressure. (This is not to argue that under certain conditions large temporary changes do not occur. For example, raised levels occur during orgasm, and Julian and Matthews (1981) report that students have shown pressures as high as 230/130 mm Hg in the stress of an oral examination!) The complexity of the regulatory mechanisms is illustrated in an account given by Gross and Dietz (1979). This begins with the following proposition:

> In the most simplified way, blood pressure is defined according to Ohm's law as voltage which is equal to the product of current multiplied by resistance. If applied to haemodynamics, current stands for flow, which is usually determined by cardiac output, thus resulting in the formula:
> Blood pressure = cardiac output × total peripheral resistance

However, it soon becomes apparent that this is a deceptively simplified account. As Figure 4.3 makes clear, a wide range of factors exist in a dynamic relationship in order to maintain blood pressure within normal limits. Indeed, so complex is this system that in only approximately ten per cent of cases of hypertension is it possible to establish a cause. In these cases the condition is secondary to known pathology, the vast majority of which involves renal disease. In the remaining 90 per cent (described as essential hypertension) the aetiology remains obscure. Given this failure to account for up to nine out of ten cases of hypertension

Figure 4.3: Various Factors Influencing the Components 'Cardiac Output (Flow)' and 'Vascular Resistance' and the Controlling Systems Responsible for the Regulation of Blood Pressure

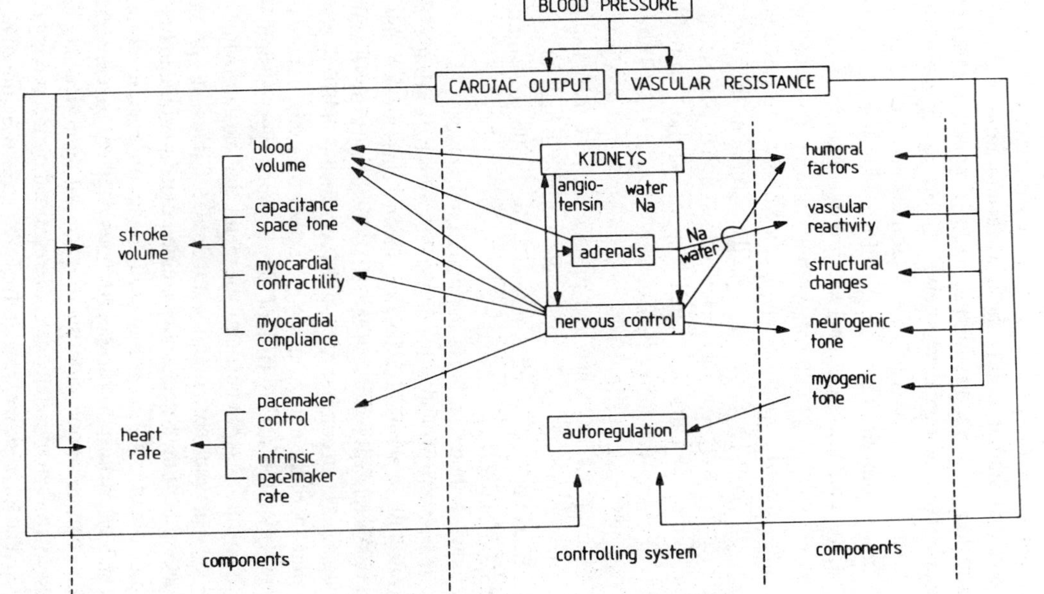

Source: 'The Significance of Volume and Cardiac Output in the Pathogenesis of Hypertension', F. Gross and R. Dietz, *Clinical Science* (1979), *57*, 59s–67s, Figure 1. Reprinted by permission of the Biochemical Society, London.

in organic terms, and given also the crucial role of the ANS in maintaining blood pressure, it is not surprising that the part played by psychological stress should have come under close scrutiny.

Stress and Essential Hypertension

According to Steptoe (1981) the medical literature of the last century contains numerous reports linking essential hypertension with various estimates of psychological well-being. Unfortunately, these early studies were often based upon very small samples and lacked even the most rudimentary controls. They are, therefore, of little more than historical interest, but emphasise the long-standing recognition of the part played by psychological factors in the aetiology and/or maintenance of raised blood pressure. Moreover, although contemporary research is less open to criticism on methodological grounds, it remains the case that while several studies point to a link between stress and hypertension, none has shown them to be causally related. One of the most widely quoted of these studies was conducted by Cobb and Rose (1973). They examined the relationship between raised blood pressure and occupational stress by comparing the incidence and prevalence of hypertension in three groups of workers; air traffic controllers working in high- and low-density traffic areas and second class airmen. The results are summarised in Tables 4.1 and 4.2.

Reviewing their findings, the authors concluded: 'In summary, it seems reasonably probable that air traffic controllers are at a higher risk of developing hypertension than are second class airmen, and that this added risk is related to working at high traffic density towers and centers.' Although this is an admirably cautious conclusion, it barely goes beyond a restatement of the data. Can we go further than this and use these data to argue that the added risk of developing hypertension is due to psychological stress? Superficially it seems that we can. After all, given that a mistake can cost literally hundreds of lives, it appears almost axiomatic that of the three groups studied those working in towers serving high-density traffic would suffer the greatest levels of stress. However, as was argued in the previous chapter, psychological stress is not to be understood in terms of stimulus alone. Rather, it must be viewed as a subjective state that is determined by the perceptions of the individual concerned. Unfortunately, Cobb and Rose offered no evidence to support their assumption that those controllers working in towers serving high-density traffic found it a highly stressful experience.

Table 4.1: Annual Incidence Rates for Hypertension Per 1,000 Men Employed as Air Traffic Controllers or Second Class Airmen

Age group (years)	Air traffic controllers	Second class airmen	
20–24	—*	—	
25–29	2	1	
30–34	2	1	
35–39	10	1	
40–44	6	—	
45–49	11	4	
50+	15	4	
		Age	
		< 40	40+
Observed (O)	28.0	16.0	12.0
Expected (E)†	5.1	2.4	2.7
O/E	5.6	6.6	4.4

Note: *The figures have been rounded off to prevent any suggestion that they are more reliable than is the case. The conventions of the National Center for Health Statistics have been used: —, the value is zero; 0, the value is greater than zero but less than 0.5.

† Expected on the basis of multiplication of the age-specific rates for second class airmen by the relevant air traffic controller populations and summing across age groups. Statistical significance is examined by the χ^2 test, assuming that the expected values represent population estimates.
Source: 'Hypertension, Peptic Ulcer, and Diabetes in Air Traffic Controllers', S. Cobb and R.M. Rose, *JAMA* (1973), *224* (4), 489–92, Table 2.

Table 4.2: Prevalence Rates Per 1,000 Air Traffic Controllers for Hypertension by Stress Level, as Measured by Traffic Density

Age group (years)	High stress	Low stress
20–24	—*	—
25–29	4	—
30–34	6	2
35–39	12	10
40–44	26	4
45–49	51	32
50+	—	36
Observed	22.0	. . .
Expected†	13.7	. . .
O/E	1.6	. . .

Note: *See footnote to Table 4.1.

† Expected on the basis of multiplication of the age-specific rates for the low-stress groups by the relevant populations for the high-stress group and summing across age groups.
Source: 'Hypertension, Peptic Ulcer, and Diabetes in Air Traffic Controllers', S. Cobb and R.M. Rose, *JAMA* (1973), 224 (4), 489–92, Table 3.

Consequently, their data cannot be said to show unequivocally that psychological stress leads to hypertension. At the same time, it would be foolish to disregard their findings, especially in the light of a study described by House, Wells, Landerman, McMichael and Kaplan (1979).

They too examined the relation between hypertension and occupational stress amongst the non-managerial work force of an American chemical factory. Data were obtained from 1809 workers (all white men) whose occupations ranged from skilled craftsmen to unskilled labourers. What makes this study exceptional is that levels of stress associated with various occupations were not assumed by the experimenters. Rather, questionnaires were employed that allowed each worker to report his own perception of the level of stress associated with five types of job pressure. These were described by the authors as follows:

> (1) *responsibility pressure* — having too much responsibility for people, process, or products and insufficient human or material assistance; (2) *quality concern* — having concern about not being able to do as good work as one could or should; (3) *role conflict* — receiving ambiguous and/or conflicting expectations from others at work; (4) *job vs. nonjob conflict* — feeling that the job interferes with non-work (e.g. family) life; and (5) *work load* — reporting a large quantity of work and frequent time pressure.

As well as cardiovascular symptoms, the study was concerned with a wide range of medical conditions of which only the former will be reported here. Data relating to hypertension were restricted to 353 subjects and, according to the authors, showed the following: '. . . clear evidence of associations between perceived stress and blood pressure and other medically assessed CHD [coronary heart disease] risk factors, after controlling a range of confounding variables.' This conclusion was based on the observation that three stress variables predicted the prevalence of hypertension. Thus, in the case of role conflict, the estimated prevalence was found to be 4.9 per cent for low levels of associated stress compared with 27.5 per cent for high levels. (For work load and job vs. non-job conflict the corresponding values were 3.2 per cent vs. 13.3 per cent, and 7.2 per cent vs. 16.5 per cent, respectively.)

Again we have evidence linking stress with hypertension, this time from a study that was designed to take account of the subjective nature of psychological stress. Yet as House *et al.* were only too aware, their results fell some way short of demonstrating that stress *causes* essential hypertension. Summarising their findings they concluded:

> Another problem, hardly unique to this study, deserves brief mention. We are interested in the effect of stress on health, but the cross-sectional nature of our data makes it impossible to establish firmly that the associations observed . . . are produced by the causal impact of stress on health rather than the reverse, or by some pattern of reciprocal causation in both directions.

This conclusion sums up the present position admirably. While experiments on laboratory animals (e.g. Folkow and Rubinstein, p. 7) and large-scale surveys of human populations indicate a link between stress and chronic raised blood pressure, a causal relationship has yet to be established. Nevertheless, the evidence linking the two is sufficiently compelling to justify asking whether psychological methods have a part to play in treating essential hypertension — at least when the condition is of relatively recent onset. It is necessary to add this last qualification, for as can be inferred from Figure 4.3, long-term hypertension may lead to structural changes in the vasculature that in turn maintain raised blood pressure. Clearly there are no *a priori* grounds for assuming that structural changes of this nature would respond to psychological intervention.

Biofeedback and Hypertension

Strictly speaking, the assumptions underlying direct feedback training make it irrelevant whether or not stress played any part in the aetiology of the patient's condition. All that is necessary is that he be given the appropriate feedback in order to bring his blood pressure under voluntary control by a process of trial and error learning. Despite sounding far too good to be true, some of the earliest research did indeed appear to show that this was the case. For example, Miller (1972) described how a single patient was taught both to raise and lower her blood pressure using the constant cuff method (p. 14). The baseline was adequate, being composed of 26 sessions spread over six weeks, followed by 37 training sessions in three months. By the end of training she had not only learned to lower her diastolic pressure from 97 mm Hg to 76 mm Hg, but had also been able to abandon anti-hypertensive medication. It is easy to see why this single case study should have caused a stir. A treatment that both reduces diastolic pressure by 21 mm Hg and frees the patient from a lifetime of taking drugs would by any standard represent a major advance. Unfortunately, no follow-up data were reported and, more importantly, this initial success seems to have failed the test of replicability, so that in 1979 Blanchard wrote: 'Miller, after his initial glowing success . . . has reported on more than 20 successive failures to obtain clinically meaningful changes in the blood pressure of hypertensives with his feedback system.' Although Miller's early work was to prove the high point in the application of direct feedback, a number of studies were subsequently reported in which more modest successes were achieved. One of the most widely quoted of these was described by Kristt and Engel (1975).

Following a five- to seven-week baseline period, five patients entered a three-week training programme in which they learned to raise and lower their blood pressures, aided by direct feedback of systolic pressure. There then followed a three-month phase during which they were required to practise the 'blood pressure lowering maneuver' and make daily records of their performances. Throughout the duration of the study patients monitored their own blood pressures four times daily. Unfortunately, complete data were obtained for only four subjects. These are shown in Table 4.3.

Table 4.3: Comparison of Pre- and Post-training Blood Pressures (mm Hg)

Patient	Pre-training SBP*	Pre-training DBP*	Post-training SBP	Post-training DBP	Decline SBP	Decline DBP	% Decline SBP	% Decline DBP
1	151	78	142	76	9†	2	5.9	2.6
2	171	93	162	92	9†	1	5.3	1.1
3	160	90	141	83	19†	7†	11.9	7.8
4	168	117	132	97	36†	20†	21.4	17.1
Mean	162.5	94.5	144.2	87.0	18.2	7.5	11.1	7.2

Note: *SBP, systolic blood pressure; DBP, diastolic blood pressure.
† $P < .01$.
Source: 'Learned Control of Blood Pressure in Patients with High Blood Pressure', D.A. Kristt and B.T. Engel, *Circulation* (1975), *51*, 370–8, Table 6.

It is interesting to observe how closely the performance of patient 4 resembles that of the single patient described by Miller (1972). Not only did her diastolic pressure fall by 20 mm Hg, but the authors reported an accompanying decrease in medication. Overall, the outcome was much less spectacular, especially in the case of patients 1 and 2, whose diastolic pressures hardly changed at all. Nevertheless, in so far as the reductions that had been achieved by the end of training were maintained at follow up, these findings were an advance on any that had been published up to that time, and the authors saw fit to claim:

> The results of this study confirm and substantially extend the findings of Benson *et al.* that patients with high blood pressure can learn to lower their SBP while in the laboratory . . . Furthermore, the results of this study show that the skills learned in the laboratory persist for at least three months.

In view of the need to show that the effects of treatment carry over into everyday life, it is hardly surprising that these findings were seen by many as yet further proof of the clinical efficacy of direct feedback. It is ironic, therefore, that they should have led other writers to ask whether the favourable outcomes owed more to the effects of non-specific factors than to direct feedback *per se*.

As well as being one of the first studies to present follow-up data, this was also one of the first in which patients were required to take an active part in treatment throughout the follow-up period. Commenting on this aspect of the study, Blanchard (1979) wrote the following:

> My own speculation (admittedly without supporting data) is that the key to the success of Kristt and Engel's approach lay in training patients in the hospital 'to use a BP cuff to perform a BP lowering maneuver' . . . Epstein and I . . . have argued elsewhere that such self-control training followed by self-management techniques is probably the optimum strategy for controlling a tonic physiologic response.

So far the concept of self-management has not been discussed, although throughout the course of this book it will become increasingly obvious that the extent to which patients actively participate in their treatment significantly influences the outcome. Unfortunately, the study conducted by Kristt and Engel lacked the controls necessary to determine the extent to which self-monitoring contributed to the overall success of their programme. However, the fact that it had some effect can be gleaned from the observation that readings made by patients 1, 2 and 3 indicated that they were able to reduce systolic pressure by an average of 14.7 mm Hg, compared with only 8.3 mm Hg when pressures were recorded by a staff physician. It is entirely possible, therefore, that some of the mean decline of 18.2/7.5 mm Hg shown in Table 4.3 was attributable to factors associated with self-monitoring rather than to direct feedback training. While this interpretation is speculative it accords with the findings of a much more sophisticated study conducted by Frankel, Patel, Horwitz, Friedewald and Gaarder (1978).

They compared the effects of a treatment package comprising diastolic feedback, EMG feedback and relaxation training, with those of sham blood pressure feedback, and no treatment. The baseline extended over a period of eight weeks, followed by a 16-week treatment phase. Thereafter, seven patients drawn from the two control conditions underwent active treatment. The design of this study was especially praiseworthy in that blood pressures were measured 'blind' and readings were taken before training (or on a different day), away from the training laboratory. The results are shown in Table 4.4.

Table 4.4: Blood Pressure Measurements During the Final Six-Weekly Visits to the Clinic in the Baseline and Experimental Periods

		Supine		Standing	
Group*	Observation period	SBP	DBP	SBP	DBP
AT primary (n = 7)	Baseline	148 (4.9)	95 (1.9)	147 (6.0)	102 (2.6)
	Active Rx	151 (6.4)	96 (3.0)	149 (7.6)	103 (3.0)
AT cross-over (n = 7)	Sham or no Rx	154 (6.0)	94 (1.1)	156 (7.9)	103 (1.5)
	Active Rx	151 (6.4)	91 (1.5)	157 (7.9)	102 (3.0)
ST (n = 7)	Baseline	150 (7.6)	95 (1.9)	150 (9.8)	102 (1.9)
	Sham Rx	149 (6.8)	93 (1.9)	149 (7.6)	101 (1.5)
NT (n = 8)	Baseline	147 (4.6)	94 (0.7)	154 (7.1)	103 (1.4)
	No Rx	152 (4.6)	95 (1.1)	157 (4.9)	105 (1.1)

Note: Data are mean (S.E.) mm Hg.
*AT, active treatment; ST, sham treatment; NT, no treatment. Note that for AT cross-over patients, the active treatment data are compared to the data of the immediately preceding final six weeks of the sham- or no-treatment protocol rather than to that of the baseline period.
Source: 'Treatment of Hypertension with Biofeedback and Relaxation Techniques', B.L. Frankel, D.J. Patel, D. Horwitz, W.T. Friedewald and K.R. Gaarder, *Psychosomatic Medicine* (1978), *40* (4), 276–93, Table 2.

Bearing in mind that this is one of the best designed and most tightly controlled studies to be found in the literature these results can only be described as disappointing. Changes were minimal, with no evidence whatsoever of a treatment effect. Data gathered in the laboratory yielded a similar outcome; the average decreases following active and sham treatment being 3/2 mm Hg and 5/2 mm Hg, respectively.

However, amidst these uniformly negative findings one patient was described who did appear to derive lasting benefit. Having shown only inconsequential changes with sham feedback, her condition improved significantly when switched to the active condition. More importantly, her improvement was maintained during the following 18 months. By the end of this period her supine and standing levels were 124/81 mm Hg and 119/84 mm Hg, respectively, compared with baseline values of 145/95 mm Hg and 132/94 mm Hg. This is not the first example of atypical improvement that has been encountered in this brief review. Table 4.3 illustrates one such individual (patient 4), and, judged in terms of immediate outcome, the single case described by Miller (1972) represents another. However, despite these observations it has to be concluded that the early promise of direct feedback has not been fulfilled, and its clinical efficacy remains unproven. The present position was illustrated by findings described by Blanchard (1979). Thirty hypertensive patients were randomly assigned to one of three conditions; direct feedback, frontalis EMG feedback, and unassisted relaxation. After four 40-minute baseline sessions, members of each group attended 12 treatment sessions spread over six to ten weeks during which time they were also required to practise at home what they had learned in the laboratory. Describing the outcome, Blanchard reported the following:

> Results show *no* significant differential effects of treatment and very small treatment effects per se. Average reduction of systolic blood pressure from pretreatment baseline to the first 2 weeks of follow-up was 6.5 mm. mercury; for diastolic blood pressure it was 2.0 mm. mercury. Thus blood pressure feedback and frontalis EMG feedback were no more effective than mere instructions to relax and try to lower blood pressure in the laboratory.

Commenting on how his own work had failed the test of replicability Blanchard concluded:

> At this point we have abandoned direct feedback of blood pressure as a psychological treatment strategy for hypertension and have moved to the exploring of some of the different relaxation techniques.

It is to an evaluation of these techniques that the next section is devoted.

Relaxation Training and Hypertension

It will be apparent that different assumptions underlie the application of direct feedback and relaxation training. While the former assumes the ability to gain control of a specific autonomic response, the latter is based on the premise that it is possible to produce a generalised reduction in SNS output, one consequence of which is a reduction in blood pressure. Reference was made in Chapter 2 to the fact that some of the earliest attempts to subject these assumptions to empirical verification were conducted by Benson and his associates (see Benson *et al.*, 1977). Typical of their work are two studies in which, following a six-week baseline period, both medicated and non-medicated patients underwent training in TM. The outcome is shown in Table 4.5.

Table 4.5: Changes in Blood Pressure of Medicated and Non-Medicated Hypertensives Following Training in TM

	Medication (*n* = 14)		Non-medication (*n* = 22)	
	SBP	DBP	SBP	DBP
Before	145.6	91.9	146.5	94.6
After	135.0	87.0	139.5	90.8
Decrease	10.6	4.9	7.0	3.8

Source: Extracted from 'Historical and Clinical Considerations of the Relaxation Response', H. Benson, J.B. Kotch, K.D. Crassweller and M.M. Greenwood, *American Scientist* (1977), *65*, 441–5.

By the end of training, both groups exhibited small, statistically significant decreases in blood pressure which, given the extended baseline period, were unlikely to be contaminated by habituation phenomena. Unfortunately, other aspects of the trial were less satisfactory and make interpretation of the results difficult. In particular, the failure to provide long-term follow-up data was a crucial omission. Without this information it is impossible to judge whether training in TM resulted in a small but stable effect (that may or may not have been specific to meditation) or a transitory placebo response. While, therefore, these results justified continued research in this area, they did not in themselves offer conclusive proof that TM possesses long-lasting anti-hypertensive properties.

The possibility that the effects attributed by Benson and his associates to TM might in fact be transitory received a measure of support from a study reported by Pollack, Case, Weber and Laragh (1977). They investigated the long-term effects of TM on a group of 20 hypertensive patients, nine of whom were receiving medication. After a three-month baseline period, pressures were measured for six months, readings being taken at least one hour after the cessation of meditation. The results are summarised in Figure 4.4.

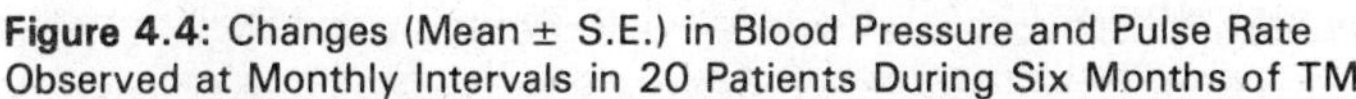

Figure 4.4: Changes (Mean ± S.E.) in Blood Pressure and Pulse Rate Observed at Monthly Intervals in 20 Patients During Six Months of TM

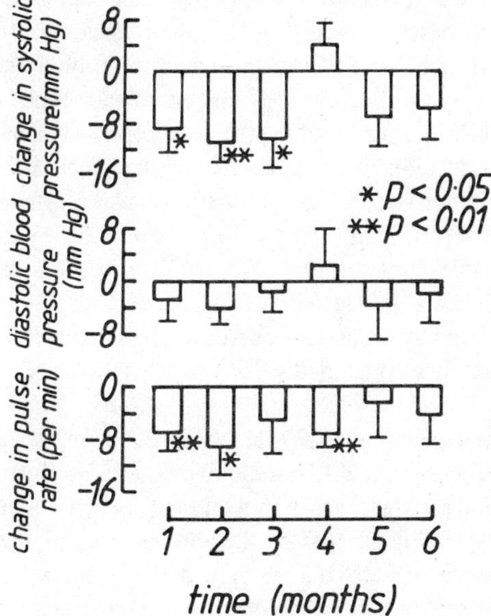

Source: 'Limitations of Transcendental Meditation in the Treatment of Essential Hypertension', A.A. Pollack, D.B. Case, M.A. Weber and J.H. Laragh, *Lancet* (1977), *1*, 71–3, Figure 1.

Although early in the trial there were significant decreases in systolic (but not diastolic) pressures and pulse rates, these improvements were no longer present by the fifth month. Furthermore, biochemical investigations showed that plasma renin activity did not change throughout the period of the study. As well as these objective measures, a subjective report was obtained from each participant towards the end of the trial. A majority claimed that they had 'an improved sense of physical well-being as well as a more relaxed and positive mental state.' The authors concluded that:

> . . . while the general feeling of wellbeing experienced by most patients may provide a useful adjunct to conventional treatments, it is unlikely that transcendental meditation contributes directly towards the lowering of blood pressure.

A somewhat different outcome was reported by Blackwell, Hanenson,

Bloomfield, Magenheim, Gartside, Nidich, Robinson and Zigler (1976). They also studied the long-term effects of TM, using as subjects a group of seven hypertensive patients, all of whom had their condition stabilised on medication. A baseline period of up to ten weeks was followed by a 12-week programme of TM, during which time blood pressures were measured weekly by medical staff and up to four times daily by the patient. By the last four weeks of the trial, six patients had undergone statistically significant reductions in blood pressure when measured at home (mean change for group, 7.5/6.1 mm Hg) compared with four when measured at the clinic (mean change for group, 4.2/1.6 mm Hg). However, a six-month follow-up showed that only two patients had maintained their improvement, although five of the six exhibited reduced levels of anxiety, as measured by a standard clinical questionnaire. Discussing their results, the authors concluded:

> . . . Our experience suggests that most subjects derive some psychological benefit from T.M.; a minority may also show sustained benefit in blood pressure, some show transitory benefit, and others none . . . The psychological benefit, the absence of drug side-effects, and the experience of self-control may make T.M. an appealing therapeutic adjunct for some but not all hypertensive individuals.

Because they give further credence to the suggestion that non-specific factors play an important part in therapies based upon psychological principles, two aspects of this study are worthy of special note. First, individual subjects differed markedly in their response to treatment and second, reductions in pressures measured by patients in their own homes were significantly greater than those recorded in the clinic by medical staff.

Overall, these studies indicate that simple programmes of relaxation training or meditation do not offer a realistic alternative to conventional treatments for hypertension. When favourable outcomes were reported they were usually too small to have clinical relevance and were often transitory and difficult to attribute to the specific effects of relaxation. To this extent the position is very similar to that of direct feedback. Indeed, were the findings described thus far the best that could be said in favour of the two treatments, it is unlikely that interest in them would have been maintained. However, there is evidence to suggest that relaxation training and biofeedback can be combined with other forms of psychological intervention to yield a treatment package of real clinical value.

Combined Behavioural Treatment of Essential Hypertension

Although investigations into the combined effects of psychological treatments are now being conducted in a number of centres, by far the most promising are those carried out by Chandra Patel and her associates. In one of her most widely quoted studies a group of 34 hypertensive patients underwent treatment which combined biofeedback, meditation and what is best described as stress management training. Because this study illustrates so many of the points that are central to this discussion, the authors' own description of their methodology is reproduced in full (Patel and North, 1975).

> All patients attended on three separate days to provide baseline B.P. The patients were then assigned at random to . . . (meditation) . . . and bio-feedback or general relaxation. Pressures were taken in the standing, sitting, and supine positions, and repeated after half an hour's rest. A random-zero sphygmomanometer was used.
>
> All blood pressures (fifth phase) were measured 'blind' by the practice nurse. Patients were asked not to change their drug therapy during the trial. The first phase of the trial consisted of twelve sessions, two a week for six weeks, B.P. being again taken in the standing, sitting and supine positions before and after the half-hour session. Active treatment consisted, first, of meetings during which the patients were shown films and slides about hypertension, the different ways in which emotion affects bodily processes, the physiology of relaxation, the concept of bio-feedback, self-control, and so on. They discussed their queries and problems freely. The rapport created between doctor and patients as well as that between the patients themselves greatly helped to strengthen the programme and ensure cooperation. Next, during individual training, patients lay on a couch or a reclining chair with legs apart and slightly rotated at the hip joint, arms by the side, shoulders flat, jaw limp, and eyes lightly closed; the head was raised to a comfortable position, but they were encouraged to lie as flat as possible. They were first asked to breathe slowly and rhythmically. Next, they were instructed to go over the different parts of the body mentally in a regular sequence, allowing each part to relax completely. Patients were instructed verbally on this methodical relaxation for ten to twelve minutes, and were then encouraged to remain relaxed for the rest of the session. Once the patient had mastered the method of relaxation, a type of transcendental meditation was introduced. Throughout the session the patient was

> connected to one of two bio-feedback instruments giving a continuous audio-signal whose pitch fell as the patient relaxed. Generally the instrument measuring electrical resistance of the skin . . . was used for the first few sessions followed by an electromyograph . . . This confirmation of relaxation was intended to encourage further relaxation. Patients were also encouraged verbally, and shown their B.P. records; they were also instructed to practise relaxation and meditation twice a day, and gradually to try to incorporate these habits into routine activities, the methods depending on individual circumstances. For example, each patient had a red disc attached to his watch to remind him to relax whenever he looked at the time, and some were told to relax before answering the telephone. Patients in the control group attended for the same number of sessions and for the same length of time. However, they were asked to relax on the couch or the reclining chair without being given specific instruction, and they were not connected to bio-feedback instruments.
>
> At the end of the trial all patients were followed up every two weeks for three months.
>
> In case the observed difference had been due to unknown factors not eliminated by randomisation we then treated the control group with . . . (meditation) . . . and bio-feedback therapy.
>
> Phase 2 of the trial began two months after the end of the follow-up for phase 1. The previous control group, now the new treatment group, attended for twelve treatment sessions as in phase 1, . . . The previously treated group were used as controls, but were seen only at the beginning and end of this phase to give B.P. readings for comparison. Only one initial and one follow-up reading was made in each group.

The outcome of the trial is shown in Figure 4.5.

In summary the results showed the following:

(1) By the end of phase 1, patients receiving treatment had undergone a mean decrease in blood pressure of 26.1/15.2 mm Hg compared with a decrease of only 8.9/4.2 mm Hg by the controls.

(2) Not all treated patients obtained the same benefit. Decreases in systolic and diastolic pressures ranged from 60 to 7 mm Hg and 30 to 1 mm Hg, respectively.

(3) Improvement was not transitory; patients treated during phase 1 had maintained their improvement by the onset of phase 2, even though no further treatment was given during the intervening five months.

(4) By the end of phase 2 the original control group was showing a

Figure 4.5: Results of Randomised Controlled Trial (Patel and North, 1975)

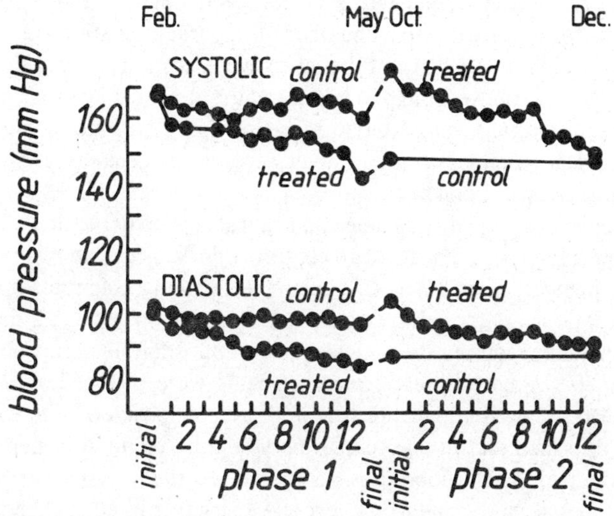

Source: 'Biofeedback-Aided Relaxation and Meditation in the Management of Hypertension', C.H. Patel, *Biofeedback and Self-Regulation* (1977), 2 (1), 1–41, Figure 2.

mean reduction in pressure almost identical to that of the group treated in phase 1.

Remembering how the effects of direct feedback training tended to disappear as the design of clinical trials improved, it is worth noting that Patel's work is generally accepted as being amongst the more sophisticated to be found in the literature. For example, the data shown in Figure 4.5 are based upon multiple readings that were taken *before* each training session by a nurse who was unaware whether the patient was receiving treatment or acting as a control. However, this is not to say that the design of the study was ideal. In particular, the lack of adequate baseline data is a potential source of bias that could have led to the effects of treatment being overestimated, although the performance of the original control group goes some way to counter this criticism. Not only did they fail to show the same decreases in pressures as those being treated during phase 1, by the time they began treatment in phase 2 they would have had ample time to become familiar with the measurement procedures. While, therefore, the provision of stable baseline data remains a paramount requirement in this kind of study, in this case it is arguable that a longer baseline period would not have significantly altered the outcome.

Although the data presented by Patel and North highlighted the potential of this form of treatment, a number of important questions remained unanswered. Not the least of these was whether its anti-hypertensive properties were robust enough to withstand the effects of factors known to be associated with raised blood pressure. In 1975, Patel published additional data which suggested that they were, at least as far as physically induced stress was concerned.

Before entering the programme and again at the end of the first phase, 32 patients (16 experimental and 16 control) were subjected to two forms of experimentally induced stress; an exercise test and a cold pressor test. The former consisted of climbing on and off a nine-inch step 25 times, while the latter required the patient to sit with his left hand in water at 4°C for 80 seconds. Baseline measurements were obtained after the patient had spent 20 minutes resting in the supine position, whereupon he was informed that in one minute he would be required to perform one of the two tasks. Blood pressures were recorded; during this one-minute interval, at the end of the test and every five minutes thereafter until they had reached their initial levels, providing that this recovery time did not exceed 40 minutes. The results are summarised in Tables 4.6 and 4.7.

Table 4.6: Absolute BP Value and Percentage of Rise: Exercise Test

Group	Initial BP	BP after test	Actual rise in BP	Percentage of rise
Treatment (*n* = 16)				
Pre-test				
Systolic	160.75	188.18	27.43	17.1
Diastolic	96.7	105.95	9.25	9.56
Post-test				
Systolic	148.1	166.91	18.81	12.7
Diastolic	86.3	90.42	4.12	4.7
Control (*n* = 16)				
Pre-test				
Systolic	161.8	191.42	29.62	18.3
Diastolic	96.75	100.56	3.81	3.9
Post-test				
Systolic	155.25	182.12	26.87	17.3
Diastolic	94.8	102.11	7.31	7.7

Source: 'Biofeedback-Aided Relaxation and Meditation in the Management of Hypertension', C.H. Patel, *Biofeedback and Self-Regulation* (1977), *2* (1), 1-41, Table 10.

Table 4.7: Absolute BP Value and Percentage of Rise: Cold Pressor Test

Group	Initial BP	BP after test	Actual rise in BP	Percentage of rise
Treatment (*n* = 16)				
Pre-test				
Systolic	153.1	172.41	19.31	12.6
Diastolic	92.5	99.81	7.31	7.9
Post-test				
Systolic	143.4	154.15	10.75	7.5
Diastolic	84.1	86.29	2.19	2.6
Control (*n* = 16)				
Pre-test				
Systolic	156.75	179.06	22.31	14.2
Diastolic	94.75	100.81	6.06	6.4
Post-test				
Systolic	151.25	185.06	33.81	22.35
Diastolic	92.5	107.06	14.56	15.74

Source: 'Biofeedback-Aided Relaxation and Meditation in the Management of Hypertension', C.H. Patel, *Biofeedback and Self-Regulation* (1977), *2* (1), 1–41, Table 11.

By demonstrating that treatment reduced the effects of the two stressors, these data undoubtedly gave added significance to the findings described by Patel and North. It might seem pedantic, therefore, to sound a note of caution about what was a necessary piece of research. However, it should be remembered that the term stress is used to cover a wide range of phenomena that can influence cardiovascular activity. While this study revealed that behavioural methods can combat the effects of one type of experimentally induced physical stress, it tells us nothing about its effectiveness in coping with the environmental and psycho-social pressures of everyday life. Certainly the tasks employed by Patel bore little resemblance to the five categories of occupational stress described by House *et al.* (1979). Clearly, therefore, the extent to which the effects described by Patel generalise into everyday life remains a crucial issue to which we shall return shortly. First, however, it is appropriate to consider one other study reported by Patel and her group.

Patel, Marmot and Terry (1981) examined the effects of the behavioural programme on a group of 99 individuals who, on screening, were found to exhibit two or more of the following coronary risk factors: serum cholesterol concentration ⩾ 6.3 mmol/l, blood pressure ⩾ 140/90 mm Hg, cigarette consumption ⩾ 10 per day. Training lasted eight weeks and there was an eight-month follow-up session. (Subsequently four-year follow-up data were reported, see p. 233.) It should be noted that, unlike the subjects in the two previous studies, none of the participants was undergoing drug therapy, thus ruling out the possibility that improvement resulted from an undetected increase in compliance with medication during the training programme (Carroll, 1984). By the end of training, the treated group had undergone a mean decline in blood pressure of 13.8/7.2 mm Hg compared with 4.0/1.4 mm Hg for the controls. At the eight-month follow-up these values were 15.3/6.8 mm Hg and 6.1/0.6 mm Hg, respectively. A similar analysis carried out on a smaller group whose initial pressures were at least 140/90 mm Hg showed that the treatment led to an initial decrease of 19.6/10.6 mm Hg and 22.4/11.5 mm Hg at eight months. Equivalent figures for controls were 8.2/3.6 mm Hg and 11.4/2.7 mm Hg. As well as measuring changes in blood pressure, a number of biochemical parameters were also investigated. This revealed that by the end of training the treated group had undergone a greater reduction in plasma concentrations of renin and aldosterone. At this stage, changes in aldosterone concentration in the treated group were significantly correlated with changes in both systolic and diastolic pressures. However, this relation had disappeared at eight months. Changes in pressure and plasma renin activity were not correlated in either group at any stage of the trial.

Without doubt, these three studies produced outcomes far more successful than any that had hitherto been attributed to the behavioural techniques. Not only did they show reductions in blood pressure large enough to be of clinical relevance, but these changes appeared to be relatively stable over time and resistant to the challenge of experimentally induced stress. What is particularly interesting is the extent to which each of the three studies complements the findings of the other two. This is in sharp contrast to the studies of direct feedback reviewed earlier, where the problem of replication was to prove such an obstacle both to research and clinical application. Usually the scientific community requires that replication should originate from an independent source, and in this respect Patel has not been well served by her peers. The literature contains very few attempts to replicate her work, although one report has been published that confirms some of her findings.

McGrady, Yonker, Tan, Fine and Woerner (1981) investigated the effects of combined EMG feedback and relaxation upon a group of 22 patients suffering from mild essential hypertension. As well as measuring blood pressure and muscle tension, changes in biochemical parameters known to be associated with hypertension were also assessed. Patients received relaxation training twice weekly for a period of eight weeks, during which time they were also required to practise the exercises twice

Table 4.8: Results of Duncan Multiple-Range Tests on Experimental and Control Pre-test and Post-test Means of Dependent Variables Yielding Significant Interaction *F* Ratios

Dependent variable	Group	Pre-test Mean	Pre-test S.D.	Post-test Mean	Post-test S.D.	Result
Systolic blood pressure	Experimental	144.41	19.83	133.18	16.77	Significant decrease
(mm Hg)	Control	140.67	19.36	139.25	14.29	No significant change
Diastolic blood pressure	Experimental	90.59	10.47	84.91	10.52	Significant decrease
(mm Hg)	Control	90.94	11.74	91.75	11.50	No significant change
EMG readings	Experimental	3.38	1.91	1.71	1.13	Significant decrease
(μ V)	Control	2.68	1.22	2.27	.69	No significant change
Urinary cortisol	Experimental	64.35	22.98	54.17	17.00	Significant decrease
(μg/24 hr)	Control	56.55	19.18	64.10	20.42	No significant change
Plasma aldosterone	Experimental	26.05	12.95	18.08	8.59	Significant decrease
(ng/100 ml)	Control	16.38	6.50	17.11	10.37	No significant change

Source: 'The Effect of Biofeedback-Assisted Relaxation Training on Blood Pressure and Selected Biochemical Parameters in Patients with Essential Hypertension', A.V. McGrady, R. Yonker, S.Y. Tan, T.H. Fine and M. Woerner, *Biofeedback and Self-Regulation* (1981), *6* (3), 343–53, Table 3.

daily for 15 minutes. The control group received no training at all, but simply attended the clinic each week in order to have their blood pressures recorded. Somewhat unusually, the baseline readings against which changes in pressures and muscle tension were measured were those taken on the patient's second visit to the clinic, while post-treatment measurements were those readings obtained on the final visit. The biochemical profile, which was measured at the commencement of the trial and at week 8 included levels of plasma and urinary cortisol, aldosterone, renin, catecholamines and vanillymandelic acid. The significant changes are shown in Table 4.8.

Overall, the outcome of this study matches those just described, the immediate post-trial decline in blood pressure of 11.2/5.7 mm Hg being very similar to that of 13.8/7.2 mm Hg reported by Patel *et al.* (1981). Moreover, in both cases the decrease in blood pressure was accompanied by decreased levels of plasma aldosterone. Once again, however, it is necessary to draw attention to methodological shortcomings; in this case the lack of an adequate baseline period and the failure to include follow-up data. It is also regrettable that, although serving as a much-needed replication study, this piece of work took us no nearer to answering the crucial question of whether the effects of treatment are maintained outside the laboratory. In the face of such consistently large laboratory effects, the last reservation might strike the reader as unduly pedantic. However, the study by Frankel *et al.* referred to earlier (p. 49) showed that small post-treatment decreases in blood pressure were reduced to almost zero when readings were made outside the training laboratory. Moreover, clinical experience convinces me that similar effects can occur even when treatment has been followed by substantial decreases.

The Problem of Generalisation

Towards the end of 1983, I was asked to treat a 46-year-old woman who for the previous three years had suffered from severe, incapacitating headache. Her medical history revealed that from the time of the birth of her second child in 1965 she had suffered from severe hypertension, with readings as high as 250/130 mm Hg being recorded. Despite intensive drug therapy the condition had never been fully controlled, and in the preceding five years she had suffered two strokes, the second of which coincided with the onset of headaches. Initially it was assumed that the two events were related. However, neurological investigations indicated that this was not so and the headaches were attributed to the effects of psychological stress. Bearing in mind the special need to reduce this patient's intake of analgesics, it was proposed that she should undergo a programme of EMG and GSR feedback-assisted relaxation training very similar to that described by Patel and North (1975). For example, as well as attending the clinic each week for a 30-minute training session, she was required to practise relaxation at home at least once a day with the aid of a portable GSR monitor. She was also encouraged to relax informally during her everyday activities and to record in a diary the location, duration and success of all attempts at relaxation. The diary was also used to record frequency, duration and intensity of headaches, as well as her use of analgesics. By the end of the tenth week she reported that she was totally free from headaches and had reduced her weekly intake of Distalgesic® from an initial level of 56 tablets to zero. The significance of this finding will be discussed in due course. However, in the context of the present discussion it is the changes that occurred in her blood pressure that are relevant. Because of her history, this was routinely measured by a nurse just before each relaxation session. Initially, it remained stable at around 170/110 mm Hg, but by week 10 there was sufficient evidence of a decline to justify continuing relaxation training. Subsequently, the trend was maintained and by week 16 blood pressure was recorded in the clinic by two independent observers at 140/85 mm Hg. Unfortunately, this is not the end of the story. Each month, as well as visiting the pain-relief clinic, this patient was routinely monitored by the specialist hypertension clinic where she had received treatment throughout her illness. Their records showed no equivalent decrease in blood pressure and by week 16 the difference between readings made in the two clinics was 20/15 mm Hg.

This particular example closely resembles a case reported by Shapiro and Surwit (1976). They described how a 35-year-old patient was treated for essential hypertension with a combination of direct feedback and relaxation training. Over a period of nine sessions his blood pressure decreased from 160/110 mm Hg to between 130/85 mm Hg and 135/95 mm Hg. However, according to Shapiro and Surwit (1976): 'Following these sessions, he returned to his physician for a second examination, and he was recorded again at 160/110.'

Why is it necessary to place quite so much emphasis on these two cases? Because they warn that even large, clinically significant reductions in blood pressure achieved in the clinic or laboratory may not generalise to other everyday environments. Failure to recognise this fact could lead to catastrophic outcomes if, on the basis of laboratory findings alone, hypertensive medication was withdrawn. So far, little research has been directed at this problem, largely because monitoring a patient's blood pressure while he is functioning in his normal environment poses severe technical problems. However, one study has employed this necessary control and this will be described shortly. First, however, it is appropriate to examine some indirect evidence which indicates that the effect of this form of treatment might in fact generalise to the outside environment.

In one of her earliest studies, Patel (1973a) presented detailed data on 20 hypertensive patients who underwent her treatment programme. Once again the outcome can only be described as impressive. The mean decrease in blood pressure was 20.4/14.2 mm Hg with only four of the group deriving no benefit. Moreover, this decrease was accompanied by an overall reduction in drug use of 41.97 per cent, with five patients being able to abandon anti-hypertensive medication completely. Detailed data relating to these five individuals are shown in Table 4.9.

Subsequently, Patel (1975) published follow-up data for all 20 patients and an untreated control group. These showed that six months after the end of training the decreases had been maintained and the overall reduction in medication had remained virtually unchanged at 40.2 per cent, compared with an increase of 5.5 per cent by the controls after three months. Commenting on the question of whether the effects of treatment extended outside the clinic, Patel (1977) argued as follows:

> Although a definite answer can only be obtained by 24-hr intraarterial recording, it should be noted that in some patients the systolic pressure was reduced by as much as 60 mm Hg. It is unlikely that a patient could reduce his blood pressure instantly by that amount.

Pursuing this line of argument it is possible to identify other equally convincing cases. Consider, for example, the blood pressure of patient 4, shown in Table 4.9. The values 220/120 mm Hg and 120/80 mm Hg both represent readings taken when the patient was not receiving medication; the former being obtained before drug therapy began, the latter after it had been discontinued. Moreover, this decrease of 100/40 mm Hg appears to have been maintained for at least the first six months of the follow-up period without any need to recommence anti-hypertensive drug therapy. Remembering also that the other four patients showed similar patterns, it does indeed appear unlikely that decreases of this magnitude and duration were specific to the clinic. Bearing these observations in mind it is interesting to note how Patel concluded the above comment:

Table 4.9: Data for 5 Patients Treated by Patel (1973) Who Were Able to Abandon Drug Therapy

Patient	Type*	Age, sex	Duration of hyper-tension (years)	Original BP (mean, mm Hg)	BP on entering trial (mean, mm Hg)	BP end of trial (mean, mm Hg)	Original drugs (mg/day)	Drugs at end of trial
1	T	39, F	20	170/130 (143)	130/100 (110)	120/83 (95)	Reserpine (0.5)	None
2	T	43, F	1½	170/120 (133)	143/ 97 (112)	110/83 (92)	Methyldopa (750)	None
3	T	44, F	14	180/110 (133)	167/100 (122)	130/85 (100)	Hydroflumethiazide (100)	None
4	E	71, F	9½	220/120 (153)	150/100 (117)	120/80 (93)	Oxprenolol (240)	None
5	E	41, F	1	160/100 (120)	150/100 (117)	110/80 (90)	Oxprenolol (160)	None

Note: T, essential hypertension following pregnancy toxemia; E, essential hypertension
Source: 'Biofeedback-Aided Relaxation and Meditation in the Management of Hypertension', C.H. Patel, *Biofeedback and Self-Regulation* (1977), *2* (1), 1–41, Part of Table 1.

. . . Morever, in a further study using similar training techniques in hypertensive patients, statistically significant reductions in both blood pressure and serum cholesterol were demonstrated (Patel, 1976a). These findings suggest that genuine, long-lasting physiological changes were taking place. In sum, it appears unlikely that the observed reductions in blood pressure were merely some transient phenomenon or an artefact of measurement.

Subsequently Agras, Southam and Taylor (1983) published data that added a measure of empirical support to this observation. They reported on 30 patients, twelve of whom had undergone relaxation training similar to that described by Patel and North. However, as well as monitoring pressures in the training environment, an ambulatory blood pressure monitor was used to obtain readings at the patients' work places. According to the authors these comprised some '24 recordings at 20-minute intervals for each individual'. The results are shown in Table 4.10.

Table 4.10: Mean Blood Pressure (mm Hg) in Clinic and at the Work Site

Location	*n*	Baseline	Post-treatment	15-month follow-up
Clinic				
Systolic				
Treatment	12	144.0 ± 16.3	128.2 ± 12.5*	131.9 ± 16.1
Control	18	141.2 ± 16.1	139.0 ± 18.7	134.8 ± 22.2
Diastolic				
Treatment	12	96.8 ± 9.2	83.2 ± 7.4‡	83.0 ± 10.7*
Control	18	94.1 ± 9.9	92.2 ± 10.6	86.8 ± 9.6
Work site				
Systolic				
Treatment	12	142.7 ± 10.0	133.6 ± 14.2†	131.2 ± 11.4
Control	18	140.0 ± 10.6	141.5 ± 14.1	134.8 ± 13.2
Diastolic				
Treatment	12	92.5 ± 9.3	86.8 ± 12.0†	85.1 ± 8.0†
Control	18	91.6 ± 7.6	93.9 ± 8.5	92.5 ± 9.0

Note: *P* values are identical between groups and within groups from baseline.
* $P < 0.05$. † $P < 0.01$. ‡ $P < 0.001$.
Source: 'Long-Term Persistence of Relaxation-Induced Blood Pressure Lowering During the Working Day', W.S. Agras, M.A. Southam and C. Barr Taylor, *Journal of Consulting and Clinical Psychology* (1983), *51* (5), 792–4, Table 1.

Summarising their data, Agras *et al.* stated: 'Thus we conclude that relaxation training may offer an enduring method to enhance blood pressure lowering in the patient who is not well controlled with standard treatment.' Bearing in mind that drug treatments remained constant across the 15-month study period this conclusion seems to be justified. Furthermore, the 'work site' readings go some way towards answering some of the doubts raised above. That said, the two individual cases described earlier indicate all too clearly that the blood pressure of the hypertensive patient may be exceedingly labile. Certainly it would not be surprising if 24-hour intra-arterial recording revealed that for some patients the anti-hypertensive properties of relaxation training are specific to the training environment.

Evaluation of the Combined Behavioural Method

Whatever doubts may remain about its generalisability, of all the behavioural methods designed to control hypertension that devised by Patel and her associates is by far the most promising. What still remains to be answered is why this should be so, and in particular why this programme has proved so superior to others with which it has much in common. For example, Frankel *et al.* (1978), Pollack *et al.* (1977), and Blackwell *et al.* (1976) all incorporated a substantial element of biofeedback, relaxation training or TM into their treatment. Yet, in the first two studies no overall reductions in blood pressure were observed, while the decreases reported by Blackwell *et al.* were negligible compared with those described by Patel. Clearly, quite apart from any specific effects of meditation or biofeedback, Patel's programme must also contain at least one other 'ingredient' that is necessary if significant and stable reductions in blood pressure are to be achieved.

A review of Patel's writings shows that like Benson (p. 24), she regards reduction in SNS activity as a key factor in this form of treatment. For example (Patel, 1973a):

> It is postulated that yogic relaxation and meditation reduces the sympathetic discharge in response to the environmental stimuli, making the neurohormonal factors concerned with the production of hypertension ineffective.

However, she also insists that for the treatment to be effective it is not enough that the patient practises relaxation for half an hour each day

(Patel, 1977). Instead he must:

> . . . incorporate relaxed attitudes into his routine activities . . . relax before answering a telephone, before an interview, examination or public speaking engagement, during a flight, when meeting strangers or waiting in a dentist's or doctor's office, and during any other personally stressful situation.

In other words not only has the patient to be taught the techniques of physical and mental relaxation, he must also be motivated to incorporate them into every aspect of his daily life. Might it be then, that motivation lies at the heart of Patel's success?

The Role of Motivation

On different occasions Patel has proposed a number of ways of maintaining the patient's motivation. These include providing him with knowledge of the disease, actively involving him in its treatment and ensuring a high level of doctor-patient interaction (Patel and North, 1975; Patel, 1977). Undoubtedly, as the account of her method reproduced on page 55 demonstrates, Patel goes to great lengths to incorporate these methods into her treatment. Indeed it is particularly revealing to observe how the normal use of the word treatment is extended to include motivational factors. Certainly this approach contrasts sharply with that adopted in some early applications of biofeedback. Then, interaction appears to have been restricted to that necessary for the therapist to link the patient to the machine, before leaving him to get on with it as best he could! However, it is one thing to recognise that a treatment programme is unique in the emphasis that it places upon motivational factors; it is quite another to demonstrate that they exert the powerful influence that Patel suggests. This requires evidence that such factors add significantly to the anti-hypertensive properties of the rest of the programme. Already, two studies have been described which indicated that this might be so. It will be recalled that Kristt and Engel (1975) and Blackwell *et al.* (1976) both achieved small but significant long-term decreases in blood pressure by using behavioural techniques. Though these studies differed in their method of training (the former using direct feedback, the latter meditation), both required patients to monitor their own blood pressures during the follow-up period. However, it was left to Sherman and Gaardner (cited by Seer, 1979) to provide the most convincing demonstration so far of the importance of patient participation. In a paper presented to the Biofeedback Society of America, they reported that an extensive analysis of the literature showed that those studies reporting the largest decrease in blood pressure were the ones with the greatest degree of patient participation. Turning to the role of doctor-patient interaction, little directly relevant research has been undertaken, though the discrepancy between Patel's findings and those of Blackwell *et al.* (p. 54) suggest that it might be an important determinant of long-term outcome. For while both treatments utilised meditation, the patients investigated by Blackwell *et al.* were taught by an outside agency rather than by their own doctor.

So far no mention has been made of the part played by biofeedback in Patel's treatment programme. In fact it appears that this too was included to maintain motivation rather than for any specific anti-hypertensive properties. For example, she speaks of changes in GSR and EMG not only enhancing relaxation but encouraging it as well (Patel and North, 1975). Any clinician who uses behavioural techniques to treat tension states will understand why it might be necessary to enhance relaxation. It is a common observation that without some form of assistance many patients find it exceedingly difficult to reach a deeply relaxed state. The reasons for this are many and varied. Some individuals appear to lack the ability to make accurate judgements about the level of tension of their muscles. Others, though only too aware of the presence of tension, do not know how to go about reducing it. An extreme example of the latter case, which has been reported in the literature, described how patients being treated for bruxism attempted to relax their jaw muscles by clenching their teeth! Moreover, if reaching a relaxed state is difficult, then maintaining it can prove well nigh impossible. As anyone who has attempted to learn meditation will be aware, all too frequently and virtually unnoticed the mind starts to wander and muscles become tense. Given the nature of these obstacles it seems logical to assume that the provision of GSR and EMG feedback would help overcome them. Not only do they provide the information that is necessary in order to achieve a relaxed state, they help maintain it by signalling subliminal increases in arousal and muscle tension as soon as they occur.

Although the use of biofeedback as an aid to relaxation is justifiable on logical grounds, the precise nature and magnitude of its effects can only be determined empirically. This was undertaken by Hafner (1982) who compared the anti-hypertensive properties of meditation plus GSR or EMG feedback with those of meditation alone. Hafner found that although both treatments led to virtually identical reductions in blood pressure, the final outcome was achieved more quickly in the combined condition. Bearing in mind the range of difficulties associated with learning to relax, these results were predictable. Quite simply, feedback made learning easier, thus enabling the effects of relaxation to be achieved more quickly. However, they also appear to question the need to include feedback in the treatment package; after all both groups achieved the same reductions in blood pressure. Why then go to the trouble and expense of providing feedback simply to speed up the process? In order to answer this question it is necessary to examine the nature of compliance in a little more detail.

Table 4.11: Compliance Rates for Different Treatments and Conditions

Advice	No. of studies	Percentage of patients who did not follow the advice		
		Range	Mean	Median
Medicine taking				
PAS and other TB drugs	20	8–76	37.5	35
Antibiotics	8	11–92	48.7	50
Psychiatric drugs	9	11–51	38.6	44
Other medicines, e.g., antacids, Iron	12	9–87	47.7	57.5
Diet	11	20–84	49.4	45
Other advice, e.g., child care, antenatal exercises	8	30–79	54.6	51
All advice	68	8–92	44.0	44.35

Source: 'Communication in the Clinical Setting', P. Ley, *British Journal of Orthodontics* (1974), *1* (4), 173–77, Table 1.

As Table 4.11 shows, the problem of compliance extends to every form of treatment and condition, even those where failure to comply has potentially lethal consequences. Although the factors affecting compliance are complex, it is possible to identify some that are relevant to this discussion. (For a more detailed account see Ley, 1974.) For example, the combination of a long-term, time-consuming treatment and a condition that is virtually free from incapacitating or unpleasant symptoms is almost guaranteed to result in low compliance. Likewise, it is frequently observed in clinical practice that the willingness of patients to persevere with a course of treatment depends in part on the immediacy of its therapeutic effect. Be it physiotherapy, a special diet or prolonged drug therapy, a regimen that is slow to produce the desired outcome is especially likely to be abandoned as ineffective. To give just one example, it is notoriously difficult to persuade depressed patients to continue tricyclic medication for the three weeks that usually elapse before its anti-depressant properties become apparent (Kessler, 1978). Consequently, compliance is likely to be enhanced by any procedure that reduces the interval between the commencement of treatment and the onset of symptomatic relief. Returning to the study described by Hafner (1982), it was just such a reduction that the provision of feedback brought about. Within the confines of the experimental laboratory this may have been of little consequence. The subject's initial commitment to participate in a relatively short experiment, aided by the presence of an enthusiastic researcher, was all that was required to ensure that he completed the training programme. However, it does not follow that this would be the case in a less-closely supervised clinical setting. Denied the early success that feedback brings about and given that the treatment is time consuming and the complaint asymptomatic, many patients might well lose their motivation and abandon therapy completely.

Accepting that motivational factors do indeed appear to play a major part in this form of therapy, one question remains. By what mechanisms do they operate: what is it that the patient is motivated to do? As we saw earlier, Patel's answer is straightforward; he is motivated to continue practising relaxation both on a formal basis and during routine activities. It is necessary to be quite clear what is implied here. Patel is arguing that although biofeedback and other forms of psychological management are necessary in order to maintain long-term compliance, it is the reduction in SNS activity (and to a lesser extent muscle tension) that deep relaxation and meditation brings about that is the active anti-hypertensive agent. It is easy to see why Patel should adopt this position. As we have seen, the short-term anti-hypertensive properties of deep relaxation are well documented and the finding that it is also associated with biochemical changes points to the possibility of longer lasting effects. However, we need to be cautious about accepting that the only effect of raised motivation is to maintain compliance. Indeed, it is arguable that Patel's programme is such as to motivate the patient in ways that, although likely to reduce blood pressure, have nothing whatsoever to do with relaxation or meditation. This point is well illustrated by asking the reader to put himself in the position of a patient undergoing this form of therapy.

On arriving at the surgery you are not handed a repeat prescription by a receptionist, even less do you have to retrieve it yourself from a box fastened to the waiting room door! Instead you are invited by the doctor to sit down and discuss the nature, causes and treatment of your illness. You are further invited to see films and slides and to meet other patients with similar problems. Moreover, once treatment begins you are not a passive recipient but an active participant. While learning to relax you are continually being encouraged by the doctor, and your newly acquired ability to control your own physiological activity is immediately made obvious through biofeedback. Finally, you are kept informed of your long-term progress by being given access to that most secret of all documents, your medical record. Faced with this form of treatment it is easy to see why you would be motivated to continue practising relaxation. However, bearing in mind what you have been taught about the nature of hypertension, it is likely that you would have been motivated to do a number of other things too. These might include losing weight, changing to a more sensible diet, avoiding sustained occupational stress and generally adopting a more appropriate life-style. In the present context this is no more than informed speculation. However, as this evaluation of biofeedback is widened to encompass more stress-related conditions it will become increasingly apparent that its *modus operandi* cannot be understood without reference to the part played by non-specific factors.

Concluding Remarks

The reader may recall that in the preface to this book it was pointed out that the results of clinical trials involving biofeedback and relaxation training are rarely straightforward and often contradictory. Few would doubt that in the case of essential hypertension this has proved to be so. Nevertheless, despite the variety of outcomes described here it is possible to draw the following conclusions.

(1) Despite reports of the occasional patient who appears to derive substantial benefit, there is no evidence that direct feedback is effective in the treatment of essential hypertension.
(2) Similarly, the reductions in blood pressure that result from short programmes of simple relaxation training or meditation are usually transient and rarely of sufficient magnitude to be of therapeutic value.
(3) A number of studies have shown that programmes which combine biofeedback and meditation with other forms of psychological management produce clinically relevant reductions in blood pressure. However, the underlying mechanisms remain obscure and in arriving at this conclusion it must be borne in mind that none of the clinical trials on which it is based met all ten criteria listed at the end of Chapter

3. In particular, the lack of adequate baseline data and failure to demonstrate unequivocally that effects observed in the laboratory or clinic generalise to everyday life require that these results be treated with guarded optimism rather than unquestioning acceptance. Moreover, even if this type of treatment survives the further investigation that such reservations demand, we should not assume that it offers a viable alternative to conventional drug therapy. As Patel (1977) has pointed out:

Although the therapy cannot be regarded as a sole treatment for established hypertension, it can form a powerful adjunct to anti-hypertensive drug therapy. It not only helps to control hypertension in those who cannot be adequately controlled on drugs alone, but it also reduces the drug requirement in a substantial number of patients.

5 RAYNAUD'S DISEASE AND CARDIAC ARRHYTHMIAS

Raynaud's Disease

This peripheral vascular disorder was first described in 1862 by the French physician Maurice Raynaud. More recently it has been defined by Thulesius (1976) as follows:

> . . . episodic attacks of decreased finger circulation characterized by white fingers, paresthesia, and a subsequent hyperemic phase with reddening of the skin and an increased cutaneous circulation. In advanced cases a continuous cyanotic phase is a predominant feature.

The condition occurs more frequently in women than men, in a ratio of approximately 5:1; is usually bilateral; and fingers are more often affected than toes. The incidence of Raynaud's disease is unclear, but one author has suggested that it may occur in up to 20 per cent of the population (Lewis, 1949). Although in most instances the condition poses no more than an unpleasant inconvenience, in a small proportion of chronic cases ulceration or ischemic gangrene may develop, making amputation necessary (Robbins, 1962). Clearly then, as with hypertension, we are dealing with a vascular condition which, if left untreated, can (albeit rarely) be severely disabling. Moreover, the similarity with hypertension does not end there, for while in some instances symptoms are secondary to known pathology, in others the aetiology is completely obscure (Robbins, 1962). This has led to the distinction being made between Raynaud's *phenomenon* and Raynaud's *disease*.

The diagnosis of Raynaud's phenomenon (or secondary Raynaud's disease) is reserved for those cases that are directly attributable to pathology of the vascular system. This may involve arterial insufficiency resulting from trauma, toxic metals, arterial occlusions, nerve lesions, connective tissue diseases or neoplasms (Sedlacek, 1983). Here the analogy with secondary hypertension is obvious. Likewise, Raynaud's disease resembles essential hypertension in that it does not appear to be secondary to any identifiable pathology. From the outset, the idiopathic nature of Raynaud's disease has been recognised, and as long ago as 1862 Raynaud (cited by Sappington, Fiorito and Brehony, 1979) concluded:

> I would say that the present state of our knowledge shows local asphyxia of the extremities ought to be considered as a neurosis, characterized by enormous exaggeration of the excitomotor energy of the gray parts of the spinal cord which control the vasomotor innervation.

In view of the fact that cutaneous blood vessels are controlled by the SNS, it is not surprising that Raynaud should seek to implicate sympathetic over-reactivity in the pathogenesis of the condition. Moreover, subsequent research, notably that of Mittelmann and Wolff (1939), has done nothing to disprove Raynaud's hypothesis. Briefly, they observed that unlike emotional distress, temperature reductions were not in themselves sufficient to produce the pain and discolouration that characterise the condition. In fact the most severe symptoms were to be found when the two factors occurred in combination. Further evidence of SNS involvement is to be found in the observation that decreases in finger temperature in response to stress are usually reduced following sympathectomy. It is against a background of such findings that modern writers have continued to echo the views of Raynaud. Thus Blanchard (1979) has described Raynaud's disease as follows:

> . . . a functional disorder of the peripheral vascular system in which the patient suffers painful episodes of vasoconstriction in the hands and sometimes the feet. During an attack, the skin blanches and is cold to the touch. Attacks are usually precipitated either by exposure to cold, such as touching a cold object, or by emotional upset.

Similarly the 14th edition of *Davidson's Principles and Practice of Medicine* (MacLeod, 1984) speaks of: '. . . peripheral vascular disturbance consisting of spasmodic contraction of the digital arteries, which is precipitated by cold, emotion and by other causative factors . . .' Despite such unanimity it must be emphasised that the aetiology of Raynaud's disease remains obscure. Like essential hypertension it is almost certainly multifactorial, involving neuro-anatomical, psychological and genetic factors. That said, there is sufficient evidence of a psychological involvement to have attracted the interest of behavioural scientists. Especially when in temperature feedback they have, so to speak, a method of treatment at their finger tips.

Temperature Feedback and Raynaud's Disease

At the end of a review of the earlier applications of temperature feedback Blanchard (1979) came to the optimistic conclusion that it offered 'a viable alternative treatment for Raynaud's disease.' This view was echoed by Yates (1980) when he stated that 'the outlook for biofeedback training with primary Raynaud's disease looks quite promising.' However, even as they were reaching these conclusions both authors were urging caution by emphasising the need for more research. And they were right to do so, for almost all the early studies were little more than anecdotal case reports with few pretensions to scientific rigour. In this context it should be noted that the total number of patients taking part in the eight studies reviewed by Blanchard was a mere 19, and in three of these studies (involving twelve of the 19 patients) no follow-up data were presented. Of the remaining seven patients for whom follow-up data were reported, five appeared to have maintained improvement for periods ranging from two to 18 months. However, even these cases present problems of interpretation, in that in four instances temperature feedback was used in conjunction with other forms of treatment. These included autogenic training, psychotherapy, hypnosis, relaxation training and EMG feedback. Thus, although the outcomes of these studies were sufficiently promising to justify further research, they were no more than that. Certainly they offered no insights into how these various methods might operate, and in particular whether temperature feedback was a necessary component of treatment. To examine these questions it is necessary to look at more recent research, although as will become obvious, even here many findings remain ambiguous and present problems of interpretation. Typical of this research was an attempt by Keefe, Surwit and Pilon (1980) to compare the effects of the following: autogenic training alone, autogenic training augmented with temperature feedback, and simple progressive relaxation training.

Once arterial disease had been excluded, a pool of 21 female patients was randomly divided to form the three treatment groups. Before treatment there was a four-week baseline period during which each patient maintained a daily record of attacks. Thereafter the appropriate training was undertaken, each group of seven patients attending three one-hour sessions within a programme lasting nine weeks in all. The methods of autogenic instruction and progressive relaxation training were similar to those described on page 26. During the nine-week training phase patients were encouraged to practise the prescribed exercise for two 20-minute sessions each day with the aid of a pre-recorded cassette containing the appropriate instructions. Patients in the combined condition received identical treatment to those undergoing autogenic training except that they also used a portable feedback monitor to practise hand-warming at home. Finally, as in the method adopted by Patel and North to treat essential hypertension (p. 55), all patients were urged to practise what they had learned in the laboratory during their daily activities and to continue to record symptoms during weeks 1 to 4 and week 9 of training. An interesting aspect of this study is that all patients were subjected to four cold-stress tests — one during the first week of the baseline period, the remainder during weeks 1, 3 and 5 of training. This required the individual to maintain digital temperature while the room was gradually cooled over a period of 25 minutes from 26°C to 17°C. During the cold challenge test changes in heart-rate as well as finger temperature were recorded. The data are shown in Figures 5.1 and 5.2.

All three treatments led to a reduction in symptoms from relatively stable baselines. However, it is regrettable that the randomisation

Figure 5.1: Mean Number of Attacks per Day Reported by all Patients During the Four Weeks Immediately Preceding Training, the First Four Weeks of Training and the Ninth Week of Training

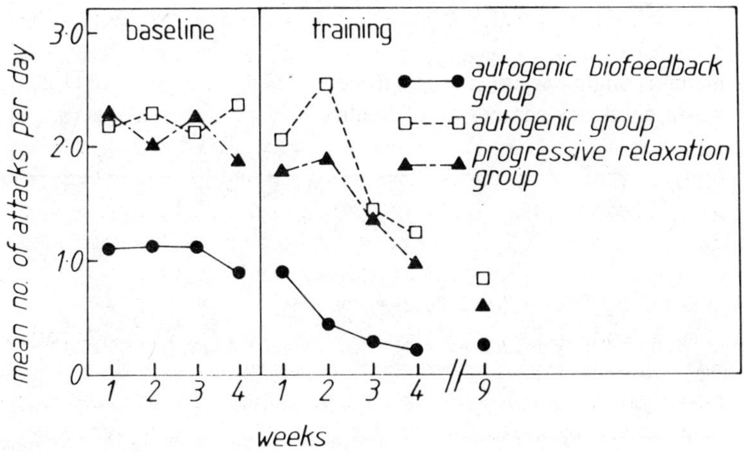

Source: 'Biofeedback, Autogenic Training, and Progressive Relaxation in the Treatment of Raynaud's Disease: A Comparative Study', F.J. Keefe, R.S. Surwit and R.N. Pilon, *Journal of Applied Behavior Analysis* (1980), *13*, 3-11, Figure 2.

Figure 5.2: Mean Digital Temperature During Pre-treatment Stress Tests (Stress Test 1) and Post-treatment Stress Tests (Stress Test 2–4). Recording of skin temperature began after a 10-min stabilisation period

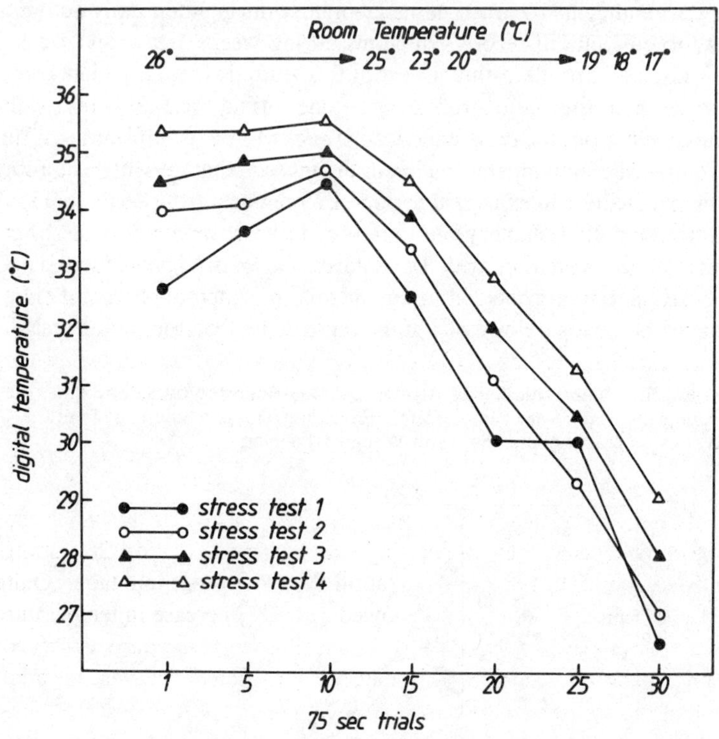

Source: 'Biofeedback, Autogenic Training, and Progressive Relaxation in the Treatment of Raynaud's Disease: A Comparative Study', F.J. Keefe, R.S. Surwit and R.N. Pilon, *Journal of Applied Behavior Analysis* (1980), *13*, 3–11, Figure 1.

procedure produced a combined treatment group that had fewer attacks than the other two groups during the baseline period, for the lack of a common starting point makes intergroup comparisons virtually impossible. Not surprisingly, the authors recognised this point but argued that:

> However, it should be pointed out, despite this problem, there was no significant difference in the cold stress performance of these two groups. It is the contention of the authors that these laboratory data

> are inherently more objective, reliable, and valid indicators of improvement than subject's self-reports . . . Furthermore these results are in agreement with previous research demonstrating that the combination of biofeedback and autogenic training is no more effective than autogenic training used alone in enhancing voluntary vasomotor control (Surwit *et al.* 1978; Keefe, 1978).

Unfortunately, as Figure 5.2 shows, data for the four stress tests were collapsed across treatment methods. Thus, while it is apparent that the average digital temperature of all 21 patients increased throughout training, we can deduce nothing about variations between the component groups. It also has to be said that there was an element of selectivity in the data adduced to support the general conclusion that biofeedback does not increase the overall efficiency of autogenic training. In fact two studies have been reported that contradict this conclusion. In the first of these, Surwit and Fenton (1980) treated two groups of seven female patients with autogenic exercises, which for one group were augmented with temperature feedback. The results showed that during the training session (while listening to a pre-recorded instruction tape) both groups exhibited small but significant increases in skin temperature. However, as Figure 5.3 makes clear, differences between the two groups began to appear when monitoring was continued for the 28 minutes immediately following the cessation of the instruction tape. Quite simply, although both groups showed a steady decrease in temperature over time, this was greater for those subjects who did not receive feedback. As the authors rightly concluded, 'for whatever reason, the addition of biofeedback to autogenic training appears to enhance voluntary vasodilation'.

The second study to suggest that temperature feedback might have a part to play in controlling Raynaud's disease is especially noteworthy in that it is one of the very few to provide long-term follow-up data. Freedman, Lynn, Ianni and Hale (1981) treated ten patients (six with Raynaud's disease and four with Raynaud's phenomenon) with 12 sessions of finger-temperature feedback. Before treatment there was a four-week baseline period during which a record of symptoms (date, time, place, perceived cause and visual description) was maintained. Identical details were obtained one and 13 months after treatment. The treatment sessions were spread over six weeks and comprised a 16-minute baseline, followed by 24 minutes of temperature feedback recorded from the distal end of the forefinger of the dominant hand. Each session ended with a second 16-minute baseline. Throughout the session room temperature

Figure 5.3: Mean Digital Temperature (Change from Baseline) For Each Five-Trial Block After the Presentation of Autogenic Instructions for all Subjects

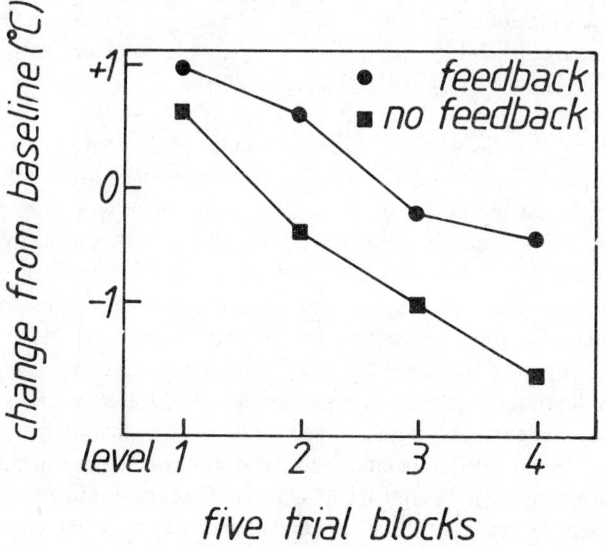

Source: 'Feedback and Instructions in the Control of Digital Skin Temperature', R.S. Surwit and C.H. Fenton, *Psychophysiology* (1980), *17* (2), 129–31, Figure 1.

was maintained at 23°C. Instructions appear to have been kept to a minimum, subjects simply being told to 'try to move the needle to the right using any mental means.' As well as finger temperature, skin conductance, EMG levels, heart and respiration rates and relative pulse volumes were recorded. At the end of each session, subjects were asked to practise whatever strategies had proved effective at least twice daily and whenever an attack seemed imminent. The various data are shown in Figure 5.4 and Table 5.1.

Figure 5.4 shows that subjects were able to control finger temperature during feedback training in the laboratory. As the authors pointed out, 'Although temperature changes were generally negative, they were significantly less negative during feedback periods than during pre- or post-feedback baselines'. The similarity between these findings and those of Surwit and Fenton is obvious and strengthens the view that temperature feedback enhances voluntary vasodilation. However, it remains unclear what mechanisms underlie this phenomenon. Previously Keefe *et al.* (1980) had argued that it reflected a general state of relaxation rather

Figure 5.4: Finger Temperature Changes, Averaged for 12 Sessions.

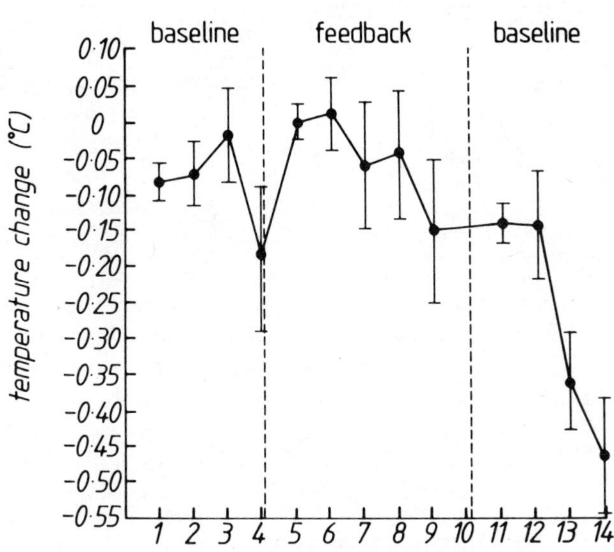

Source: 'Biofeedback Treatment of Raynaud's Disease and Phenomenon', R.R. Freedman, S.J. Lynn, P. Ianni and P.A. Hale, *Biofeedback and Self-Regulation* (1981), *6* (3), 355–65, Figure 1.

than acquired control of a specific autonomic response. However, Freedman *et al.* found no consistent relationship between finger temperature and other physiological measures. They concluded that these findings made it 'unlikely that changes in finger temperature were due to general physical relaxation.'

Evaluation

It will be immediately apparent that the body of research devoted to the behavioural control of Raynaud's disease lacks both the quality and quantity of that relating to essential hypertension. This is hardly surprising. While severe Raynaud's disease may inconvenience the sufferer, it rarely, if ever, poses the major threat associated with uncontrolled hypertension. Nevertheless, the studies described here do nothing to weaken the optimism that characterised Blanchard's review of earlier research. In particular, the long-term follow-up data described by Freedman *et al.* (Table 5.1) are especially interesting. An overall reduction in attacks

Table 5.1: Immediate and Long-term Outcome for 10 Raynaud's Sufferers Treated with Biofeedback

Age, sex		Diagnosis	Duration (years)	Number of attacks per week: Pre-treatment	First follow-up	1-year follow-up
40,	F	Raynaud's disease	7	14	4	3
34,	F	Raynaud's disease	22	28	0.25	1
45,	F	Raynaud's disease	10	14	1	1
49,	F	Raynaud's disease	3	28	0	0
49,	F	Raynaud's disease	10	28	2	2
28,	F	Raynaud's disease	3	21	—	0.58
37,	M	Raynaud's phenomenon (traumatic vibration disease)	8	28	0.25	1
35,	F	Raynaud's phenomenon (scleroderma)	3	21	7	7
66,	M	Raynaud's phenomenon (carpal tunnel syndrome)	12	2	0.06	0.25
19,	F	Raynaud's phenomeonon (scleroderma)	7	28	0	0
Means			8.5	21.2	1.6	1.6

Source: 'Biofeedback Treatment of Raynaud's Disease and Phenomenon', R.R. Freedman, S.J. Lynn, P. Ianni and P.A. Hale, *Biofeedback and Self-Regulation* (1981), *6* (3), 355–65, Table 1.

of more than 92 per cent appears to offer quite powerful support for their treatment programme; especially as in all ten cases the condition was long-standing. It may come as a surprise, therefore, to learn that Blanchard's optimism is not universally shared. For example, Sappington *et al.* (1979) have argued as follows:

> Although many researchers in the area seem to be convinced that biofeedback is an effective symptomatic treatment in Raynaud's disease . . . the body of knowledge amassed to date in support of that belief is sketchy at best.

Subsequently this pessimistic view was echoed by Carroll (1984) when, in a more general review of the clinical application of biofeedback, he wrote:

> While biofeedback may yet prove of value in the context of cardiac arrhythmias, there is little to commend the use of biofeedback for Raynaud's disease. Here, even the early case studies offer only the most marginal support; only a fraction of the patients treated seem to have gained lasting benefit.

Curiously, in reaching this conclusion Carroll made no mention of the work of Freedman *et al.* However, it is unlikely that it would have led him substantially to alter his views, for like Sappington *et al.*, Carroll largely based his criticism on the fact that none of the studies described to date were adequately controlled. This is valid criticism, for it is generally recognised that like other cardiovascular symptoms, Raynaud's disease is susceptible to the effects of suggestion. Indeed, as long ago as 1945, Lipkin, McDevitt, Schwartz and Duryee achieved both objective and subjective relief by treating Raynaud's disease with a variety of inert procedures, including saline injections and sham iontotherapy. It is, of course, arguable that the gains reported by Freedman *et al.* were far larger and longer lasting than those that are normally associated with a placebo response. Certainly the placebo effect is rarely robust enough to be fully maintained over such a long period. However, even if this argument were to be accepted in its entirety, the case for appropriate controls would remain.

At the end of the preceding chapter it was argued at some length that the favourable outcomes reported by Patel could have reflected changes in patients' life styles rather than the anti-hypertensive property of meditation. With only a little imagination it is possible to offer a similar interpretation of the data described here. Consider, for example, the observation by Freedman *et al.* that their follow-up data were recorded when the average daily temperature was 17.2°F below that of the baseline period. On the face of it this appears to be yet one more piece of evidence pointing to the potency of the treatment; certainly this was the view taken by Freedman *et al.* However, might it not just be possible that a combination of unfavourable climatic conditions, daily recording of symptoms and new-found responsibility for their own well-being led patients to take more care to keep warm and to avoid inappropriate behaviours? While such an interpretation may appear facile, it underlines the need for further fully controlled studies in order to 'help determine the "active ingredients" of biofeedback as well as the most efficacious behavioural treatments for peripheral vasospastic disorders' (Freedman *et al.* 1981).

Concluding Remarks

This brief review has much in common with the more detailed evaluations of biofeedback and relaxation training discussed in the preceding chapter. It is possible to identify anecdotal case reports, laboratory investigations and at least one long-term study which indicate that Raynaud's disease may respond to behavioural treatments. Yet, like those relating to essential hypertension, the data must be treated with caution. In particular the problem of small samples and lack of necessary controls means that even when significant effects have been reported, the underlying mechanisms cannot be unequivocally specified. Given then that so many questions remain to be answered, can we justify treating Raynaud's disease by behavioural techniques? Perhaps the best way to deal with this question is to adopt a pragmatic approach and consider the alternatives.

In general, drug therapy is unsuccessful and is frequently associated with unacceptable side effects. (It should also be noted that the quality of research into the pharmacological control of Raynaud's disease has, if anything, proved to be even less satisfactory than its behavioural counterparts. Freedman *et al.* (1981) reported that they were unable to find in the literature a single controlled trial of any compound.) We have already seen that sympathectomy can reduce symptoms, though in a significant proportion of cases they return within two years (Verrill, 1984). Moreover, it has to be conceded that this is a hazardous procedure, which carries a recognised risk of permanent neurological deficit. Indeed, many authorities now favour chemical methods when seeking to achieve symptomatic relief by sympathetic blockade. For example, Hannington-Kiff (1984) has suggested that repeated guanethidine blocks offer an alternative to surgical excision of the regional sympathetic ganglia. Although less hazardous than surgical procedures, it is appropriate to point out that Hannington-Kiff listed eight disadvantages associated with this method of treatment. Judged against this background, and bearing in mind that the condition seldom demands immediate action, a behavioural approach to the treatment of Raynaud's disease does appear to be justified. Its efficacy is no less well established than that of drug therapy and, moreover, it is non-invasive and free from side effects. Certainly a combination of temperature feedback and relaxation training carries none of the hazards associated with surgical excisions and, to a lesser extent, chemical blocks.

Cardiac Arrhythmias

Basically, the heart is a large, hollow, muscular organ that is divided into four chambers; the right and left atria and the right and left ventricles. At the junction of the vena cava lies the sino-atrial node (SAN), a collection of specialised cells that undergo regular depolarisation, thus acting as the heart's pacemaker. Although the SAN has its own intrinsic rate of depolarisation, this is open to modulation by input from both the sympathetic and parasympathetic branches of the ANS. Normally parasympathetic activity (by way of the vagus nerve) is dominant, and reduces the depolarisation rate from 80–90 per minute to give a normal heart rate in the range of 60–80 beats per minute (bpm). Depolarisation of the SAN initiates an impulse that stimulates the atrial muscle and causes it to contract. This activity stimulates the atrio-ventricular (AVN) node, which in turn activates (by way of the atrio-ventricular bundle) the ventricle muscle and causes it to contract. The complete cardiac cycle is illustrated in Figure 5.5.

Figure 5.5: The Cardiac Cycle

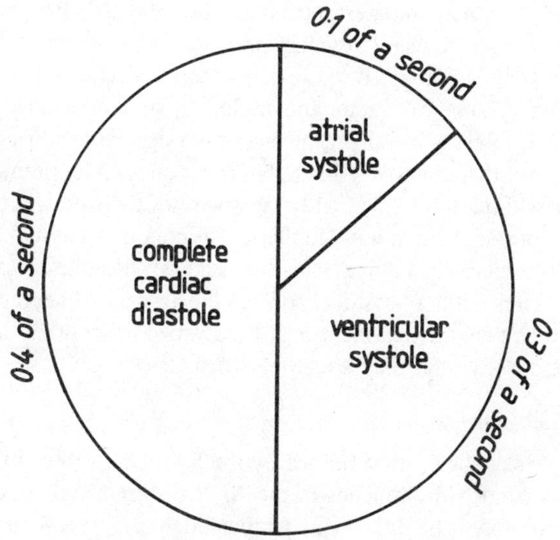

As Figure 5.5 makes clear, maintenance of regular heart-rate depends upon a sequence of events, each with its own temporal characteristics. Arrhythmias occur when this sequence becomes disturbed. Reference to any textbook of cardiology shows that many arrhythmias have been described, most with a variety of causes. However, this discussion will be confined to the two that have been shown to respond most readily to behavioural control. These are premature ventricular contractions (PVCs) and sinus tachycardia.

Premature Ventricular Contractions (PVCs)

Although normally the cardiac cycle is initiated by impulses generated in the SAN, under certain circumstances a heart beat may also result from an impulse generated at another site. Should this occur then the smooth sequence of events illustrated in Figure 5.5 is likely to be disrupted. One such example is the PVC, which is defined as an impulse arising in the ventricular muscle that typically occurs some 0.3 seconds after the previous sinus beat and is usually followed by a refractory pause. (For an elaboration of this simplified account see Jordan, 1979.) The precise aetiology of PVCs is unclear, although their frequency is likely to be increased in the presence of organic heart disease. They pose a particular threat in myocardial infarction, when an unusually premature beat may initiate ventricular fibrillation (de Bono and Julian, 1984). However, in many instances premature beats occur in the absence of underlying pathology. In these cases their occurrence has been linked to a wide range of precipitants including smoking, intake of coffee and alcohol, stress and conflict, mental or physical fatigue, irregular sleep and digestive disturbances. Although it is not unusual for premature beats to occur without the individual being aware of their presence, they are on occasions associated with unpleasant symptoms. These may include faintness, dizziness, sweating, nausea, weakness, breathlessness and acute anxiety. Thus while PVCs occurring in the absence of heart disease are regarded as benign, treatment may be deemed appropriate in order to ease the distress that they sometimes produce.

Sinus Tachycardia

Although heart beats are initiated by the SAN, their rate is maintained by inputs from both branches of the ANS. Consequently, excess sympathetic activity is likely to be accompanied by an increase in heart rate. The term 'sinus tachycardia' is applied when this rate exceeds an arbitrarily defined value of 100 bpm. Like PVCs, sinus tachycardia is associated with both organic and non-organic factors. The former include congestive heart failure, fever, anaemia and hyperactivity of the thyroid gland. Amongst the non-organic factors are high levels of anxiety, dietary effects and drug reactions. However, sinus tachycardia differs from PVCs in that apart from a marked increase in rate, the ECG is usually normal.

Cardiac Arrhythmias and Biofeedback

As was pointed in Chapter 2, much early research into biofeedback arose from the suggestion that it enabled autonomic activity to be brought under voluntary control. In fact a great deal of this research was specifically concerned with the question of whether animals and humans could learn to control heart rate. Given the excitement that these studies engendered, it is perhaps not surprising that their clinical significance began to be investigated. A decade later, Blanchard (1979) summarised the state of this area of clinical research in the following manner: 'In the treatment of PVCs and tachycardia by biofeedback of heart rate, there is very suggestive evidence of efficacy and utility . . . For other arrhythmias, it is too early to say.'

At the outset it must be recognised that many of the criticisms levelled at research into the behavioural control of Raynaud's disease apply with equal force here. While Blanchard reviewed five studies, the total number of patients treated was only 16, and follow-up ranged from none to 18 months. That said, his cautiously optimistic conclusion has been echoed by two other authors not renowned for believing their geese to be swans (Yates, 1980; Carroll, 1984).

Premature Ventricular Contractions and Biofeedback

In principle it would be possible to translate the abnormal ECG pattern associated with PVCs into a form whereby a patient could be made aware of premature beats as they occurred. However, this method has not found favour when biofeedback has been applied to the control of cardiac arrhythmias. Instead, whatever the nature of the disturbance, treatment has almost always concentrated on teaching the patient to control heart rate. The outstanding example of this approach was described by Weiss and Engel (1971) who trained eight patients (six with a history of heart disease and all known to suffer from PVCs) to increase and decrease heart rate, alternate increasing and decreasing heart rate within the same session, and maintain heart rate within given limits. (In this condition feedback did enable the patient to detect PVCs as they occurred.) Training was carried out with the patient lying on a bed in a sound-proof room, the required response being signalled by two coloured lights. A third light was used to provide feedback; i.e. 'it was on when the patient was producing the correct heart rate (HR) response'. A second source of feedback came from a meter so that, 'whenever the patient was performing correctly, the meter arm moved, and when he performed incorrectly it stopped'. Each session lasted 80 minutes, which included a 10-minute baseline and 34 minutes of training. Between one and three sessions were carried out each day and each of the four conditions was taught for approximately 10 sessions. Each patient underwent regular electrocardiographic monitoring on the ward, and was told in detail about the nature

Table 5.2: Ratios of Sessions During Which Each Patient Performed Successfully to Total Number of Sessions for Each Contingency

Patient	Speed	Slow	Different-ial	CRF	Range 1:1 On	Range 1:1 Off	Range 1:3 On	Range 1:3 Off	Range 1:7 On	Range 1:7 Off
1 (Study 1)	4/9	4/6	7/9	5/6	—	—	—	—	—	—
1 (Study 2)	—	—	—	8/10	3/5	4/5	2/4	3/4	2/4	2/4
2	11/14	5/7	9/9	10/10	2/2	2/2	2/2	2/2	3/3	3/3
3	5/11	9/10	8/10	2/3*	4/4*	4/4*	3/4*	3/4*	5/5*	5/5*
4	6/10	5/10	10/10	5/5	11/11	11/11	7/7	7/7	—	—
5	1/10	9/9	12/14	15/15	—	—	—	—	—	—
6	1/6	5/11	—	13/16	—	—	—	—	—	—
7	2/8	7/10	—	2/4	—	—	—	—	—	—
8	—	16/18	—	15/15	—	—	—	—	—	—

Note: During the range session, successful performance was defined as maintenance of HR within the correct range for more than 50% of the time.

*Slow.

Source: 'Operant Conditioning of Heart Rate in Patients with Premature Ventricular Contractions', T. Weiss and B.T. Engel, *Psychosomatic Medicine* (1971), *33* (4), 301–21, Table 1.

of the experiment. He was also allowed to inspect his heart rate data throughout the trial.

Table 5.2 shows that all eight patients were able to exert some degree of control over heart rate, though there was considerable variability within the group. Changes in PVCs were less straightforward. Not all patients showed significant reductions and, of the five who did, reductions occurred at different phases of training (Table 5.3). On the other hand it is important to recognise that not only were these reductions recorded away from the training environment, in four cases they were maintained over follow-up periods of up to 21 months.

Table 5.3: Premature Ventricular Contraction Frequencies (PVCs/Min) on Ward During Different Phases of Study

Patient	Speeding	Slowing	Differential	Range or PVC avoidance
1	10.7	7.6	2.0	0.8
2	1.4	2.3	1.1	0.5
3	34.4	30.0	12.4	—
4	6.6	5.7	5.0	2.1
5	10.2	6.6	4.9	3.8
6	3.1	7.1	—	6.5
7	16.6	4.7	—	9.4
8	—	15.2	—	10.2

Source: 'Operant Conditioning of Heart Rate in Patients with Premature Ventricular Contractions', T. Weiss and B.T. Engel, *Psychosomatic Medicine* (1971), *33* (4), 301–21, Table 2.

Subsequently, Engel and Bleecker (1974) described the outcome of a five-year follow-up on one of these patients, as follows: 'The patient we have followed was reported then to have 1 to 6 PVC/min, two months after study. After about five years her PVCs continue to be rare, and she does not require any antiarrhythmic medication.' They then went on to describe the effects of treating one further patient with PVCs in the manner described above. The patient was a 27-year-old woman who suffered from Marfan's syndrome. From the age of 20 she had experienced progressive congestive heart failure which, when she was 25, was controlled by mitral valve replacement. However, she continued to have up to 20 PVCs/min and failed to respond to drug therapy. By the end of training these had decreased to less than 0.5 PVCs/min, this gain being maintained over a nine-month follow-up period and confirmed by several continuous 10-hour recordings made outside the laboratory. At the time these findings were reported the patient was described as active and requiring no anti-arrhythmic medications. However, the time that had elapsed since the cessation of training was not stated.

Sinus Tachycardia and Biofeedback

While it is possible to question the logic of using heart-rate feedback to treat PVCs, no such reservations apply in the case of sinus tachycardia. It is surprising, therefore, that so far clinical trials appear to have been restricted to uncontrolled, single case studies. For example, as well as the patient described earlier, Engel and Bleecker (1974) presented details of a 53-year-old woman with persistent sinus tachycardia that had not responded to drug therapy. Past medical records showed that over the preceding four years her pulse rate never fell below 80 bpm and had averaged 106 bpm across 50 observations. Training in heart slowing was spread over 21 sessions, with feedback gradually being reduced across sessions from continuous to 14 per cent. The results showed that heart rate fell from 86.3 bpm early in training to 68.5 bpm during the later sessions. Independent measures made outside the laboratory showed that heart rate was maintained 'at about 75 bpm'. Several other single-subject studies have produced similar outcomes. For example, Figure 5.6 illustrates reduction in the heart rate of a 50-year-old man with a 26-year history of tachycardia who was treated by Scott, Blanchard, Edmunson and Young (1973).

In this instance training was in heart-rate reduction, correct responses being reinforced with money. Unfortunately performance outside the laboratory does not appear to have been monitored, either during training or at long-term follow-up. More recently Janssen (1983) has replicated the findings of Engel and Bleecker (1974), although again only one patient was treated. After eight sessions of feedback training the heart rate of a 23-year-old man with a history of sinus tachycardia had dropped from 103 bpm to 66 bpm. Follow-up at 1 and twelve months showed that improvement had stabilised at 68 and 73 bpm respectively.

Evaluation

We saw earlier that while Blanchard recognised that the studies described here offered suggestive evidence of efficacy and utility, he also underlined the need for controlled studies. Regrettably, little has changed since 1979 when Blanchard presented his review of the literature. Indeed, some four years later Engel and Baile (1983) were still forced to conclude that: 'Although there are sufficient data now available to warrant further study, and in some cases clinical trials, none of these procedures has been

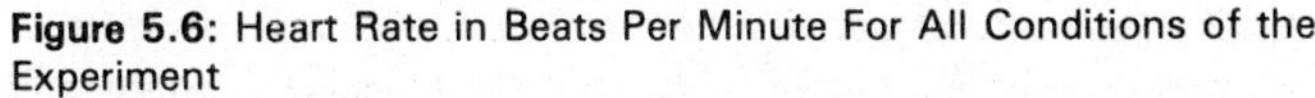

Figure 5.6: Heart Rate in Beats Per Minute For All Conditions of the Experiment

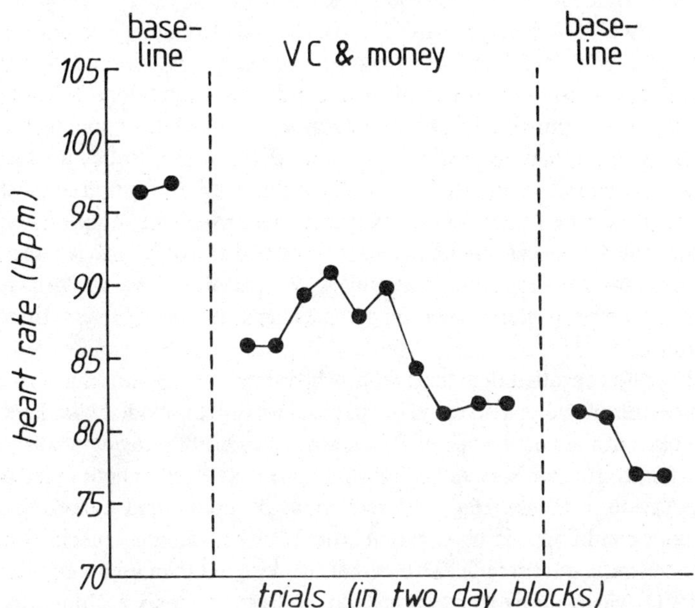

Source: 'A Shaping Procedure for Heart-Rate Control in Chronic Tachycardia', R.W. Scott, E.B. Blanchard, E.D. Edmunson and L.D. Young, *Perceptual and Motor Skills* (1973), *37*, 327–38, Figure 5.

established with sufficient reliability to justify calling them established treatments.'

Given that so many authorities have recognised the promise inherent in this approach to the treatment of cardiac disorders, it is pertinent to ask why more sophisticated clinical trials have not been forthcoming. We shall return to this question later. First, however, what of the case studies described above?

Despite methodological shortcomings, the study of PVCs described by Weiss and Engel (1971) contained many admirable features. In particular the fact that monitoring of improvement took place away from the training laboratory and was subsequently subjected to independent verification means that the improvement noted in four patients ought not to be too readily dismissed. However, for reasons that have already been elaborated, it cannot be unequivocally asserted that this improvement was specific to biofeedback. Like essential hypertension and Raynaud's disease, PVCs and sinus tachycardia are conditions that frequently respond to changes in emotional state, life style and environmental factors. Indeed, in his substantial textbook *Diseases of the Heart*, Friedberg (1966) lists elimination of tobacco and alcohol, adequate sleep, relaxation and exercise, and even psychotherapy alongside pharmacological control as methods of treating the two conditions. Clearly, therefore, a sophisticated programme of biofeedback training, such as that described by Weiss and Engel, offers ample opportunities for non-specific factors to operate. Unfortunately the lack of appropriate controls makes it impossible to specify the extent to which these factors contributed to the successful applications described above. However, there are grounds for suggesting that they may have played a part. Not the least of these is the nature of the feedback that Weiss and Engel employed.

It will be recalled that apart from when they were required to maintain heart rate within a given range, patients were not provided with direct feedback of the occurrence of PVCs. As Yates (1980) has pointed out, it is far from clear why the ability to control heart rate should lead to a reduction in PVCs. Had such reductions been confined to the range training condition this observation would, of course, lose much of its force. However, Table 5.3 shows that this was not the case; frequency of PVCs varied across conditions and, moreover, this variability was not uniform across subjects. Clearly, therefore, if the argument that improvement was non-specific is to be refuted, it becomes necessary to explain why feedback of PVCs was no more effective than heart-rate feedback. Not surprisingly, Engel has recognised this difficulty and suggested that more than one mechanism might be involved in PVC control. For example, Engel and Baile (1983) described how:

> In our laboratory two patients were seen whom we had trained to slow their ventricular rates and who had reduced frequencies of PVCs during periods when they were slowing their ventricular rates. Pharmacological studies revealed that in one case this effect was associated with a reduction in sympathetic tone whereas in the other case this effect was associated with an increase in vagal tone.

That is, control of heart rate may act in two ways to reduce frequency of PVCs; by decreasing sympathetic tone or by increasing vagal tone. While this is an interesting hypothesis, much more supporting empirical evidence is required before it can be accepted as anything more than that. Certainly the outcome of a pharmacological investigation involving only two patients falls some way short of proof that the reductions in PVCs that Weiss and Engel reported were specific to biofeedback training.

In many ways the status of heart-rate feedback is identical to that of the techniques devised to treat essential hypertension or Raynaud's disease. While each has been associated with clinically significant outcomes, in none of them has the active treatment component been unequivocally identified. However, there is one important practical aspect in which this application of biofeedback differs from the other two. That is the demand that it makes on resources. Although the programme described by Patel and North (p. 55) is wide ranging, it is relatively simple and involves only a few visits to the GP's surgery. Likewise the temperature feedback training programmes outlined in the preceding section are inexpensive both in terms of equipment and technical staff. Contrast this with the methods that Weiss and Engel employed to treat arrhythmias. Not only were patients required to take part in as many as 50 training sessions, treatment was carried out on an in-patient basis and required complex monitoring equipment. Given the heavy demand on resources that this would entail it is perhaps not surprising that large-scale clinical trials have not been forthcoming. In the first place they would be extremely expensive to mount. Furthermore, even if they showed biofeedback to be an effective method of treating PVCs and sinus tachycardia, it is unlikely that it would find other than a very limited place in clinical practice. It must be remembered that while these arrhythmias may occasion distress, they rarely pose a serious threat to the otherwise healthy patient. As Friedberg (1966) has pointed out: 'The presence of premature beats per se without associated heart disease rarely has significance as to longevity, or as to suitability for life insurance, military service or employability.'

Very few cardiologists would seek to justify treating such a condition with a procedure as costly as heart-rate feedback training. Moreover, in those instances where organic heart disease makes the control of PVCs or sinus tachycardia desirable, less expensive methods of treatment are usually available. Thus as Steptoe (1981) has argued: '. . . unless robust and stable responses can be generated in a greatly abbreviated treatment time, it is unlikely that biofeedback will be recommended as an alternative, or even an adjunct to pharmacological interventions with the problem.' Given the technical difficulties inherent in heart-rate feedback training, it is hard to envisage such advances occurring.

Concluding Remarks

It was pointed out in the preface to this book that one reason for dealing in depth with the behavioural control of cardiovascular disorders is that they provide a background against which other applications of biofeedback can be described and evaluated. This is an appropriate point, therefore, to pause and examine some conclusions that emerged from the preceding chapters. Undoubtedly one of the most interesting features of the discussion was the shift in emphasis that occurred as more empirical findings were presented. Originally the case for using biofeedback and relaxation training in a clinical setting was argued almost entirely in reductionist terms. Biofeedback was said to operate by providing the information necessary for specific autonomic responses to be brought under voluntary control by a process of operant conditioning. Similarly the value of meditation and relaxation training as methods of combating the pathological consequences of stress lie in their power to produce 'physiological changes, characteristic of an integrated hypothalamic response' (p. 24). Given this theoretical orientation, it is hardly surprising that a great deal of research into the two forms of treatment adopted a similar approach. Thus, studies were described that measured changes in respiratory rate, muscle tension, and levels of serum cholesterol, plasma renin, plasma aldosterone and urinary cortisol. However, even as these studies were being evaluated, such decidedly non-neurophysiological concepts as motivation, compliance, self-control and life style were also beginning to enter the discussion.

At this point we need to be clear why it became necessary to widen the conceptual framework within which biofeedback and relaxation training were evaluated. Quite simply the data demanded it. Recall the different outcomes reported by Kristt and Engel (1975) and Frankel *et al.* (1978); or by Patel and North (1975) and Pollack *et al.* (1977). Only when non-physiological factors were taken into account was it possible to reconcile these contradictory findings. With hindsight none of this should occasion surprise. As we have seen, efficient functioning of the cardiovascular system depends on a subtle interplay of genetic, anatomical, physiological and psychological factors. Thus it was always naïve to imagine that we could reverse cardiovascular dysfunction simply by training the sufferer to control just one of these components. This does not, of course, mean that relaxation training and/or biofeedback have no part to play in the treatment of these conditions. Indeed, we have already seen that a combined behavioural approach offers a safe first-line treatment of mild essential hypertension and Raynaud's disease.

What it does mean is that we should not necessarily expect high success rates and that when favourable outcomes are achieved, we must beware of uncritically attributing them to acquired control of the ANS. At least that is the position with cardiovascular dysfunction. When we come to address the efficacy of biofeedback in controlling headache, the problem is, if anything, even more complex.

6 BIOFEEDBACK AND PAIN

It has already been shown that evaluating the efficacy of biofeedback and relaxation training poses some formidable methodological problems, many of which were illustrated in the previous chapters. When we attempt to assess how conditions involving long-standing pain respond to treatment, however, we are faced with two additional difficulties. The first is of a technical nature and relates to the problem of how we measure the effects of treatment. The second is less readily obvious and arises from the fact that for some patients relief from pain can cause more problems than it solves.

The Measurement of Pain

In any clinical trial it is necessary to define the independent and dependent variables. To take a simple example, an investigator might wish to determine the relationship between blood pressure and dosage of a beta-blocking drug. In this case the independent variable is drug dosage and the dependent variable is blood pressure. Apart from technical details, such as which Korotkov sound represents diastolic pressure, this study presents no problems in defining the dependent variable; systolic and diastolic pressures are universally accepted as the appropriate measure. However, when we come to investigate pain states, the choice of dependent variable is much less obvious. Consider another simple hypothetical study, this time designed to test the effect of transcutaneous nerve stimulation (TNS) on chronic low-back pain. In this case there is no objective measure of pain that is analogous to systolic and diastolic blood pressure. Pain is a subjective experience, the nature and intensity of which is known only to the sufferer. Whatever the depth of our clinical judgement and however sophisticated our diagnostic equipment, estimates of another's pain can only be arrived at indirectly. This would be difficult enough were pain a mere physical sensation. As we shall see, however, it is much more than that.

Chronic Pain

The very earliest theories of pain are summarised in the following quotation by Descartes, taken from Melzack (1973).

> If for example fire . . . comes near the foot . . . the minute particles of this fire, which as you know move with great velocity, have the power to set in motion the spot of the skin of the foot which they touch, and by this means pulling upon the delicate thread . . . which is attached to the spot of the skin, they open up at the same instant the pore . . . against which the delicate thread ends, just as by pulling at one end of a rope one makes to strike at the same instant a bell which hangs at the other end.

With the development of scientific anatomy and physiology, the Cartesian view of pain gave way to more sophisticated theories. Yet despite their increased sophistication, most remained wedded to the basic concept of pain as a purely sensory phenomenon, caused by neural activity travelling unmodified from the site of the injury to a specific pain centre located in the brain. However, as pain became a subject of research in its own right it was soon apparent that this was a grossly oversimplified view. Evidence emerged from both the clinic and the psychophysiological laboratory which showed that the perception of pain relies upon a complex feedback system in which the original neural activity is open to modulation at all levels of the CNS. Thus the final perceptual experience described as pain depends upon the interaction of many factors amongst which psychological variables such as anxiety, mood, attention and past experience all play a part. (For a detailed account the reader is referred to the Gate-control theory of Melzack and Wall, 1982.) At a very simple level, we are all aware of how non-organic factors can affect pain; a headache that is almost unbearable when we are alone and depressed may fade into insignificance if we are joined by someone whose company we value. More objectively, Melzack and Torgerson (1971) have demonstrated the multi-dimensional nature of pain by analysing the language used by sufferers to describe their symptoms. They observed that as well as a sensory component, variously described as 'burning', 'aching', 'throbbing' or 'stabbing', pain was also described in terms of its affective qualities, such as 'punishing', 'exhausting' and 'terrifying'. Quite apart from pointing to the presence of the psychological dimension, the initial interest in the language of pain has led a number of workers to examine the possibility of using subjective descriptions to aid diagnosis. So far this work has proved promising rather than definitive, although one finding is particularly relevant to this chapter. Agnew and Merskey (1976) found that patients with pain of proven organic aetiology used words from the sensory category more frequently than did those whose pain was psychiatric in origin. They also noted a trend for patients with mixed diagnoses (organic and psychiatric) to use affective descriptors more frequently than those with a purely organic diagnosis.

Unless we recognise the complex nature of pain, trials designed to evaluate treatment are likely to produce data that at best will be incomplete and at worst, downright misleading. Consider the hypothetical trial of TNS. There is evidence that this form of therapy acts by modulating sensory input at a relatively low level within the CNS. Therefore, a patient whose chronic pain contained a large affective component would be unlikely to gain lasting relief from this type of treatment. Within the context of a clinical trial, such an outcome could easily lead us to reject TNS, when in fact concomitant anti-depressant therapy (or confining the treatment to non-depressed patients) might well reveal a significant clinical effect. Clearly, the choice of measuring device becomes crucial if this kind of ambiguity is to be avoided. In the above example a scale that takes account of both the sensory and affective components is called for. Regrettably, the literature shows that all too frequently little attention is paid to this aspect of research. It is not uncommon to find that an investigator has specified the placement of an EMG electrode to the nearest millimetre, yet at the same time has measured pain in a wholly atheoretical and cavalier fashion. Moreover, the problems thus created are not confined to evaluating the outcome of a specific trial. The failure to adopt a universally acceptable index of pain makes inter-trial comparisons virtually impossible. For example, it is meaningless to ask if a treatment that reduces the frequency of headaches from four per week to one is more effective than one that leads a patient to reduce his drug consumption by 62 per cent.

Chronic Pain and Secondary Gain

Although gain may become a feature of virtually any chronic condition, its relationship to pain has attracted particular attention. Consider the following case history described by Bokan, Ries and Katon (1981).

A middle-aged woman was referred to the University of Washington

Pain Clinic for evaluation and treatment of headaches and medication detoxification. No organic etiology was uncovered for her headaches, and detoxification proceeded uneventfully until the patient became suicidal after a few weeks. The patient's husband at that time confessed to having an extramarital affair. Once the affair was brought into the light of couples counseling, pieces of the puzzle began fitting together for the patient — how her husband's seemingly solicitous attitude and encouragement to seek medical help and take medications had led her to be either asleep most of the time or toxic enough to be socially inappropriate. This allowed the husband not only the opportunity to pursue his affair, but also sympathy from the couple's social network, thus tertiary gain. One could speculate that the original headache symptoms were an attempt to hold the husband in the marriage and hence were attempts at secondary gain. With these factors identified and dealt with in therapy the headaches and suicidal features subsided and the patient and her husband were able to work on their marriage.

This case report offers a particularly powerful demonstration of how chronic pain may be maintained by factors that have nothing to do with organic pathology. However, it is only during the last two decades that the role of gain in maintaining pain behaviour has been systematically investigated. The outcome of this research has led a number of authors to argue that instead of focusing on the sensory aspects of chronic pain we should concern ourselves with the pain-related behaviours exhibited by the patient (Fordyce, 1978; Roberts, 1983). Their analysis has been carried out within the framework of operant conditioning, the basic premise being that 'Pain behaviors followed contingently by reinforcing consequences may continue to occur into the future after the originating nociception has healed or abated' (Fordyce, 1983). In other words, a patient may continue to present with pain because they are being reinforced for doing so by a process of operant conditioning. For example, he is likely to attract sympathy and attention from his friends and doctor. He may be excused from undertaking work that he doesn't enjoy or even be allowed to give up work completely (and receive financial compensation for doing so). Moreover, attempts to treat his condition may further reinforce the very symptoms that they were designed to cure. It is all too common to meet chronic pain sufferers who regularly take large doses of addictive pain killers and psychotropic drugs. (Of the last 20 patients referred to me for assessment, three had been taking dipipanone hydrochloride, and 18 had been taking benzodiazepines for at least six months.) Here pain behaviour is doubly reinforced. Not only do many patients come to enjoy the state of mind that these drugs induce, but they almost all find their withdrawal symptoms deeply aversive.

In the above examples it was the patient who benefited from maintaining his symptoms. However, as the case described by Bokan *et al.* (1981) demonstrates, other people may also achieve gains from the patient's misfortune. Although pain is a private experience it occurs in a social setting, most commonly involving the family. Consequently, as the condition becomes increasingly chronic it may begin to affect the whole family dynamic. A spouse who once filled the role of housewife may now become the breadwinner and decision maker. Sexual incompatibility may be legitimised and a whole range of role-reversals become established. In so far as these changes are advantageous to the non-sick partner, then she too has a vested interest in maintaining the *status quo*. At this point it is worth mentioning that of all the ideas that I put to medical students this one attracts the most hostility. As one first-year student recently wrote:

> Personally I find it offensive to suggest that a wife would deliberately try to keep her husband sick just so that she could carry on going out to work and avoid sex. I am sure if I was married and found myself in this position I would do all I could to make him better.

Given the idealism that characterises most young medical students this indignant response is understandable. However, it demonstrates a misunderstanding of how gain operates to maintain behaviour. Only very rarely does the individual systematically work out the behaviours necessary to maintain his role as a patient. Likewise (though the account given by Bokan *et al.* might imply otherwise) a husband does not deliberately encourage his wife to take ever increasing doses of drugs in order to safeguard his extra-marital affairs. Rather these behaviours develop over a period of time and, more importantly, they tend to be acquired without awareness. Thus, returning to the example provided by Bokan *et al.* (1981), they emphasised that 'in the authors' experience, most of these gains involve an unconscious or non-volitional mechanism'. That learning can occur in this manner, given the right conditions, was neatly argued by Fordyce (1983), as follows:

> In the United States . . . people from Arkansas, when they speak, rarely sound like people from Massachusetts. They sound like people from Arkansas, and more particularly, like the specific speaking styles

of their parents. That kind of learning was not intentional, nor did it require the person to be aware that learning was under way for it to occur.

At this stage it would have been open to my critical first-year medical student to argue that it is one thing to show that learning can occur without awareness, it is quite another to show that such learning influences pain behaviour in the way that learning theorists suggest. This is a difficult argument to counter for, like pain, learning cannot be viewed directly. However, it is possible to defend the operant model on two grounds. First, case histories such as those described by Bokan *et al.* frequently cannot be adequately interpreted within any other conceptual framework. Second, as was outlined on page 29, a number of studies have shown that, by applying this model, some chronic sufferers whose condition has proved resistant to conventional therapies can be successfully treated and rehabilitated.

This is an appropriate point to refer to a somewhat different group of patients, whose symptoms are also associated with gain. Unlike the individuals described above, their pain is not due to organic pathology or physical injury, but appears to result from severe psychological trauma. This condition, variously referred to as conversion hysteria and hysterical neurosis, was first described in 1895 by Breuer and Freud when they published *Studies on Hysteria*. According to Bond (1979):

> An hysterical neurosis is one in which the symptoms have the function of reducing excessive levels of emotion and where the individual concerned is unaware of the connection between physical symptoms and underlying conflicts.

The conditions that have been ascribed to conversion hysteria are wide ranging and as well as pain include the following: amnesia, paralysis, disorders of gait, deafness, mutism and blindness (Gelder, Gath and Mayou, 1983). In some conditions diagnosis is difficult, though in the case of pain a psychogenic aetiology is often indicated by the presence of the following five factors: (1) The onset of pain is preceded by high levels of emotional stress. (2) The distribution of the pain does not conform to the known innervation of the site. (3) Pain is both poorly located and unaffected by changes in activity or position. (4) The reaction of the patient is atypical, in that while he may describe his pain as excruciating he does so in a relaxed, carefree manner, frequently referred to as *belle indifference*. (5) Despite claiming that the pain dominates his whole life, the patient often refuses any treatment that involves even the mildest discomfort.

By now it should be clear that biofeedback is not going to help patients whose symptoms have become associated with a large element of gain. Quite simply, an individual whose pain serves to maintain a supply of addictive drugs or preserve his marriage is not going to 'get better' just because we teach him to relax his forehead each time a machine starts to click! Indeed, not only will biofeedback prove ineffective in such cases, it is contra-indicated, for by subjecting the patient to yet another 'specialist' procedure involving complex machines, we confirm his status as a chronically sick person, both in his own eyes and in those of his family. This danger was clearly stated by Turner and Chapman (1982):

> We believe there may be a danger for psychotherapists in the use of biofeedback with chronic pain patients even though these methods seem on the surface to give scientific credence and respectability to psychotherapy. To the extent that preoccupation with physiology leads to ignoring the complex nature of chronic pain problems, the psychotherapist assumes a position little different from that of physicians using nerve blocks, surgeries or transcutaneous electrical stimulation . . . The therapist eager to find problems suitable for biofeedback therapy may unwittingly collude in the process of somatization by delivering a physiologically focussed treatment that legitimates the patient's denial of life problems. In the long run this may support rather than weaken pain chronicity.

Obviously this comment applies to any chronic illness. However, because pain cannot be observed directly, secondary gain poses particular problems for the research to be described here. All too often it is exceedingly difficult to establish whether a patient failed to respond to treatment because it was fundamentally ineffective, or if secondary gain was acting to maintain pain-related behaviour. Clearly, this is yet one more factor to take into account when we come to evaluate the behavioural control of headache.

Headache

Unlike hypertension, headache is a complaint from which we all suffer at some time or other. The two conditions also differ in that although frequent headache makes us all too aware of its presence, it is almost invariably benign. For example, Blau (1982) has estimated the incidence per general practice of primary cerebral tumour to be in the order of only one case every five to ten years. Yet despite its commonplace and benign nature, Simpson (1984) was still able to write that headache remains 'certainly the commonest, probably the most ambiguous and sometimes the most difficult clinical problem in medicine'. Just how common is reflected in DHSS statistics, which show that in 1979 almost half a million working days were lost through migraine alone (Blau, 1982). Moreover, this figure must inevitably underestimate the size of the problem. Given the benign nature of the complaint and the ready availability of simple analgesics, it is safe to assume that many sufferers see no need to seek medical advice. Although it is impossible to give a precise estimate of the number of cases that never find their way into DHSS statistics, a study conducted by Waters and O'Connor (1971) suggests that it is considerable. They found that only 23 per cent of female migraine sufferers had consulted their doctor about headache during the previous year and that 46 per cent had never done so at any time during their lives.

Returning to the comment made by Simpson, it isn't necessary to delve very deeply into the literature in order to see why headache should be regarded as an ambiguous clinical problem. For although in everyday conversation we speak of headache as if it were a single entity, it has, in fact, been attributed to a multiplicity of causes. For example, Budzynski (1983) listed no fewer than 15 categories of headache (or, to be more precise, head pain) including the following: muscle contraction or tension headache; vascular headache of the migraine type; cranial neuralgias; and referred pain from dental, ocular, aural, nasal, and sinus structures. However, it is not so much the large number of conditions that are associated with headache that creates problems as the fact that many of them are imprecisely and ambiguously defined.

Discussing the problem of differential diagnosis, Blau (1982) pointed out that 90 per cent of all headaches encountered in general neurological out-patient clinics are due to migraine, tension or muscle contraction. From the point of view of the present discussion this is reassuring, for it is just these conditions that have been most widely investigated and treated by the use of behavioural techniques. However, even when the discussion is confined to these common varieties of headache, the problem of definition remains. Consider the following definition of migraine, produced in 1969 by the World Federation of Neurology.

A familial disorder characterised by recurrent attacks of headache

> widely variable in intensity, frequency and duration. Attacks are commonly unilateral and are usually associated with anorexia, nausea and vomiting. In some cases they are preceded by, or associated with, neurological and mood disturbances. All the above characteristics are not necessarily present in each attack or in each patient.

Unfortunately, as Waters (1982) has pointed out, although this statement has the appearance of a definition, it is in fact too ambiguous to be of scientific value. The inclusion of words such as 'commonly', 'usually', and 'in some cases' leaves open to doubt what constitutes a true case of migraine, and even if the clinician or researcher overcomes these ambiguities, he is unlikely to survive the *coup de grâce* contained in the final sentence! Similar problems are encountered when dealing with tension headache, for which the picture is even more confused. For while in some cases the diagnostic labels 'tension headache' and 'muscle contraction headache' are used synonymously, in others they are intended to signify different conditions. For example, Budzynski uses the labels 'tension (muscle contraction) headache' and 'muscle contraction (tension) headache' interchangeably (Budzynski, 1983; p. 193). This approach accords with that of the Ad-Hoc Committee on the Classification of Headache (1962), which defined tension headache thus: '. . . associated with sustained contraction of skeletal muscles in the absence of permanent structural change, usually as part of the individual's reaction during life stress.'

Blau (1982), on the other hand, has argued that it is necessary to distinguish between muscle contraction and tension headaches. He defined the former as follows: 'that caused by a painful, tender muscle or a muscle spasm adjacent to a painful site — for example, cervical spondylosis or a painful temporomandibular joint.' Tension headache he regarded as 'commonly a symptom of anxiety or depression', characterised as follows:

> a continuous symmetrical headache, often described as an awareness or discomfort at the vertex, forehead, occiput, in a coronal distribution or all over the head, not associated with visual or gastrointestinal symptoms. The ache lasts of the order of hours, often throughout the waking period, rarely interferes with daily activities and is unaffected by analgesics, although it may respond to sedatives.

Finally, Carroll (1984) drew on the work of Olton and Noonberg (1980) to arrive at a three-part definition in which the term 'tension' refers to the following:

(1) . . . the subjectively experienced symptoms described typically as a 'tightness' or 'pressure' usually of the forehead, but sometimes located at the back of the head and neck.
(2) . . . the contracted state of the head muscles involved, usually the forehead frontalis muscles.
(3) . . . the social circumstances and emotional milieu associated with the occurrence of such headaches.

It would be difficult to produce a better illustration of the confusion and ambiguity that surround this particular diagnostic category. For quite apart from the inclusion of words such as 'usually' and 'often', the term 'tense' is variously used to describe a subjective sensation, the state of the musculature, the prevailing social atmosphere and the emotional state of the individual. Moreover, it is far from clear whether just one, some, or all of these elements need to be present in order to arrive at a diagnosis of tension headache.

Why is the question of definition such an important issue? Quite simply, without clear diagnostic criteria it is exceedingly difficult to interpret the outcome of experimental studies. Just as the use of non-standardised measures of pain makes it virtually impossible to compare outcomes, so it is with ill-defined diagnostic criteria. It was with a heavy heart therefore that I read in a recent review article (Haynes, Cuevas and Gannon, 1982) the following:

> . . . none of the (69) studies reviewed evaluated diagnostic reliability by having more than one judge independently diagnose subjects . . . Therefore, in examining the published research on muscle-contraction headache one must be exceedingly cautious in attempting to infer etiological factors because there is no guarantee that the subjects in these studies were, in fact, suffering from muscle-contraction headache.

It is to an evaluation of some of the more important of these studies that we now turn.

Tension Headaches

Despite the problem of arriving at a universally accepted definition, many clinicians and researchers act on the assumption that a significant proportion of all headaches are the direct result of sustained contraction of the scalp and neck muscles in response to psychological stress. It is hardly surprising, therefore, that much research has focused on the relation between EMG activity and headache. Broadly speaking, this research has been directed at two separate, though closely related issues. The first concerns the extent to which sufferers are able to utilise EMG feedback in order to learn to control their symptoms. The second has been aimed at gaining a deeper understanding of the aetiology and nature of tension headaches; usually by testing one or more of the following four hypotheses.

(1) During headache-free periods chronic sufferers will exhibit above-average resting levels of tension in the head and neck muscles, and/or
(2) Will show above-average increases in tension in these muscles when subjected to stress.
(3) During headaches tension in the head and neck muscles will be increased and,
(4) Reduction in headache during EMG-feedback training will be accompanied by a corresponding decrease in tension.

The outcome of these tests will be examined in detail shortly. First let us turn to the question of clinical efficacy.

Clinical Efficacy of EMG Feedback

Despite being one of the earliest attempts to demonstrate the clinical efficacy of frontalis EMG feedback, a study conducted by Budzynski, Stoyva, Adler and Mullaney (1973) remains one of the most interesting and influential to be found in the literature. The eighteen subjects that participated had been recruited through advertisements placed in a local newspaper. Initially all applicants completed a 22-item questionnaire in order to screen out those whose headaches appeared not to be due to muscle contraction. The remainder were then given a medical and psychiatric examination in order to eliminate those suffering from neurological and other organic disorders and to confirm the diagnosis of tension headache (described by the authors as 'a dull ''band like'' pain located bi-laterally in the occipital region, although it is often felt in the forehead region as well'). Throughout the two weeks preceding treatment each participant kept a diary in which headache intensity was recorded each waking hour on a six-point scale. During this period two frontalis EMG readings were taken in order to establish baseline levels. On commencing treatment participants were divided into three groups. Group A members learned to relax the frontalis muscles with the aid of EMG feedback, whereas those in group B were simply told to relax while receiving pseudofeedback in the form of a tape recording of the EMG output generated by group A subjects, which they were informed served as a focus of attention. Group C members received no treatment, but like groups A and B continued to fill in the headache diary. Training consisted of 16 sessions, 'ideally' two per week, followed by a three-month follow-up. Throughout training members of groups A and B were required to practise at home for two 15–20 minute periods each day, the procedure that they performed in the laboratory. The changes in frontalis EMG and headache ratings that occurred over the trial are shown in Figures 6.1 and 6.2 respectively.

Figure 6.1: Mean Frontalis EMG Levels Across Sessions. Group A, true feedback; group B, pseudofeedback

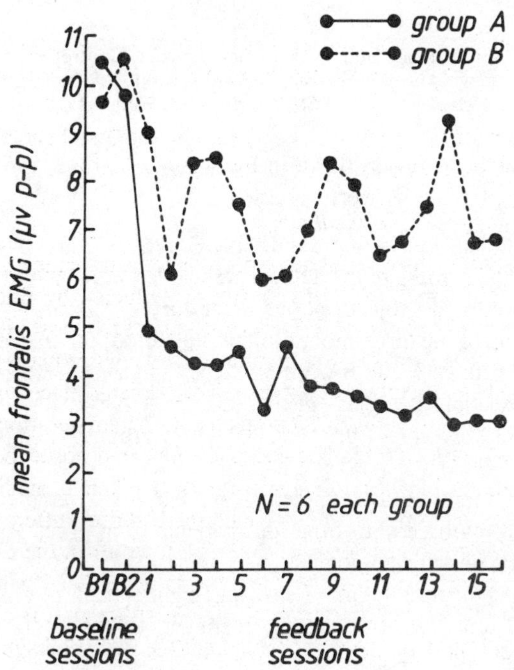

Source: 'EMG Biofeedback and Tension Headache: A Controlled Outcome Study', T.H. Budzynski, J.M. Stoyva, C.S. Adler and D.J. Mullaney, *Psychosomatic Medicine* (1973), *35* (6), 484–96, Figure 3.

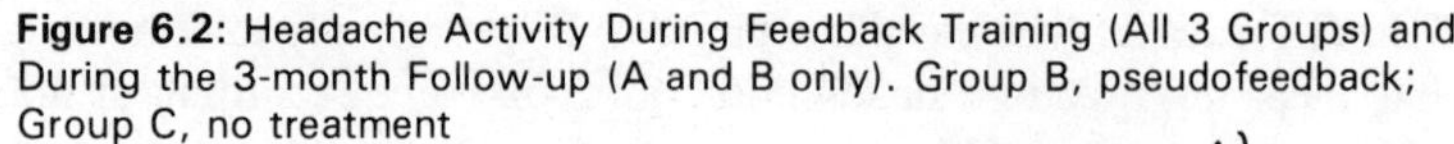

Figure 6.2: Headache Activity During Feedback Training (All 3 Groups) and During the 3-month Follow-up (A and B only). Group B, pseudofeedback; Group C, no treatment

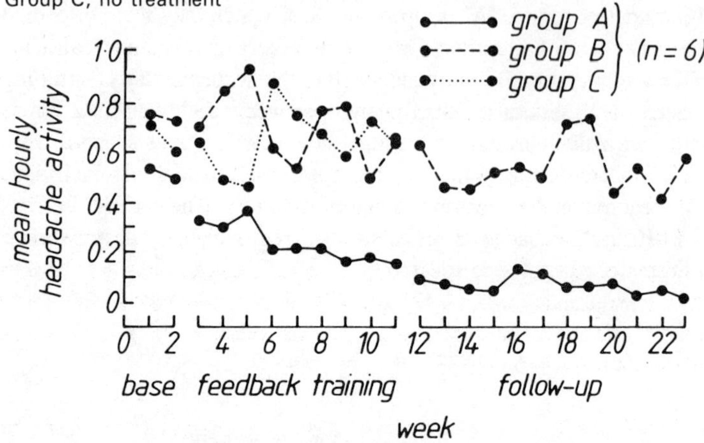

Source: 'EMG Biofeedback and Tension Headache: A Controlled Outcome Study', T.H. Budzynski, J.M. Stoyva, C.S. Adler and D.J. Mullaney, *Psychosomatic Medicine* (1973), *35* (6), 484–96, Figure 4.

As well as the changes shown in Figures 6.1 and 6.2, a number of other important findings were reported.

(1) Pre-treatment levels of frontalis EMG averaged just over 10 μV p-p, which according to the authors was 'at least double those shown by young normal subjects in our laboratory'.
(2) At the end of the three-month follow-up period, the frontalis EMG values for groups A and B were 3.92 and 8.43 μV p-p, respectively.
(3) The correlations between weekly headache activity and weekly frontalis EMG levels were +0.90 and −0.05 for groups A and B, respectively.
(4) Eighteen months after completing training, improvement had been maintained by three out of the four patients from group A whom it had proved possible to contact.
(5) Following the three-month follow-up, eight patients (3 group B and 5 group C) underwent the active treatment. Of these, six (2 group B) 'showed significant decreases in headache scores'.

Quite clearly these results show that frontalis EMG feedback was associated with reductions in headache that were both clinically significant and, in the handful of cases that were followed up, long lasting. Moreover, this initial success was not to fail the test of replication; similar studies described by Wickramasekera (1972, 1973) and Kondo and Canter (1977) were but a few of many that confirmed the efficacy of this form of biofeedback.

At this point the position appears to be straightforward, with none of the conflicting reports that characterised the behavioural treatment of essential hypertension. It is hardly surprising, therefore, that this particular application came to be regarded by many as the jewel in the crown of biofeedback. Unfortunately, this state of affairs was not to last. For at the same time that controlled trials were confirming the clinical efficacy of frontalis EMG feedback, others were undermining the theoretical assumptions upon which it was based. Indeed, as we shall see, it is hardly an exaggeration to say that for every study that confirmed one or other of the four hypotheses outlined earlier, it is possible to cite another that failed to do so.

(1) Chronic sufferers will have above average head and neck EMG resting levels during headache-free periods. The finding of Budzynski *et al.* (1973) that pre-treatment frontalis EMG activity of patients was at least twice that of controls is frequently cited as evidence to support this hypothesis (e.g. Budzynski, 1983). However, it would be unwise to attach much importance to this observation, for other than that they were 'young and normal', no details were provided to show that the control subjects were appropriate. No such criticism can be made of a well-designed study by van Boxtel and van der Ven (1978). They compared EMG activity of seven subjects known to suffer from tension headaches with that of eleven controls, both at rest and while under mental stress. Subjects were undergraduates who were recruited through a newspaper advertisement. Headache sufferers were 'extensively interviewed about frequency and nature of symptoms' and screening procedures included an eye-test and EEG, a sinus X-ray and blood pressure measurements. EMGs were recorded from four muscle sites (frontalis, trapezius, temporalis and forearm flexors) on four occasions, three with the subject at rest, the fourth while he was studying a three-page text prior to taking an examination. The results are shown in Figure 6.3.

These results confirmed those of Budzynski *et al.* (1973) in that compared with controls the headache group showed consistently higher resting levels of frontalis EMG activity. This difference was not observed in measures taken at other muscle sites, although the authors stated that recordings from the forearm 'suggested a difference in activity'. This is an interesting finding, for while other researchers have reported above-average frontalis activity in tension headache sufferers (Vaughn, Pall

Figure 6.3: Integrated EMG (μV^2) per 5-min Period in the Four Experimental Sessions. ●, headache group; ○, control group

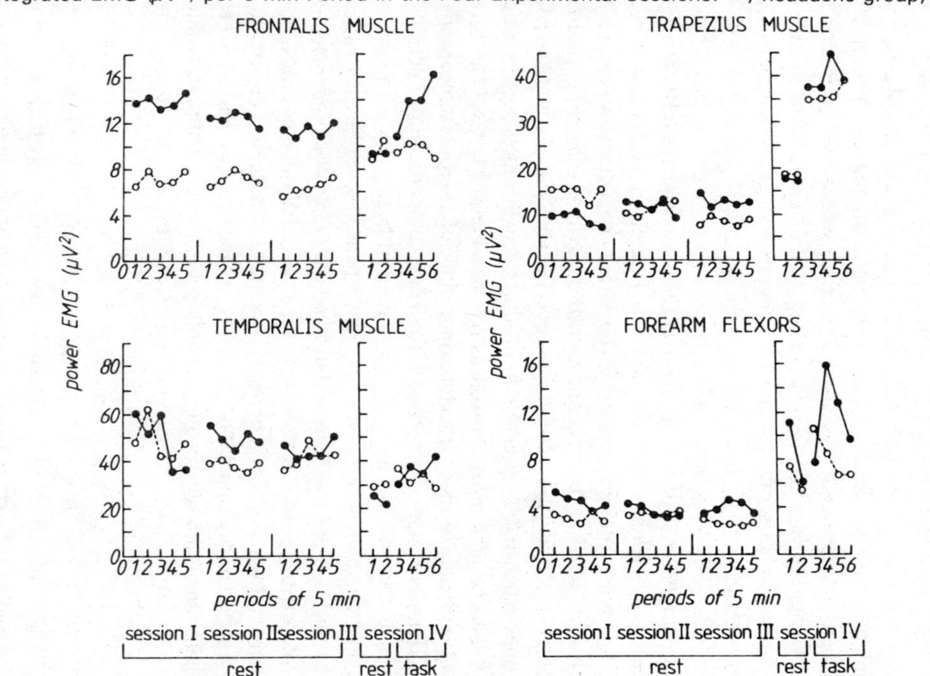

Source: 'Differential EMG Activity in Subjects with Muscle Contraction Headaches Related to Mental Effort', A. van Boxtel and R. van der Ven, *Headache* (1978), *17*, 233–37, Figure 1.

Table 6.1: Mean Baseline EMG Values (μV/s) for Migraine Patients, Muscle-Contraction Headache Patients and Controls

Patients	Non-headache Frontalis	Non-headache Neck	Headache Frontalis	Headache Neck
Migraine	48.7 ± 29.7	20.4 ± 15.1	56.1 ± 28.1	27.9 ± 28.3
Muscle-contraction	26.9 ± 17.3	14.6 ± 8.4	31.8 ± 22.8	14.6 ± 9.2
Controls	26.9 ± 9.3	8.3 ± 4.1		

Source: 'Muscle Contraction and Migraine Headache: Psychophysiologic Comparison', D.A. Bakal and J.A. Kaganov, *Headache* (1977), *17*, 208–15, Table 1.

and Haynes, 1977), few have demonstrated this degree of specificity. By doing so they appeared to offer a powerful demonstration that tension headaches are in fact associated with contraction of specific cranial muscles, thus providing the rationale for treating such headaches with frontalis EMG feedback. It was doubly unfortunate, therefore, that about the same time Bakal and Kaganov (1977) produced quite different findings.

The design of the latter study is especially interesting on three counts. First, as well as a headache-free control group, migraine sufferers were also included. Second, each headache sufferer attended the laboratory twice, once when free from symptoms and once while experiencing a severe headache, and third, as well as recording EMG levels from the neck and frontalis muscles, vasodilation of the right and left superficial temporal arteries was also monitored. The EMG data are shown in Table 6.1.

When symptom-free, migraine sufferers exhibited significantly greater frontalis activity than did the tension headache sufferers or controls, *whose levels were identical*. Furthermore, unlike the patients studied by van Boxtel and van der Ven (1978), both headache groups were found to have raised levels of neck EMG activity. Commenting on their findings, Bakal and Kaganov argued as follows:

> The failure of muscle contraction headache patients to differ in frontalis EMG activity from controls should caution those who assume an invariable relationship between muscle contraction headache and increased EMG activity.

Undoubtedly their own findings (along with a similar outcome reported by Sutton and Belar, 1982) justified this note of caution. At the same time they were not wholly incompatible with the assumption underlying the treatment of tension headache with frontalis EMG feedback. This assumption would be satisfied by a demonstration of abnormal contraction

Figure 6.4: Integrated EMG (MV/min) for 20 Trials

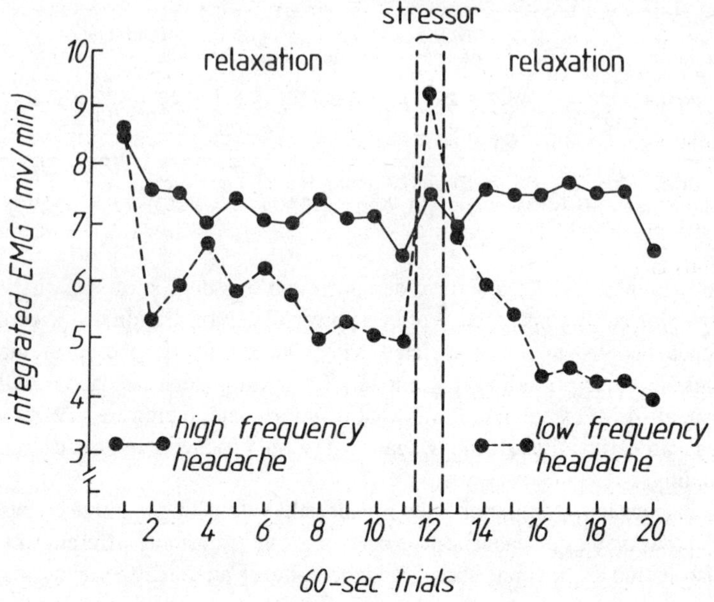

Source: 'Frontalis EMG Response to Stress in Subjects with Frequent Muscle-Contraction Headaches', R. Vaughn, M.L. Pall and S.N. Haynes, *Headache* (1977), *16*, 313–17, Figure 1.

when the sufferer is under stress or experiencing a headache or both. Here again, however, the results of experimental investigations were to prove equivocal.

(2) Chronic sufferers will show above-average increases in head and neck EMG activity when subjected to stress. A study by van Boxtel and van der Ven (1978) that offered some support for this hypothesis was described in the previous section. As Figure 6.3 shows, they found that unlike controls, headache patients showed sharp increases in frontalis activity during the 20-minute study period. No such trend was observed in recordings made from either the trapezius or the temporalis muscles. However, other studies have failed to replicate these findings. For example, Vaughn *et al.* (1977) compared the frontalis EMG levels of undergraduates with high and low frequencies of tension headaches, both at rest and under stress. Initial selection was by questionnaire, followed by screening aimed at excluding migraine sufferers. During the stress phase the subject was required to subtract silently from 300 in steps of

13 for 60 seconds. The results are shown in Figure 6.4.

While Figure 6.4 indicates that the group with a high frequency of headaches had higher resting levels than did the controls, it also shows that it was the latter group that showed the greater response to stress. It is arguable that, because they began from a higher baseline, the failure of the high-frequency group to show an equivalent increase represents nothing more than a ceiling effect. However, as Figure 6.4 makes clear, in order to sustain this interpretation it would be necessary to further argue that the high-frequency group had a lower ceiling than did the controls.

(3) During headaches tension in the head and neck muscles will increase. One of the earliest tests of this hypothesis was conducted by Tunis and Wolff (1954), in what remains one of the most wide-ranging studies to be reported. As well as measuring EMG activity of tension-headache sufferers both in the presence and absence of symptoms, they also recorded concomitant changes in extracranial pulse-wave activity of the cranial arteries, thus providing an index of vasoconstriction as well as muscle contraction. Data from 10 subjects revealed that during a right temporal muscle-contraction headache there was a 'tenfold increase of the average amplitude of action potentials from muscles in the right temporal region as compared with records during headache-free periods'. However, although providing a clear confirmation of the hypothesis under test, other findings emerged that were equally important. First, although headaches were associated with increased muscle contraction, they were also accompanied by an increase in vasoconstriction, and even during headache-free periods there was a tendency for tension-headache sufferers to be more vasoconstricted than controls. Second, it transpired that although brief episodes of either temporal artery constriction or contraction of temporal muscle alone rarely resulted in headache, the concurrence of the two more commonly did so. Tunis and Wolff summarised these findings as follows:

> In short, sustained skeletal muscle contraction in itself, if sufficiently forceful and sustained, can be painful. However, if in addition there is vasoconstriction of the relevant nutrient arteries, the amount and duration of skeletal muscle contraction necessary for pain production need be far less, and the intensity of the resultant pain from muscle contraction may be greater. It is likely that the large group of normotensive and hypertensive persons with headaches associated with emotional conflict, tension, and contraction of the cranial and cervical

> muscles are those most likely to exhibit the combination of muscle contraction and vasoconstriction. Again, however, it is unnecessary to assume that both factors must always be present to induce headache.

The importance of these findings ought not to be underestimated for they indicated that any attempt to investigate the relation between headache and muscle contraction needs to take account of concomitant changes in vascular activity. However, even when such changes have been taken into account, conflicting findings have emerged.

It will be recalled that, as well as measuring changes in EMG activity both in the absence and presence of symptoms, Bakal and Kaganov (1977) also monitored pulse velocities in the superficial temporal arteries. In the context of the present discussion the most relevant finding was that, unlike Tunis and Wolff, they observed only small, non-significant increases in frontalis EMG activity during tension headaches (Table 6.1). It is also worth noting that when challenged with bursts of white noise, both groups of headache sufferers (but not controls) showed increased vasoconstriction. One other finding worthy of mention is that reported by Haynes, Griffin, Mooney and Parise (1975), who observed a significant increase in frontalis EMG during headaches. However, this was small (5.37 mV/min compared with a baseline of 4.19 mV/min), with several subjects failing to show any increase.

(4) Reduction in headache associated with EMG feedback training will be accompanied by a corresponding decrease in tension in the head and neck muscles. Given the number of reports of the efficacy of EMG feedback, it is reasonable to expect there to be a wealth of data against which this hypothesis could be tested. Yet surprisingly few authors included any data showing changes in EMG levels as the treatment progressed. Moreover, those studies in which these data were obtained produced just about every possible outcome. For example, Budzynski *et al.* (1973) reported a correlation of 0.90 between headache activity and EMG level. Cox, Freundlich and Meyer (1975) found this correlation to be only 0.42 and, despite accounting for only 18 per cent of the variance, this was large when compared with the findings of Epstein and Abel (1977). They studied the relation between frontalis EMG and headache activity in six sufferers of tension headache. In only one case was concordance between levels of EMG and headache activity established, and in one patient decrease in headache was accompanied by increased EMG activity! Similarly Epstein, Abel, Collins, Parker and Cinciripini (1978) reported that correlations between head pain and EMG activity varied between

0.11 and 0.74 for different subjects.

Faced with this large body of conflicting data, it would be understandable if by now the reader too had become more than a little tight headed and vasoconstricted! Perhaps, therefore, we should stand back and review the position so far. We started with the simple premise that tension headaches are caused by contraction of the head and neck muscles, possibly in response to stress. Given this premise it followed that frontalis EMG feedback training should bring relief from symptoms, and this has been shown to be the case. However, as the preceding section illustrates, the initial premise has proved to be a gross oversimplification, and a summary of what EMG studies have revealed about the aetiology and nature of tension headache has to take the following form. Although some sufferers do have high resting levels of muscle tension, others do not, though many exhibit a significant degree of vasoconstriction. Moreover, when high resting levels are observed, they may not necessarily involve the head muscles. Further, the degree of increased contraction found in response to stress is highly variable and may not occur at all. Likewise, while some sufferers show very large increases in EMG activity during headaches, in others increases are either small and irregular, or totally absent — and in any case they are not invariably accompanied by headaches. Finally, the relation between reduction in headache and EMG activity following feedback training may be considerable, relatively small or non-existent.

Perhaps the first thing to be said about this summary is that it should occasion no great surprise. An examination of the various studies described in the previous section shows them to have differed not only in the criteria by which tension headache sufferers were selected, but also in a number of crucial details of experimental design. For example, investigations into the effects of stress differed both in the nature and duration of the stress-inducing task, while the site at which EMG changes were monitored also varied, as did the measures used to assess changes in pain. Add to these differences the failure of most investigators to take into account the effects of vasoconstriction and the reason for so much confusion and contradiction becomes apparent. Indeed, it is arguable that the only conclusion that can be drawn with any degree of certainty is that in many cases a diagnosis of tension headache will at best be over-simplistic and at worst downright misleading. However, this assertion immediately faces us with a paradox. Put simply, if many patients diagnosed as suffering from tension headache are not in fact the victims of increased cranial muscle contraction, then why should frontalis EMG feedback have proved such an effective method of treating them? Given that EMG feedback does nothing to the patient other than inform him of the level of tension in his muscles, there can only be two answers to this question. It achieves its effect either through the relaxation process, or via non-specific psychological factors.

Non-specific Factors in EMG Feedback

The power of even quite unexceptional psychological factors to affect headache is part of the clinician's everyday experience and was clearly demonstrated by Carrobles, Cardona and Santacreu (1981), who observed that many sufferers showed sufficient improvement during a non-treatment baseline period to render subsequent treatment unnecessary. Similar findings were described by Kewman and Roberts (1980). They found that merely requiring patients to keep detailed records of their symptoms was sufficient to lead to a decrease in both the frequency and intensity of migraine headaches. Faced with such findings it is easy to see how the favourable outcome achieved by Budzynski *et al.* (1973) might owe more to non-specific factors than to the newly acquired ability of sufferers to control the activity of a particular muscle. Like the programme devised by Patel and North to treat essential hypertension, that described by Budzynski *et al.* appears to have been designed to maximise the effects of such factors. For example, patients were told the likely cause of their headaches and the rationale underlying EMG feedback. At the same time their own role in treatment was emphasised. ('This will involve a great deal of work on your part, both here in the lab. and also at home.') Moreover, having been given a positive expectation of a favourable outcome, ('The goal of this study is to learn to relax your muscles so that the tension level never gets too high, and you no longer get headaches.') they were then made responsible for charting their own progress by regularly filling in the headache diary.

Generally speaking, attempts to determine the contribution made by non-specific factors have compared the effects of feedback with those of treatments that also utilised the monitoring equipment, but without providing feedback. An example of this method (Budzynski *et al.*, 1973) has already been described, and in this case the results were unequivocal; the effects of pseudofeedback were minimal. A somewhat different approach was adopted by Kondo and Canter (1977), who used false feedback to estimate the placebo effect. This consisted of a recorded tone that the subject was led to believe represented true feedback. Thus, all 20 participants were told the following: '. . . the pitch of the tone indicated muscle tension level and that their task was to find a way to decrease the pitch of the tone and keep it as low as possible.' After a

10- to 14-day baseline period, each subject attended ten 20-minute training sessions spread over 15 days; equal numbers of subjects received either true or false feedback. The results are shown in Table 6.2.

Although these data demonstrate the clear superiority of true feedback, they also show a small but significant improvement by the placebo

Table 6.2: Mean Number of Headaches Per Person Per 5-Day Block During the 10 Days Before Training and the 15 Days of Training

	Pre-training days		Training days		
Group	10–6	5–1	1–5	6–10	11–15
Feedback					
Mean	5.2	5.4	3.4	1.4	1.0
S.D.	1.54	1.71	.96	.50	.93
False Feedback					
Mean	4.5	5.4	4.4	3.8	3.5
S.D.	1.50	1.07	.96	1.13	.96

Note: Persons with tension-plus-migraine, mixed headaches could differentiate the two types and reported only tension headaches. S.D., standard deviation.
Source: 'True and False Electromyographic Feedback: Effect on Tension Headache', C. Kondo and A. Canter, *Journal of Abnormal Psychology* (1977), *86*, 93–5, Table 1.

group. This improvement was maintained by two of the five subjects who were available at a twelve-month follow-up (compared with four out of five who had received true feedback). Generally speaking these results are typical of those of other studies that employed this methodology. Thus, it appears that the established efficacy of EMG feedback training is more than a transitory placebo effect. Consequently, we must turn to the second general question to which this review is directed. Is feedback from a specific site necessary or are equally good results attainable by a programme of relaxation training such as that devised by Benson and his associates?

Relaxation Training and EMG Feedback Compared

Typical of this area of research is a study described by Haynes *et al.* (1975), who compared the effects of frontalis EMG feedback with those of simple relaxation training. Subjects were university students 'demonstrating distinct, frequently occurring "tension-headache" syndromes' to the extent that 'all but two had consulted a physician about their headaches'. Throughout the two weeks preceding treatment all patients maintained a headache diary and rated occurrences and intensity on an 11-point scale every two hours between 10.00 am and 10.00 pm.

Figure 6.5: Mean Headache Rate (Headaches/Week) for the 2-week Pretreatment Phase, the Week Following Treatment and at Follow-up, as a Function of Intervention Procedure

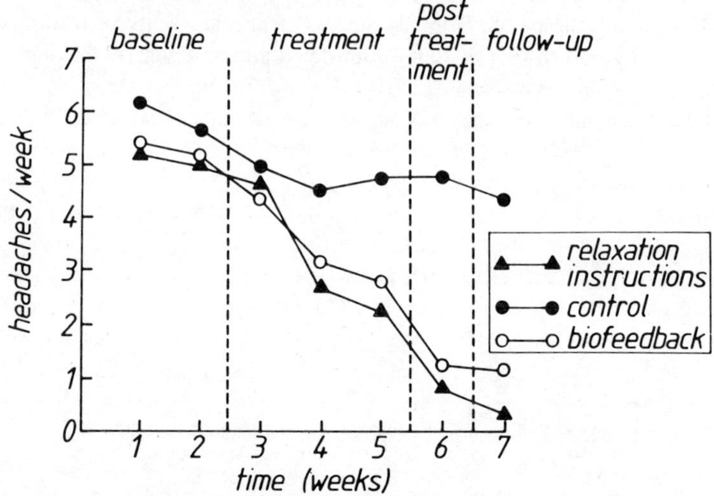

Source: 'Electromyographic Biofeedback and Relaxation Instructions in the Treatment of Muscle Contraction Headaches', S.N. Haynes, P. Griffin, D. Mooney and M. Parise, *Behavior Therapy* (1975), *6*, 672–8, Figure 1.

Thereafter, eight patients were assigned to the two treatment conditions, the remaining five acting as controls. Treatment, which occurred twice weekly for three weeks, consisted of either feedback or taped relaxation techniques. Control subjects were told to relax but received no instruction on how to do so. All subjects were encouraged to utilise what had been learned in the laboratory in order to prevent or terminate headaches and maintained headache diaries throughout the treatment period and for one week thereafter. Follow-up data were obtained by telephone some six months later. The results are shown in Figure 6.5.

While these results confirmed that frontalis EMG feedback is associated with significant and relatively long-lasting relief from headache, they also showed that virtually identical relief can be obtained by simple relaxation training. Furthermore, several other studies that addressed this problem produced almost identical outcomes. For example Cox *et al.* (1975) compared the effects of frontalis EMG feedback, relaxation training and a pharmacologically inert capsule. Both training groups showed significant decreases in headache behaviour that were not significantly different from each other. Likewise, Chesney and Shelton (1976) found that the effects of relaxation training were not enhanced by adding EMG feedback, both treatments proving superior to feedback alone.

How are these results to be interpreted? At the very least they show that although EMG feedback is effective in reducing tension headache, it is not unique among behavioural techniques in doing so. Once again, however, other evidence can be cited that makes it necessary to qualify this conclusion. For example, in the study described by Budzynski *et al.* (1973), the control patients underwent relaxation training and were treated in a virtually identical manner to those receiving feedback, yet only when they were switched to the feedback condition did they show significant improvement. Clearly, this is one case of EMG feedback proving effective where relaxation training alone had failed to do so. A further example is to be found in a study reported by Hutchings and Reinking (1976), who compared the effects of frontalis EMG feedback with those of relaxation training and a combination of the two. Eighteen subjects participated in the trial; to enter the trial they had to experience at least three headaches a week and provide 'a written physician's statement that [their] head pain was due to tension headaches', and take part in an interview 'to ascertain the acceptability of [their] headache profile in the study'. Throughout a 28-day baseline period all subjects recorded their headache activity on a 24-hour basis and, commendably, also attended three sessions at which frontalis EMG was recorded. Each of the three treatment conditions consisted of ten training sessions and thereafter all subjects continued to record their headache activity for 28 days, during which time three more EMG recordings were made. The results are shown in Figures 6.6 and 6.7. (Note that the four points plotted along the abscissa are based upon mean values of measures made during (1) the baseline period (pre), (2) the first and second half of treatment (exper-1 and exper-2, respectively) and (3) the follow-up period (post).)

Yet again we have proof of the power of EMG feedback to reduce headache, which in this case was not matched by relaxation training. Discussing their findings, the authors concluded as follows: 'Thus, verbal relaxation methods work, but they do not seem as effective as EMG-assisted methods in terms of speed of effect or extent of headache-activity reduction.'

This study was given added interest when subsequently the authors reported that six months after the end of training the inclusion of feedback in the treatment no longer predicted outcome. In a summary of their two studies, Reinking and Hutchings (1981) concluded:

> By this time, there was no longer any evidence of a treatment effect.

Figure 6.6: Mean Composite Headache Scores for Treatment Conditions over Experimental Periods

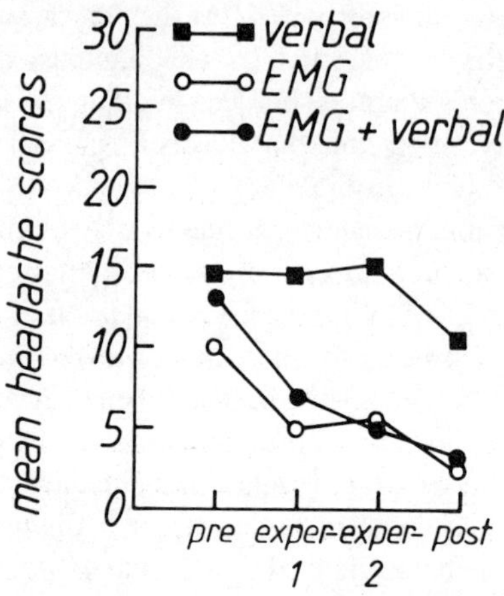

Source: 'Tension Headaches What Form of Therapy is most Effective?', D.F. Hutchings and R.H. Reinking, *Biofeedback and Self-Regulation (1976), 1* (2), 183–90, Figure 1.

Figure 6.7: Mean EMG (μV/min) for Treatment Conditions over Experimental Periods

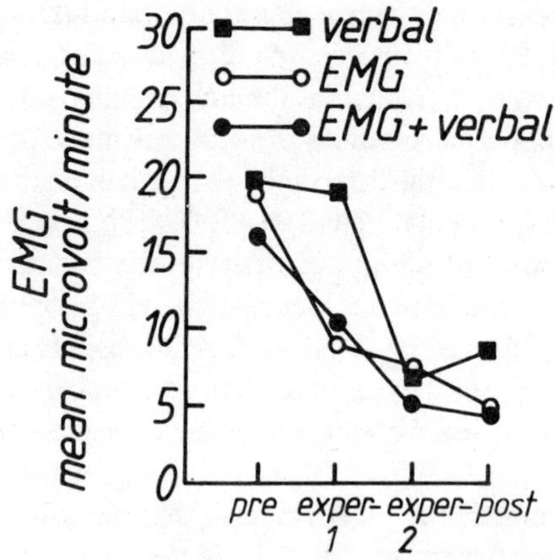

Source: 'Tension Headaches What Form of Therapy is most Effective?', D.F. Hutchings and R.H. Reinking, *Biofeedback and Self-Regulation (1976), 1* (2), 183–90, Figure 2.

> All treatment conditions were equally represented in the continued success reports. Apparently, whatever had produced the earlier favourable results was no longer effective . . . Thus it seemed that type of treatment was relevant to initial therapy success but continuation of relaxation practice was necessary if initial gains were to be maintained.

Again we are left with a series of experiments which show that there is no simple solution to the question that they were supposed to answer. For what they demonstrate is that on some occasions frontalis EMG feedback is no more effective than relaxation training, while on others it is. This position was neatly encapsulated in a paper published in 1982 by Blanchard and his associates, when they concluded that 'the machines *may* be necessary *some* of the time for *some* of the patients'. An attempt will be made to elaborate on this conclusion after the behavioural control of migraine has been discussed.

Migraine

It is often assumed that migraine is a contemporary disease, arising from the stresses, strains and self-indulgences that characterise modern industrial society. In fact this is not so, for while there are grounds for linking migraine with stress, it is by no means a 20th-century phenomenon. As Waters (1982) has pointed out, the earliest descriptions of 'sick headache' go back some 5000 years, and the account given by Hippocrates of a periodic headache with visual disturbances and vomiting has much in common with that to be found in many modern textbooks. Given that migraine has been known and described for so long, it is surprising that apart from the work of Waters and his associates, few reliable epidemiological surveys have been reported. What information is available has been summarised in a number of places (Adams, Feuerstein and Fowler, 1980; Waters, 1982, 1986) and shows migraine to be:

(1) More common in women than men, and less prevalent with increasing age (Table 6.3)
(2) Not strongly associated with a previous history of allergy or hypertension
(3) Contrary to common belief, unrelated to intelligence or social class.

Classic Migraine

The difficulty in defining migraine in a scientifically acceptable manner

Table 6.3: Prevalences of Migraine (per cent, based on clinical diagnosis) in Previous Year in Community Survey in Pontypridd, Wales, in 1968

	Age group (years)			
	21	35	55	75
Men	16.8	16.4	12.6	4.9
Women	30.1	26.0	16.6	10.3

Source: 'The Epidemiology of Headache', W.E. Waters, from *Seminars in Neurology* (Thieme-Stratton, 1982), *2* (1), 1–8, Table 4.

was outlined in the introduction to this chapter. Various authorities have attempted to overcome this problem by devising diagnostic systems that employ a number of sub-categories. For example, Blau (1982) has proposed a six-fold classification which, excluding neuralgic migraine, comprises common, classical, complete, complicated and visual migraine and migraine with unresolved complications. However, almost all research has relied upon a simpler classification that only distinguishes between classic and common migraine. Consequently this convention will be adopted in the remainder of this chapter.

The term classic migraine refers to that condition in which headache is preceded by a prodromal phase. (It is the presence of prodromal symptoms that distinguishes classic from common migraine.) The prodromal phase may last for up to 12 hours, during which marked changes in mood frequently occur and range from near euphoria at one extreme to a state of mild depression at the other. Along with these changes many sufferers develop a craving for certain foods, especially sweets and carbohydrates. Towards the end of this phase aura may develop, the most common symptom being disturbed vision, described by Simpson (1984) as 'a sensation of white or coloured lights, scintillating spots, wavy lines or defects in the visual fields'. The visual defect frequently takes the form of an enlarged blind spot, so that a colleague recently described how he recognised the onset of an attack by his inability to see both of his patient's eyes simultaneously. Less frequently aura is associated with motor disturbances and may involve numbness in the hands and around the mouth. Aura usually lasts for 25 to 30 minutes before giving way to the headache phase. This often begins as a mild localised discomfort that almost inevitably develops into an intense throbbing pain which is frequently confined to one side of the head. The pain is exacerbated by movement and many sufferers prefer to avoid bright lights. During this phase nausea is common and like the headache may persist for 2 to 3 days, though it is more frequent for both symptoms to have subsided within 12 hours.

If a single definition that embraces every aspect of migraine has proved elusive, then so too has a satisfactory account of its pathogenesis. Without doubt the failure to provide a complete theoretical account of migraine is due in no small measure to the fact that, like essential hypertension, its onset is associated with a wide range of seemingly unrelated factors. These include diet, hormonal changes, abnormal sensory input, oversleeping and psychological stress. Moreover, the picture is further complicated by the fact that not all sufferers are affected by the same precipitating factors and a given precipitant does not always provoke an attack in a vulnerable individual. The capricious nature of the relation between migraine and its precipitants is nowhere more clearly illustrated than in the case of environmental stress. No clinician who works with migraine sufferers can fail to have met the individual who announces that he is shortly to take a complete break in 'a little cottage ten miles from anywhere', only to learn subsequently that the first week of this country idyll was spent in a darkened room, with a bottle of painkillers by the bed! Faced with such observations, it is perhaps understandable that Kruk and Pycock (1983) should go so far as to assert that 'Neither the biological mediators nor the precipitating causes of migraine are known.' However, this is surely an over-pessimistic view, for while our knowledge of the pathogenesis of migraine is incomplete, the vascular theory accords with many of the observed facts.

The Vascular Theory of Migraine

Put simply, the vascular theory relates the symptoms of migraine to changes in cranial blood vessels; aura is attributed to cortical ischaemia resulting from vasoconstriction of the intra- and extra-cranial arteries, and headache to a rebound vasodilation that leads to hyperaemia. Although most authorities would accept this general interpretation, there is rather less unanimity when it comes to defining the biochemical mechanisms that must underlie these vascular changes. However, even here it is widely accepted that fluctuations in serotonin levels play a major part. For example, Mathew, Ho, Kralik, Taylor and Claghorn (1980) have suggested that:

> Increase in plasma catecholamines can account for a number of important biochemical changes occurring during the course of a migraine headache. Increase in free fatty acids, especially arachidonic acid, has been named as a key event; free fatty acids have been reported to cause platelet clumping with subsequent release of serotonin which leads to the prodromal phase of migraine headache characterized by vasoconstriction.

The theory then moves on to account for the ensuing vasodilation in a similar manner; the key mechanism in this case is a decrease in serotonin. This process was summarised by Adams *et al.* (1980) who, drawing on the work of Fanchamps (1974), proposed the following:

> A subsequent depletion of platelet serotonin levels decreases the normal tonus of the arteries, particularly the external carotid, a process that results in a passive distention of the arterial walls. In conjunction with the activity of serotonin, plasmakinin is synthesised, permeates the vessel walls and the perivascular tissue, and presumably reduces the pain threshold of the receptors in the affected vessels.

Support for this interpretation comes from both laboratory experiments and clinical observation. For example, O'Brien (1971) reported that the prodromal phase is accompanied by a 20 per cent reduction in cerebral blood flow, though it has to be added that not every attempt to link such reductions with raised levels of serotonin has proved successful. While animal studies show that intra-carotid injection of serotonin leads to decreased intra- and extra-cranial blood-flow, Lance, Anthony and Gonski (1967) failed to replicate this finding in humans; vasoconstriction being confined to the external carotid. On the other hand, the clinical observation that methysergide (a serotonin inhibitor) offers prophylactic relief points to the involvement of serotonin in the onset of migraine. Likewise the presumed association between serotonin depletion, vasodilation and headache accords with the following findings: (1) plasma serotonin levels fall by up to 72 per cent during the headache phase (Anthony, Hinterberger and Lance, 1967) and (2) it is possible to induce an attack by injecting reserpine, which is known to lead to a marked reduction in the amount of stored serotonin (Kruk and Pycock, 1983).

At this point it must be emphasised that the summary presented here is no more than a simple outline of a complex theoretical model that is still being developed. Yet even this brief account illustrates how the vascular theory enables us to deal systematically with what is by any criterion a complex and capricious phenomenon. Certainly most pharmacological treatments appear to be based upon an implicit acceptance of the theory. Reference has already been made to the prophylactic use of the serotonin inhibitor methysergide while many sufferers are prescribed ergotamine for its vasconstrictive properties. However, in the context of this discussion the importance of the vascular theory lies in the emphasis that it places upon systems controlled by the ANS. For in doing so, it offers a possible link between neurophysiological models and those that emphasise the role of psychological stress.

Migraine and Stress

Although differing in the emphasis that they place upon the role of psychological stress in the pathogenesis of migraine, most authorities accept that its effect cannot be ignored. For example, Mitchell and White (1977) saw it as probably the major factor, arguing as follows:

> . . . the majority of migraine attacks are precipitated by strong cognitive and emotional reactivity (whether covert or overt) to increased work pressure, . . . and problems involving financial, career or social position.

On the other hand, a more conservative approach was adopted by Blau (1982) who stated that:

> Patients and doctors act in collusion in overemphasising the stresses of modern life and hard work . . . Nevertheless, a proportion of migraineurs have their attacks provoked by anxiety or stress, in the family or at work.

Apart from denying that they collude with their patients, most clinicians would agree with one or other of these assertions. After all it is common for patients to attribute at least some of their attacks to emotional upheavals. In this instance clinical impression appears to be confirmed by large-scale surveys. For example, a retrospective study by Selby and Lance (1960) revealed that 67 per cent of 388 cases of headache were associated with emotional factors. There is of course a problem in assessing the reliability of such data, in that the patient's recall of the circumstances surrounding past attacks is open to all the subjective biases that can creep into the conventional clinical interview. This need not be an insurmountable obstacle when the patient attributes his attacks to some physical factor such as diet, for he can be challenged with the appropriate substance under controlled conditions. (It is interesting to note that where this has been done, the ability of sufferers to identify precipitating factors does not appear to be all that reliable. Moffett, Swash and Scott (1974) described a double-blind experiment in which 25 migraineurs who claimed that their attacks were provoked by chocolate were asked to eat two varieties, only one of which contained cocoa. The results showed that not only did this procedure induce very few attacks, but they were just as likely to occur following administration of the placebo substance.)

Unfortunately, it is far less easy to conduct an equivalent investigation when stress is suspected of being the key factor. As was pointed out in Chapter 4, experimentally induced stress lacks the long-term threat

Table 6.4: Factors Acting as Direct Precipitants of Headaches; Retrospective Enquiry

Factor	Men			Women		
	Classic migraine	Common migraine	Non-migraine headache	Classic migraine	Common migraine	Non-migraine headache
Alcohol	7	4	8	3	2	3
Diet (cheese, chocolate especially)	7	1	0	6	6	1
Hunger	10	8	9	8	7	5
Loss of sleep or oversleeping	10	10	7	7	3	2
Anger, frustration	12	8	8	13	14	8
Work problems	18	15	13	14	11	11
Personal problems	20	12	11	14	16	8
Relief of strain	8	5	3	13	10	3
Environment, weather, lighting, etc.	7	7	6	6	1	3
Psychological stress evident at onset of first migraine (excluding onset at menarche)	16	13	—	9	13	—

Source: 'Psychological Aspects of Migraine', R. Henryk-Gutt and W.L. Rees, *Journal of Psychosomatic Research* (1973), *17*, 141–53, Table 4.

Table 6.5: Prospective Enquiry

	Men		Women	
	Classic migraine	Common migraine	Classic migraine	Common migraine
No. reporting no migraine attacks	9	12	10	12
No. not returning for follow up	2	2	3	1
No. of subjects reporting attacks	14	11	12	12
Total no. of attacks in 2 months	29	20	41	31
Alcohol	2	1	0	0
Food	0	1	0	0
Hunger	0	1	0	0
Menstruation	—	—	0	3
Physical environment	2	0	2	1
Anxiety, overwork and other emotional strain	10	7	13 }	14
Anger and resentment	3	5	5 }	
Relief of strain	2	1	2	0
No cause apparent	10	5	15	10
No. of attacks appearing to have psychological precipitant	15 (50%)	13 (65%)	23 (56%)	10 (45%)

Note: Overall average, 54% migraine attacks coincide with emotional stress
Source: 'Psychological Aspects of Migraine', R. Henryk-Gutt and W.L. Rees, *Journal of Psychosomatic Research* (1973), *17*, 141–53, Table 5.

and uncertainty which is characteristic of that encountered in real life. In this case we have little choice but to rely on survey methods and take care to obtain prospective as well as retrospective data. One of the most widely quoted of these was conducted by Henryk-Gutt and Rees (1973), who compared 100 migraine sufferers (50 classic and 50 common) with non-migraine headache sufferers and headache-free controls.

Migraine sufferers were identified by means of a questionnaire administered to almost 2000 civil servants within the age range 16 to 65 years and social class range 1 to 5. Assessment took two forms; all participants completed the Eysenck Personality Inventory (EPI; Eysenck and Eysenck, 1964), the Minnesota Multiphasic Personality Inventory (MMPI; 1962) and the Buss-Durkee Hostility/Guilt Inventory (Buss and Durkee, 1957), before attending a semi-structured interview. As well as obtaining social, medical and psychological data, the interview was designed to elicit any factors that the participant believed had been responsible for precipitating headaches in the past. Additionally, migraine sufferers took part in a two-month prospective study in which they noted 'any unusual or special events coinciding in time with the attacks, as well as their emotional state around the time of the attack'.

As well as the data shown in Tables 6.4 and 6.5, the study revealed that compared with controls, migraine sufferers were more likely to:

(1) Suffer nervous symptoms or emotional difficulties
(2) Seek medical consultations for emotional symptoms
(3) 'Bottle up' anger and resentment, and exhibit an inability to express these feelings appropriately, and
(4) Display a lack of assertiveness and experience more mood swings, both in response to stress and for no identifiable reason.

The headache data go a long way towards confirming what most clinicians have long recognised, that is, along with a number of physical agents, psycho-social factors may precipitate an attack of migraine. However, as was seen to be the case with hypertension, the link between stress and migraine proved to be far from straightforward.

Common sense might dictate that if stress is a major precipitant of migraine, then the typical sufferer will be the individual who lives and works under conditions of extreme and prolonged pressure. In fact this did not prove to be the case; the amount of life stress described by migraineurs and controls proving to be virtually identical. Henryk-Gutt and Rees resolved this paradox by proposing that the defining characteristic of migraine sufferers was not the number of stressful encounters that they experienced, but their reaction to them. Drawing on the interview material and psychometric data they argued that:

> These findings suggest that migraine subjects are predisposed, by constitutional and not by environmental factors, to experience a greater than average reaction to a given quantity of stress. This would link with the objective findings of higher 'N' scores in the EPI and increase of emotional reactivity as shown on the other psychometric tests, in the migraine groups.

Finally, they concluded that:

> these findings are evidence for increased reactivity of the autonomic nervous system in migraine subjects and . . . this may provide a predisposing factor for the development of migraine attacks.

Despite the fact that a subsequent study by Philips (1976) failed to confirm that migraine sufferers have raised 'N' scores on the EPI, this was an important conclusion. For as Yates (1980) has argued, the finding that migraine sufferers are characterised by ANS lability fits well with the vascular theory, pointing out that:

> Exaggerated cranial artery responsiveness, cranial vascular variability, and general instability of the ANS have been shown to be present in migraine patients in remission.

Although the hypothesis that a labile ANS underlies the association between psychological stress and migraine has a number of weaknesses, these are certainly no more than par for this particular course. Consequently it is predictable that behavioural scientists should have directed their attention to the treatment of migraine. After all, it is easy to see why relaxation training, by virtue of its power to reduce SNS activity, might offer prophylactic relief. Similarly, in line with the vascular theory, direct feedback of changes in cranial blood-flow (a method which, though logically plausible, has so far attracted little interest from clinicians — see Budzynski, 1983), might enable the sufferer to learn to abort attacks when they occur. It is surprising, therefore, that both of these techniques were overshadowed by a form of biofeedback that, initially, was based on no theoretical foundations whatsoever. This is the method used to treat Raynaud's disease in which the patient is provided with temperature feedback.

Temperature Feedback and Migraine

The use of temperature feedback arose out of one of those serendipitous observations that are so common in medicine; Sargent, Walters and Green (1973) describe how its application was suggested by the following:

> . . . the experience of a research subject who, during the spontaneous recovery from a migraine attack, demonstrated considerable flushing in her hands with an accompanying 10°F rise in 2 min. Knowledge of this event quickly spread throughout the laboratory and prompted two individuals with migraine to volunteer for training in hand temperature control. One was wholly successful and learned to eliminate migraine for the most part. The other had a partially beneficial result, and she was able to somewhat alleviate headache intensity and reduce frequency of headache.

Obviously proof of the efficacy of hand-warming requires more than the casual description of the three cases outlined above and it was not long before a number of clinical trials were reported, all of which confirmed the original observations of Sargent *et al*. Moreover, it appeared to matter little whether the sufferer was trained to raise the temperature of his hand in absolute terms or relative to that of his forehead. Unfortunately, there is little to be gained from describing these studies in detail, for they were deficient both in design and data presentation. However, in 1976, Turin and Johnson described a small-scale study which, although not ideal in every respect, allowed some of the claims made for this form of treatment to be evaluated.

Seven migraine sufferers participated in the trial, which employed a partial cross-over design to compare the effects of hand-warming with those of hand-cooling. The characteristics of the subjects varied greatly, ranging from a 58-year-old chemist with a 50-year history of migraine at one extreme, to a 20-year-old undergraduate with a three-year history at the other. Before training there was a four- to six-week baseline period during which all subjects maintained a detailed headache diary. Thereafter feedback training took place twice weekly for a six- to 14-week period. Each session lasted 45 minutes, the first 25 minutes being an acclimatisation/baseline period during which the subject sat quietly with the thermistor attached to the index finger of the dominant hand, without receiving feedback. During the 20-minute feedback session subjects were simply instructed to try 'any nonphysical means to change their finger temperature', and other than being told to 'check the effectiveness of any given strategy by attending to the feedback meter', no advice on how the required change might be brought about was given. All subjects were required to practise their chosen strategy at home and to continue keeping the headache diary throughout the period of treatment. Of the seven subjects, four received training in finger-warming only, while the remaining three underwent six weeks of finger-cooling followed by a similar period of finger-warming. In every case subjects were led to believe that the procedure that they were undertaking was of therapeutic value.

Temperature data were compiled for each session by comparing the average temperature over the last five minutes of the baseline period with that of the whole 20-minute feedback session. Representative data from the warming condition are shown in Table 6.6.

Table 6.6: Changes in Finger Warming (Measured in °C)

Subject	Mean deviation from baseline Session 1	Session 10	Difference*
1	0.3	0.1	0.2
2	−1.3	1.2	2.5
3	−0.1	0.3	0.4
4	−0.1	1.7	1.9
5	0.1	0.4	0.3
6	0.4	0.5	0.1
7	−0.3	0.1	0.4

* $P < 0.025$ (Wilcoxon test).
Source: 'Biofeedback Therapy for Migraine Headaches', A. Turin and W.G. Johnson, *Archives of General Psychiatry* (1976), *33*, 517–19, Table 2.

By the tenth session all seven subjects had learned to perform the hand-warming manoeuvre, although in most cases the increases were small. The cooling condition followed a similar course, for although one subject was unable to perform this task at all, the other two achieved modest reductions of 0.35°C and 0.45°C. A comparable analysis of the headache diaries showed that, over the course of the trial, frequency and duration of attacks declined significantly, with an accompanying reduction in medication of more than 50 per cent. Once again, as with the treatment of essential hypertension, it is possible to point to one subject (a woman) who achieved an outstanding result, and by the end of training was free of symptoms and required no medication. Commenting on the performance of this individual, the authors remarked that: 'This was quite impressive as the subject had a 16-year history of migraines and reported that her condition had been gradually worsening during the year preceding the study.' Unfortunately we do not know how long this improvement was maintained, for it is a regrettable feature of this study that no long-term follow-up data were reported. Nevertheless, the finding that all seven patients had improved by the end of training confirmed the serendipitous observations described by Sargent *et al.* (1973). Moreover, this confirmation was given added significance by the performance of the three subjects who underwent both forms of treatment. Only when switched to the warming phase did they begin to show improvement; the condition of one of them having deteriorated during the cooling phase. Turin and Johnson regarded these latter observations as powerful evidence that the improvement which accompanied handwarming was more than a transient, machine-oriented placebo response. Undoubtedly, their data are consistent with this interpretation. However, as was argued in Chapter 5, the fact that placebo effects are controlled is not in itself proof that clinically significant improvement is specific to the treatment under investigation. Indeed, in this case there are features of the data that raise doubts as to whether hand-warming *per se* played any part in the significant relief that these patients enjoyed.

Returning to Table 6.6, it is striking that even by the tenth session most subjects were able to achieve only very small increases in temperature. Intuitively, it seems unlikely that changes of this magnitude could lead to the reduction of symptoms that was achieved. Moreover, the degree of hand-warming control and relief from migraine did not appear to be correlated. For example, the individual data contained in the original report showed that by the end of the programme patients 3 and 4 had improved to an almost identical degree. Yet, as Table 6.6 reveals, they differed markedly in their hand-warming ability. Clearly such findings demand consideration when we theorise on the nature of the mechanisms that underlie the hand-warming phenomenon.

The Sympathetic-Control Hypothesis

Some early attempts to explain the therapeutic effects of hand-warming were based upon a simple hydraulic model. This assumes that hand-warming is achieved by increasing the supply of blood to the hand, thus producing a corresponding decrease in the supply to the cranial region. Consequently, by redistributing blood to the periphery, the painful effects of vasodilation are avoided. Clearly the lack of correlation between change in finger temperature and symptomatic relief offers no support for this hypothesis; nor does the observation by Sargent *et al.* (1973)

that sufferers who attempted to increase the volume of blood in their hands by placing them in warm water rarely obtained relief. It is hardly surprising, therefore, that the hydraulic model was rejected by Sargent *et al.*, who proposed instead the sympathetic-control hypothesis, arguing as follows:

> . . . it seems reasonable to hypothesize that autogenic-feedback training for hand-warming is effective in amelioration of migraine, because patients are learning to 'turn off' excessive sympathetic outflow. Since the sympathetic control centers for vascular behaviour are located in subcortical structures, it seems that the attack on vascular dysfunction in the head is linked to a general relaxation of sympathetic outflow, rather than through hydraulic maneuvering of blood in various portions of the body.

Bearing in mind the role of the ANS in controlling the behaviour of the cardiovascular system, and given also the effects of relaxation on CNS activity, this does indeed seem a reasonable hypothesis. Not only is it internally consistent, it accords with the behavioural findings of Henryk-Gutt and Rees and closely resembles the explanations advanced by both Benson and Patel to account for the anti-hypertensive properties of the relaxation response. And herein lies a problem; for in accepting the sympathetic-control hypothesis we are again faced with the question of whether hand-warming is anything more than an esoteric way of teaching the patient to relax. Given the question, it comes as no surprise to learn that one of the earliest attempts to resolve it was undertaken by Edward Blanchard and his associates (Blanchard, Theobald, Williamson, Silver and Brown, 1978).

Subjects were recruited through newspaper and TV advertisements, followed by personal interviews in which the diagnosis of migraine was confirmed, whereupon three groups of ten patients, matched for frequency and intensity of headaches were assembled. Before treatment all participants maintained detailed headache diaries; they then underwent either feedback training or relaxation training or acted as a waiting-list control. Feedback training resembled that described by Sargent *et al.*, in that as well as receiving temperature feedback, subjects also underwent autogenic training. Relaxation training was similar to that devised by Jacobson, although here too an element of autogenic training was included. In both cases patients were asked to practise the relevant exercises for approximately 30 minutes each day. All 20 patients attended two 50-minute training sessions each week for a period of six weeks, during which time they continued to fill in headache diaries. The ten control subjects were told only that they would eventually receive whichever treatment seemed superior and in the meantime were telephoned to remind them to continue recording their headaches. A number of indices were employed to measure the effects of treatment, so that by the end of the trial the authors were able to conclude that: '. . . treated patients were having fewer headaches, and when they did have them, the headaches tended to be less painful and debilitating. Moreover, treated patients were taking less analgesic medication.'

It is worth noting that the control group also showed a significant decrease in number of headaches, though there was no equivalent improvement on the other indices. The frequency data are summarised in Figure 6.8.

Figure 6.8: Weekly Values for Average Number of Headaches per Week for each Group throughout Study, for two Expanded Treatment Groups at Last Week of Treatment, and for Follow-up Data at One, Two and Three Months

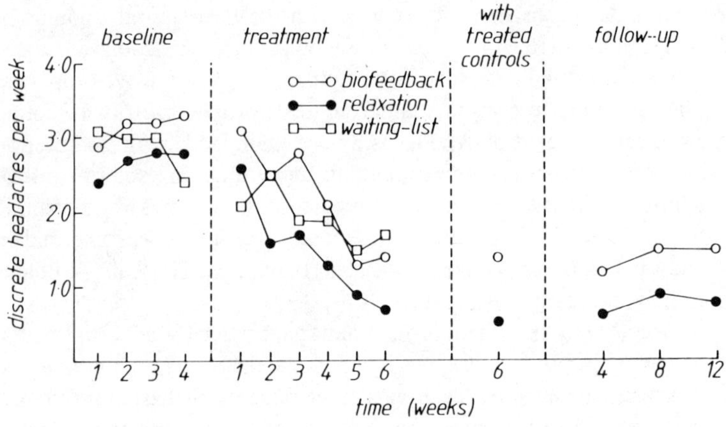

Source: 'Temperature Biofeedback in the Treatment of Migraine Headaches', E.B. Blanchard, D.E. Theobald, D.A. Williamson, B.V. Silver and D.A. Brown, *Archives of General Psychiatry* (1978), *35*, 581–8, Figure 2.

These data offer yet further proof of the efficacy of the technique first described by Sargent *et al.* (1973). Moreover, a one-year follow-up study of 18 of the patients revealed that most of the improvement had been maintained (Silver, Blanchard, Williamson, Theobald and

Brown, 1979). However, more significant was the finding that both at the cessation of training and one year later progressive relaxation proved equally effective. This latter finding led Blanchard *et al.* to conclude that: 'These results lead one to suspect that the final common pathway by which both treatments act is teaching the patient to relax and assume a more calm, relaxed attitude.' Subsequently, a number of authoritative reviews have echoed this conclusion and it is now widely accepted that virtually nothing is obtained by hand-warming that cannot be achieved by relaxation training (Turner and Chapman, 1982; Schuman, 1982; Carroll, 1984). What is especially interesting about these reviews is that, as well as pointing out the key role of relaxation in reducing symptoms, they go on to implicate other psychological factors in the final outcome. Thus Blanchard *et al.* speak of the patient learning not only to relax, but also to assume a more relaxed *attitude*. Likewise Schuman (1982) draws attention to the sense of control over pain that this form of treatment offers. Most interesting of all, however, is that even while they were espousing the sympathetic-control hypothesis, Sargent *et al.* (1973) were emphasising the role of other less-clearly defined psychological factors. As well as speculating on the role of subcortical structures they also argued as follows:

> The authors think that an important trend is beginning to take place in the areas of psychosomatic disorders and medicine. This is the increasing involvement of the patient in his own treatment. The traditional doctor-patient relationship is giving way slowly to a shared responsibility in which the patient is helped to become aware of his problems, both physical and emotional, and can therefore become a responsible partner in going toward psychosomatic and physical health.

It is striking how closely this conclusion accords with the remarks that ended Chapter 4. It was proposed then that the programme devised by Patel and her associates contained elements which, although included to motivate the patients to continue practising relaxation, would also motivate them to undertake other anti-hypertensive behaviours that had nothing to do with reducing SNS output. At the same time it was admitted that while the validity of this argument appeared self-evident, it could not be supported by empirical data. It is reassuring, therefore, to find that at least one study has examined how far the behavioural control of migraine is in fact a multi-factorial phenomenon.

Starting from the position that most migraine attacks are precipitated by strong cognitive and emotional reactivity, Mitchell and White (1977) argued that single behavioural treatments (be they relaxation training, biofeedback, or autogenic training):

> . . . not only ignore each individual's response variation to particular features of the environment, but also ignore the specific physical, situational, and psychological antecedent stressors that are now believed to be critical in the production of migraine headache.

They then went on to describe a four-stage programme of behavioural self-management that involved the following:

> teaching people to analyze and identify problems in their own personal environments and behaviours (both overt and covert), to work out their own management strategies, and to self-apply control techniques aimed at modifying both their environment and their reactions to that environment.

As the preceding discussion makes clear, there are good grounds for believing that any one of these activities might be accompanied by relief from symptoms. What makes this study particularly valuable is that Mitchell and White employed a type of multiple-baseline design that enabled the contribution of each phase of training to be examined separately.

Twelve patients began a 48-week trial, during the first 12-week phase of which all twelve simply recorded their migraine attacks. At the end of phase 1 three of them were informed that recording of symptoms had in the past been shown to be of therapeutic value, and they were asked to continue recording their attacks for the next 36 weeks. The remaining nine were then seen in a group setting and

> . . . were provided with a rationale for migraine which described the biochemical basis of migraine and asserted that they were susceptible to migraine headaches because of certain predisposing factors, namely, genetic and constitutional, and that there was nothing that they could do to control the onset of migraine once this biochemical process had started. In addition, they were told that, since the biochemical process was precipitated by frequent, intense, and disruptive emotions in response to situations and people perceived as stressful in their everyday lives, they could, by becoming more aware of and by monitoring these stress events, gradually reduce the number of migraine headaches over a period of time.

This constituted phase 2, which also lasted twelve weeks, at the end of which six patients began phase 3, in which they were instructed in skill acquisition. This consisted of training in progressive muscle relaxation, 'mental and differential relaxation, and self-desensitization'. Following a further 12 weeks, three of these patients returned for phase 4 training, which was a more advanced form of what had been acquired during phase 3, and included assertion training and habit reversal (for details see Mitchell, Piatkowska and White, 1974; Mitchell and White, 1974). The results are shown in Figure 6.9.

Figure 6.9: Changes in Migraine Frequency with Increments to Training in Behavioural Self-Management. Note: SR, self-recording only; SM, self-monitoring only; SMS_1, self-recording, self-monitoring and skill acquisition stage one; $SMS_{1,2}$, self-recording, self-monitoring and skill acquisition stages one and two

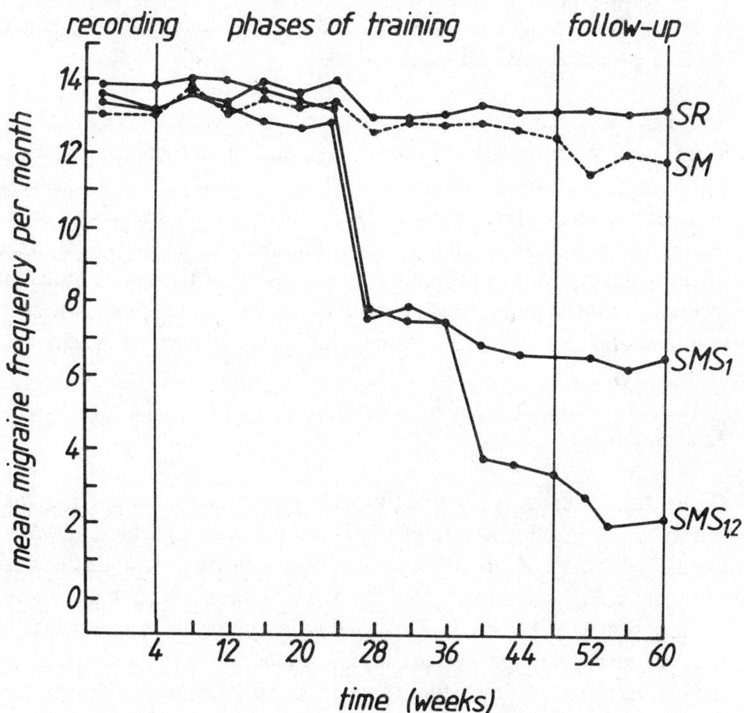

Source: 'Behavioural Self-Management: An Application to the Problem of Migraine Headaches', K.R. Mitchell and R.G. White, *Behavior Therapy* (1977), *8*, 213–21, Figure 1.

These results differ from those described by Blanchard *et al.* (1978) and by Kewman and Roberts (1980) in that self-recording of symptoms did not lead to a reduction in the frequency of attacks. It was only with skill acquisition training that any improvement occurred and, as Figure 6.9 makes clear, this was greater after the advanced training programme. The authors summarised their results as follows:

> Significant reductions in the frequency of migraine episodes occurred only when individuals were taught problem-appropriate control skills and a self-management paradigm to facilitate their self-application. As the range of skills learned increased, the additional flexibility provided greater control over antecedent stimuli and further reduced the frequency of migraine headaches . . . training has enabled the individuals concerned to modify and adapt more effectively both their environment and their reactions to their environment, and thus remain reasonably composed and better able to cope with those situations previously perceived as stressful.

Like virtually all the research discussed in this section, this study can be criticised on a number of grounds. The size of the sample was small, no account was taken of the order in which the various treatments were introduced into the programme, and the follow-up period was barely adequate. Yet despite these shortcomings this remains an important piece of research. As well as providing further proof of the vulnerability of migraine to behavioural treatments, it offers some clues as to how such treatments operate. We shall return to this study at the end of the chapter.

Evaluation

Given the complexity, ambiguity and downright contradiction that characterises much of the research described in this chapter, it would be understandable if this application of biofeedback were to be dismissed as an inadequately investigated form of treatment with nothing to offer chronic headache sufferers. Yet it would be unfortunate if this was to become the prevailing view. For amidst all the confusion and ambiguity that characterises the literature reviewed here, one fact stands out. For some patients at least, biofeedback works. The picture only begins to become unclear when we attempt to predict which patients will benefit and why. At the outset it needs emphasising that this inability to provide satisfactory answers to these questions is due in no small measure to the lack of a satisfactory definition of the illness, rather than a failure to conduct acceptable research into the treatment. Many doctors are, of course, aware of the problem of definition and also recognise that headache is far too complex a problem to lend itself to simple explanation. After all they are frequently no better placed to predict how and why a chronic headache sufferer will respond to some well-established analgesics. Consequently, referrals for biofeedback training are usually made on purely pragmatic grounds, especially as the methods described here are safe, non-invasive and free from side-effects. However, such an approach to treatment is both inefficient and unscientific and even the most sympathetic referring doctor is justified in asking if there are *any* headache sufferers for whom biofeedback is specifically indicated. In the case of EMG feedback I believe that there are.

EMG-Feedback and Tension Headache

It will be recalled that Tunis and Wolff (p. 113) described a group of headache sufferers whose symptoms are due to forceful and sustained muscle contraction. The evidence reviewed here suggests that although such individuals would benefit from EMG feedback treatment many would obtain equal relief from progressive relaxation training. However, there are some who undoubtedly would not. These are the individuals described on page 69 who simply do not know how to relax certain muscles. Although in such cases the role of EMG feedback seems self-evident, a case history helps to illustrate the point.

Recently I was asked to see a 52-year-old executive suffering from chronic head and neck pain. Neurological and X-ray investigations revealed only mild degenerative changes of the cervical vertebrae, all of which were commensurate with the patient's age. Although such changes can produce quite severe pain, the physicians felt that in this case its intensity and distribution were incompatible with such limited pathology. Consequently, I was asked to give an opinion as to whether psychological problems might be a contributing factor. An interview revealed nothing untoward; certainly there was no evidence at all that the patient was using his pain for secondary gain. However, what did emerge during the accompanying physical examination was that the neck and shoulder muscles were in an almost permanent state of spasm. This phenomenon is not uncommon and, as we have seen, led Blau to distinguish between muscle-contraction and tension headaches. Interestingly, the patient was quite unaware that his muscles were tense, even when it was pointed out to him, so it was hardly surprising that he was unable to relax them. However, during 12 weekly sessions of EMG feedback training, each lasting 30 minutes, he gradually learned to reduce EMG activity and reported a concomitant reduction in pain. Given the underlying pathology, total relief was neither expected nor achieved. Nevertheless, by the end of treatment the patient was emphatic that he had derived substantial benefit. A follow-up interview suggested that non-specific factors had played little part in his improvement; his role in the family, self-image and range of activities had not changed. Rather, in his words, 'I am doing the same things I did before treatment, but now it doesn't hurt as much'. Almost certainly, this was a case of EMG feedback training proving effective in its own right and to play down its role on the grounds that the patient had merely learned to relax his neck muscles is to miss the point. Without feedback he was quite unable to do so.

What then of the patients who are able to learn to relax unaided? In these cases the only possible grounds for providing EMG feedback would be to speed up the learning process and to mobilise non-specific factors. However, these effects should not be undervalued. We saw earlier how biofeedback might contribute to the behavioural control of hypertension by increasing the rate at which the patient learns to relax, thus helping to maintain motivation during the early stages of treatment. Similar effects on the rate of learning have been described by Budzynski (1983) when EMG feedback was used to teach headache sufferers to relax their head muscles. Moreover clinical observations suggest that in the treatment of chronic headache, its non-specific effects do not end there.

In Chapter 4, a chronic hypertensive patient was described who showed dramatic improvement from long-standing headache after biofeedback-assisted relaxation training. A two-year follow-up showed that she had remained pain free and had no need whatsoever of analgesics. As part of the follow-up one of my senior students spent an hour with her so that she could give her own impressions of the treatment. Interestingly, biofeedback did not feature prominently in her comments. Rather, most of the discussion centred on how she was now able to control her pain, without having recourse to drugs. For example:

> . . . For me the most important part was that for the first time I wasn't just an invalid, but was shown how to cure myself . . . The family never thought I would make it [a family outing], but I knew I would . . . I called at the surgery for my blood-pressure tablets and they gave me a repeat prescription for pain-killers as well. I told them, 'I don't need those any more!'

It is interesting to observe how closely this patient's report approximates to the aims of the four-stage programme devised by Mitchell and White (p. 136). It requires no great knowledge of the gate-control theory to recognise how such changes in attitudes and self-perception would contribute to a favourable outcome. It was interesting, therefore, to learn that although biofeedback and relaxation did not dominate the follow-up interview, 'she still practised relaxation for 20 minutes each day without fail.' We were even more interested to learn that she had acquired a feedback monitor of her own, in order to 'remind myself from time to time that I really am in charge'. She then went on to add that it also reminded her of how, when she first came to the clinic, '*the machine really convinced me I was getting somewhere*'. As was emphasised in the preface, anecdotal case histories have a different status to data derived from tightly controlled double-blind studies and rightly, they have only limited relevance to clinical trials designed to demonstrate efficacy. However, they are extremely relevant when, having established the efficacy of a treatment, we seek to understand its *modus operandi*. It is significant, therefore, to find that not only did the comments made by this patient echo what many others have told us at our routine debriefing sessions, they were also very similar to other published accounts. For example, Budzynski (1983; discussing a tension-headache sufferer treated by Reeves, 1976) wrote the following:

> Interestingly, this client reported that just talking about the stressful situations with the therapist (during the baseline period) did *not* help. On the other hand, the positive cognitions such as 'I can handle this', 'I can relax', etc were quite effective. In other words, the deliberate substitution of positive for negative self-statements was required to reduce headache. Based on our experience with headache patients at our private clinic, . . . we have found that the systematic modification of maladaptive thought patterns is more effective when backed by the patient's *demonstrated ability to relax* [my italics]. Therefore, we prefer to develop in the patient the relaxation skills first and then begin the cognitive skills training.

As the review of the benzodiazepines in Chapter 1 made all too clear, when different patients make virtually identical comments about their treatment we ignore what they tell us at our peril. What these patients were telling us was that, for them, biofeedback was a significant component of the treatment package, especially in the early stages of training. Moreover, the fact that this was because it 'convinced me I was getting somewhere', or 'demonstrated my ability to relax', should not lead us into the trap of dismissing it as a mere placebo. Rather, it should direct us to a more considered view of what precisely we mean by the term placebo in this context. We shall return to this question in the final chapter.

Temperature Feedback and Migraine

In certain respects, what was said about EMG feedback applies equally to the use of temperature feedback in the treatment of migraine. Thus, while numerous studies have shown that hand-warming may lead to significant relief, the benefit is often no greater than that achieved by relaxation alone. However, despite these similarities, the two cases are not identical. There is no group of migraineurs analagous to those tension-headache sufferers who need EMG feedback in order to learn to relax a specific group of muscles. To be sure there will be many who find it difficult or even impossible to relax unaided. However, there is no convincing evidence that temperature-feedback training is a more effective aid than a combination of EMG and GSR feedback. In fact my own clinical experience indicates that the latter form of training is much more acceptable to patients. Once they have been given an account of the pathogenesis of migraine it is not difficult to convince them of the logic underlying EMG and GSR feedback. Only rarely has this proved to be the case with temperature feedback; even the most detailed explanation seldom seems to convince the patient that hand-warming 'makes sense'. Add to this the long pre-treatment acclimatisation period necessary for temperature to stabilise and the fact that many patients find it impossible to produce other than the smallest increase (Table 6.6), and it becomes difficult to advance a case for this particular type of feedback. In fairness, it has to be said that this conclusion would not be shared by those who pioneered the clinical application of temperature feedback. Thus, in a recent review Green and Green (1983) claimed that: 'After using a variety of feedback modalities over a period of several years, we feel that for educating people in prevention no form of biofeedback is more useful than temperature training.'

It is unclear why such widely differing outcomes should have occurred, although the admirably detailed account that the authors gave of their training programme shows that it consists of much more than simple temperature feedback. Autogenic training, breathing exercises and EMG feedback are also included and their contribution should not be underestimated. Until it is proved otherwise, their presence will continue to sustain the widely held view that temperature feedback brings nothing to the treatment of migraine that cannot be achieved by other behavioural techniques based upon relaxation.

Concluding Remarks

This chapter began with a quotation by Simpson (1984) that headache remains 'probably the most ambiguous and sometimes the most difficult clinical problem in medicine'. The discussion that followed did nothing to challenge that assertion. Yet out of the confusion and contradiction that characterised many of the studies described here, a number of findings emerged which carried forward this evaluation of the current status of biofeedback. Chapter 5 ended with the argument that the effects of biofeedback and relaxation training in the treatment of essential hypertension are at least in part non-specific. At the same time it was acknowledged that this argument owed more to informed speculation than to empirical evidence. This is not so in the case of headache. Numerous examples have been described where symptomatic relief was not directly related to the changes in EMG activity resulting from feedback training. Additionally, the various anecdotal case reports described here highlight the importance of non-specific factors. Given that all the conditions described so far appear to be associated, to some extent, with psychological factors, this conclusion is unremarkable. However, it is a conclusion that all too often is misunderstood by clinical colleagues. This is not surprising, for within the medical profession the terms 'non-specific' and 'placebo' are often used synonymously. Other than making clear that this is not what is implied here, a detailed appraisal of this important issue will be delayed until the final chapter. However, it would be remiss to end this discussion of pain without briefly addressing two further issues.

For the reasons set out in the preface, this chapter has been confined to the behavioural control of headache. This is not meant to imply that behavioural methods cannot be applied to the treatment of a much wider range of chronic pain states. Indeed, within the last few years various forms of biofeedback have been used to treat the following problems: causalgia (Blanchard, 1979a), dysmenorrhea (Dietvorst and Osborne, 1978), low-back pain (Nouwen and Solinger, 1979), phantom limb pain (Sherman, Gall and Gormly, 1979), rheumatoid arthritis (Achterberg, McGraw and Lawlis, 1981), temporomandibular joint pain (Dahlström, Carlsson, Gale and Jansson, 1984) and pain due to Tietze's syndrome (Jones and Evans, 1980). While these studies are interesting, describing them in detail would add little to what has already been said. Virtually all showed that a proportion of patients treated derived benefit. Equally, however, it was rarely possible to specify precisely the underlying mechanisms, although most authors had to invoke non-specific factors to account fully for their findings.

Finally, a brief mention should be made of alpha-wave feedback. Many early workers seemed to regard this technique as the most appropriate form of biofeedback for treating pain. However, early enthusiasm rapidly dwindled in the face of research findings and it is generally accepted that there is no evidence that pain can be controlled by alpha-wave feedback (Schuman, 1982; Basmajian, 1983). (Feedback of EEG activity is, however, still used in the treatment of certain forms of epilepsy — for reviews of varying complexity see Yates (1980), Basmajian (1983) and Carroll (1984).)

Up to this point this evaluation of biofeedback has been confined to the treatment of what may be loosely described as stress-related conditions. However, it would be wrong to assume that biofeedback has no clinical value outside the control of such conditions. In fact, a number of applications have been described where comparison with relaxation training would be wholly irrelevant. Notable amongst these is the use of EMG feedback in the rehabilitation of stroke patients. Here the problem is not one of teaching a psychologically stressed individual to relax; rather, it involves attempting to restore tone to groups of muscles that have become flaccid as a result of physical trauma. The next section begins with an evaluation of this and other applications of biofeedback, all of which involve some form of muscle retraining.

7 CEREBROVASCULAR ACCIDENTS (STROKE)

The Faber Medical Dictionary (1975) defines stroke as 'A sudden and severe attack, as of apoplexy.' In turn, apoplexy is defined as 'loss of cerebral function due to haemorrhage or thrombosis of a cerebral vessel'. According to Simpson (1984), intracranial vascular lesions are the third commonest cause of death in Western countries. The annual incidence of cerebrovascular accidents (CVAs) is in excess of 1 per cent in the population over 65 years old. Put another way, in any one year, two people out of every 1000 will suffer an initial stroke, and one will die of a stroke. Depending upon the site of the lesion, the stroke victim may suffer a wide range of sensory and motor deficits. However, the area most commonly affected is that supplied by the middle cerebral artery. Consequently, one of the most frequent presentations is paralysis (either total or partial) of the side of the body contralateral to the site of the lesion. Almost without exception nothing can be done to reverse the course of a CVA, so that treatment is aimed at preventing further attacks and minimising the effects of residual deficits. As was pointed out in Chapter 4, by far the most important prophylactic measure is to control hypertension, usually by pharmacological means. Rehabilitation, on the other hand, relies on a combination of physical therapy and psychological support. Here the aim is to restore muscle function and maintain the patient's morale and motivation. The approach to rehabilitation was summarised by Simpson (1984) as follows;

> Early institution of treatment is essential. In the period immediately following a stroke, passive movements of limbs should be practised. Supervised exercises and encouragement should later aim at the development of mobility. Few patients, no matter how severe their original hemiplegia, cannot be taught to walk again. Later the patient should be guided in the performance of the activities of everyday living. Modifications of dress, housing, baths, lavatories and kitchen equipment may enable the patient to cope at home.

Although these are highly desirable objectives, they are often difficult to achieve. Most people who suffer a stroke find it a frightening and depressing experience. In virtually a couple of hours the sufferer may be transformed from an active member of society into a semi-paralysed patient with limited powers of speech. It is not surprising, therefore, that many such individuals become demoralised. Certainly it is easy to understand why many see little point in trying to develop movement in a limb that, as well as appearing totally flaccid, may also fail to respond to sensory input. Against this background, it is understandable why Yates (1980) should have suggested the following role for EMG feedback: 'The effect of demonstrating to a patient with apparent total paralysis that residual function remains and can be ''seen'' to be able to be varied by voluntary effort can be quite dramatic.' This observation alone would appear to justify incorporating an element of EMG feedback training into the conventional rehabilitation programme. However, some authorities have pressed the case much more strongly than this. Indeed, Basmajian, Regenos and Baker (1977) have gone so far as to claim that 'The most dramatic application of electromyographic biofeedback in this decade has been for stroke patients.'

EMG Feedback and Stroke Rehabilitation

Most reviews of this area of biofeedback training identify a study by Andrews (1964) as one of the first of any real consequence. He used needle electrodes to feed back EMG activity from the biceps and triceps to 20 hemiplegic patients whose condition had ceased to respond to conventional therapy. Initially, feedback was from the unaffected contralateral side. This provided a 'target' measure of EMG output that the patient then tried to reproduce in the affected muscles. If no activity was observed, the limb was passively moved through a range of normal movements, the patient being required to try to maintain the EMG activity thus produced. According to Andrews, the first ten patients 'all responded by developing within a period of three minutes many motor unit action potentials capable of producing strong voluntary controlled action of that muscle'. By any standards this was a remarkable observation. However, it needs pointing out that it was not supported by quantitative data, and no assessment of long-term outcome appears to have been made. Thus, the clinical relevance of the study remained undemonstrated, and it is best viewed as the starting point for subsequent research.

One of the most widely quoted studies of this application of biofeedback was described by Basmajian, Kukulka, Narayan and Takebe (1975). They compared the effectiveness of EMG feedback with that of conventional physical therapy in the treatment of foot-drop following stroke. Twenty adult volunteers were allocated at random to form the

Table 7.1: Characteristics of Group One and Group Two Patients

	Group 1, 10 patients (physical therapy only)				Group 2, 10 patients (physical therapy and biofeedback)		
Case	Age (years), Sex	Duration (months)	Recovery stage	Case	Age (years), Sex	Duration (months)	Recovery stage
1	62, F	36	1	11	48, F	24	1
2	58, F	12	2	12	53, M	4	2
3	37, F	20	2	13	60, M	65	2
4	47, F	50	2	14	52, F	27	2
5	56, M	36	2	15	52, M	12	2
6	63, M	120	3	16	38, F	5	1
7	44, F	4	1	17	62, M	10	2
8	47, M	21	2	18	30, M	48	3
9	47, M	120	3	19	45, M	6	3
10	45, F	28	3	20	58, F	24	3
Average	50.6	44.7			50.8	22.5	

Source: 'Biofeedback Treatment of Foot-Drop After Stroke Compared with Standard Rehabilitation Technique: Effects on Voluntary Control and Strength', J.V. Basmajin, C.G. Kukulka, M.G. Narayan and K. Takebe, *Archives of Physical Medicine and Rehabilitation (1975), 56,* 231–6, Table 1

two groups shown in Table 7.1. In order to enter the trial, subjects had to satisfy the following five criteria:

> (1) a cerebrovascular accident at least three months before; (2) residual foot dorsiflexion paresis; (3) a minimum passive dorsiflexion from complete plantarflexion to neutral position (90°); (4) ability to ambulate with or without a cane and/or short leg brace; and (5) no receptive aphasia.

Patients receiving conventional therapy underwent a total of fifteen 40-minute sessions of standard physical exercises aimed at facilitating ankle dorsiflexion. Identical training was given to the feedback group, except that the duration of the exercises was halved. The remaining 20 minutes were spent in EMG feedback training, which was done 'with the patient seated in a comfortable chair and with the knee in varying positions'. Outcome was assessed by comparing strength of dorsiflexion and active range of motion (ROM) measured two days before and two days after training. The results are shown in Table 7.2.

Follow-up examinations, which focused upon gait pattern, were carried out four to 16 weeks after completion of training. These results

Table 7.2: Changes in Range of Motion and Strength for Group 1 and Group 2 Patients After Training

Group 1, 10 patients (physical therapy only)			Group 2, 10 patients (physical therapy and biofeedback)		
Case	Motion (degrees)	Strength (kg)	Case	Motion (degrees)	Strength (kg)
1	−2	−1.30	11	20	2.60
2	15	0.25	12	7	4.10
3	12	1.60	13	−4	1.50
4	21	3.55	14	14	2.55
5	4	0.00	15	26	1.75
6	2	2.00	16	17	2.05
7	−3	0.25	17	2	4.70
8	11	2.10	18	16	2.05
9	−3	−1.00	19	5	0.90
10	0	3.25	20	5	2.30
Average	5.7	1.07		10.8	2.45

Source: 'Biofeedback Treatment of Foot-Drop After Stroke Compared with Standard Rehabilitation Technique: Effects on Voluntary Control and Strength', J.V. Basmajian, C.G. Kukulka, M.G. Narayan and K. Takebe, *Archives of Physical Medicine and Rehabilitation* (1975), *56*, 231–6, Table 3.

are shown in Table 7.3. Although it was assumed that the condition of the patients had stabilised, it is interesting to note that most of those receiving physical therapy showed improved performance on all three measures. Commenting on this finding, Basmajian *et al.* stated that: 'The improvement displayed by even the first group of patients suggests that a potential for functional improvement exists that is often unexploited.' However, they went on to point out that the patients receiving EMG feedback achieved increases in strength and range of movement that were approximately twice those noted above (Table 7.2). Thus, they concluded that: 'The addition of biofeedback facilitates the process. Four patients in the biofeedback group achieved and retained conscious control of dorsiflexion; three of them are now able to walk without the use of their short leg brace.'

If the work of Andrews (1964) was instrumental in arousing interest in this application of biofeedback, then it was this study that was responsible for taking it out of the laboratory and into the clinic. However, it has not gone uncriticised, especially on methodological and statistical grounds (Fish, Mayer and Herman, 1976). For example, it was unfortunate that the initial randomisation procedure produced groups that differed significantly in the mean duration from time of stroke. This leaves open the possibility that the superior outcome of the group treated with biofeedback represented nothing more than that their condition was of

Table 7.3: Gait Analysis (Dorsiflexion Control During Gait; as detailed in note)

	Group 1 (physical therapy only)					Group 2 (physical therapy and biofeedback)			
Case	Start of training	End of training	Follow-up	Time (weeks)*	Case	Start of training	End of training	Follow-up	Time (weeks)*
1	0	1	1	4	11	0	1	1	16
2	0	1	1	4	12	1	2	2	16
3	1	1	1	15	13	1	2	3	12
4	1	3	3	5	14	1	2	2	9
5	1	2	2	4	15	1	2	2	9
6	1	3	3	4	16	1	2	2	6
7	1	1			17	2	4	4	16
8	2	3	3	16	18	2	4		
9	2	2	2	4	19	2	4	4	6
10	3	3			20	3	4	4	8

Note: 0 — no dorsiflexion: complete foot drop; constant toe dragging. 1 — Trace dorsiflexion: primarily reflexive in flexion synergy; constant toe dragging. 2 — Poor dorsiflexion: continues to drag toes during swing through occasionally, entire sole down in early stance (foot flat). 3 — Fair dorsiflexion; occasional heel-toe gait pattern; most frequently, entire sole down in early stance. 4 — Good dorsiflexion: good heel-toe gait pattern; when patient tires, reverts to toe drag and/or foot flat. 5 — Normal heel-toe gait pattern

* Time in weeks since end of training.

Source: 'Biofeedback Treatment of Foot-Drop After Stroke Compared with Standard Rehabilitation Technique: Effects on Voluntary Control and Strength', J.V. Basmajian, C.G. Kukulka, M.G. Narayan and K. Takebe, *Archives of Physical Medicine and Rehabilitation* (1975), *56,* 231-6, Table 5.

more recent onset. Indeed, Burnside, Tobias and Bursill (1979) have reported that the difference in strength of the two groups (Table 7.2) becomes statistically insignificant when the effect of duration is partialled out. Clearly, therefore, promising as the findings of Basmajian *et al.* undoubtedly were, there was a need for them to be replicated before EMG feedback training could be said to have a major role in the rehabilitation of stroke victims.

An early attempt at replication was described by Burnside *et al.* (1979), who measured the effects of adding EMG feedback training to a programme of standard physical therapy designed to treat foot-drop. The two treatment groups each comprised eleven elderly subjects, matched for age, duration of illness and initial muscle strength. Treatment consisted of twelve 15-minute sessions of exercises designed to increase range of movement and muscle strength. In the experimental condition, EMG feedback was provided throughout each session. Control subjects also had the apparatus attached to their leg muscles, but no feedback was provided. The following three measures were employed to evaluate outcome; range of ankle movement (ROM), muscle strength and gait. Assessments, which were carried out 'blind', took place immediately after treatment and at a six-week follow-up. Unfortunately no quantitative data were presented, the description of outcome being confined to between-group comparisons of the number of patients who improved on the three measures at each of the two assessment points. These are shown in Table 7.4.

Table 7.4: Comparison of the Number of Patients From Each Group Showing Improvement Post-Treatment and 6-Week Follow-Up

Test	1st	2nd
ROM	E = C	E > C
Muscle strength	E > C	E > C
Gait	E = C	E > C

Source: Extracted from 'Electromyographic Feedback in the Remobilisation of Stroke Patients', I.G. Burnside, H.S. Tobias and D. Bursill, in *Research in Psychology and Medicine, 2,* eds D.J. Oborne, M.M. Gruneberg and J.R. Eiser (Academic Press, 1979), 462–8.

Discussing their findings, Burnside *et al.* concluded that:

> we feel justified in recommending the use of EMG feedback as a potentially valuable technique in the repertoire of therapists treating patients who have suffered a stroke . . .

Given the superiority of the treated group at follow-up this conclusion has some validity. However, the lack of detailed quantitative data severely restricts the conclusions that can be drawn from this study.

More recently Binder, Moll and Wolf (1981) studied two groups of five hemiplegic patients (matched for age and duration of illness) suffering from residual motor deficits in the lower extremities. All ten patients received a total of twelve 40-minute treatment sessions spread over a period of four weeks. For the control group treatment consisted entirely of standard therapeutic exercises. The experimental group was identically treated except that the exercises were combined with EMG feedback training. According to the authors, feedback was included in order to:

> (1) initiate a contraction when he was unable voluntarily to produce muscle activity, (2) maintain an active muscle contraction when the strength of a muscle contraction began to improve, (3) relax a muscle contraction when the patient was unable voluntarily to reduce muscular activity either in a hypertonic antagonist or in an agonist following an active contraction, and (4) improve or maintain motivation by providing feedback to the patient as soon as an activity was performed.

Because of these different objectives, the muscle groups targeted for training varied across trials and included the quadriceps femoris, hamstrings, anterior tibialis and gastrocnemius. Several outcome measures were employed, including ROM and timed ambulation for 50 metres on both smooth and carpeted level surfaces. All assessments were carried out 'blind' one week before treatment began and one week after it concluded. The results are summarised in Tables 7.5 and 7.6.

In one respect the data shown in Table 7.5 resemble those described by Basmajian *et al.* That is, both groups showed an increased range of ankle movement following training. However, in this instance, adding EMG feedback to conventional physical therapy did not lead to further improvement. On the other hand it did seem to facilitate performance on the timed ambulation test (Table 7.6). Binder *et al.* offered two possible explanations of this outcome:

> First, the novel electronic device used may have increased the motivation of the experimental group. Second, the speed and accuracy with which EMG biofeedback provided information to the patient during the training session may have facilitated the integration of sensory cues and motor output during ambulation.

Table 7.5: Pre-test to Post-test Changes in Active Ankle Range of Motion While Seated

Experimental Group		Control Group	
Patient	Active ankle ROM (°)	Patient	Active ankle ROM (°)
1	+11.7	6	+19.6
2	+18.0	7	+19.0
3	+ 9.0	8	+16.3
4	+12.6	9	+ 3.3
5	+25.6	10	+29.0
Mean (± S.D.)	+15.38 (±6.58)		+17.44 (±0.25)

Source: 'Evaluation of Electromyographic Biofeedback as an Adjunct to Therapeutic Exercise in Treating the Lower Extremities of Hemiplegic Patients', S.A. Binder, C.B. Moll and S.L. Wolf, *Physical Therapy,* (1981), *61* (6), 886–93, Reprinted with permission of the American Physical Therapy Association.

Table 7.6: Pre-test to Post-test Changes in Timed Ambulation

Patient	Improvement (sec)	
	Smooth surface	Carpeted surface
Experimental		
1	− 2.0	17.0
2	−36.0	6.0
3	25.0	11.5
4	98.0	59.0
5	19.0	15.0
Mean (± S.D.)	18.8 (±49.61)	21.7* (±21.26)
Control		
6	− 2.5	2.0
7	5.0	− 1.0
8	− 8.0	− 6.5
9	−15.0	−24.0
10	−41.0	−28.0
Mean (± S.D.)	−10.9 (±17.65)	−11.5 (±13.66)

*$P < 0.01$
Source: 'Evaluation of Electromyographic Biofeedback as an Adjunct to Therapeutic Exercise in Treating the Lower Extremities of Hemiplegic Patients', S.A. Binder, C.B. Moll and S.L. Wolf, *Physical Therapy* (1981), *61* (6), 886–93. Reprinted with permission of the American Physical Therapy Association

These are both plausible interpretations. However, it is again necessary to point to some difficulties raised by the data. First, the superior outcome achieved by the experimental group partly reflects the fact that in all but two instances the performance of the controls had worsened by the end of treatment. Second, because no pretreatment baseline scores were reported, it is unclear whether the improvement exhibited by the experimental group was clinically significant. However, it is worth noting that only in the carpeted condition was this improvement *statistically* significant. It seems likely, therefore, that relative to pre-treatment performance, the gains associated with EMG feedback were not necessarily all that remarkable.

Not infrequently it proves particularly difficult to restore function to a limb in which loss of muscle power is compounded by a loss of sensation. Indeed, according to Skelly and Kenedi (1982), Basmajian specifically excluded such patients from his studies 'because their prognosis was considered to be so poor'. Clearly, the case for utilising EMG feedback would be strengthened by a demonstration that it was effective in treating this type of dual dysfunction. Skelly and Kenedi (1982) sought to achieve this by comparing the degree of improvement of hemiplegic patients with or without sensory loss. Twenty subjects (eleven with sensory loss) participated in the trial all having: (1) suffered a CVA at least six months prior to the study; (2) full passive range of shoulder movement; (3) limited active elevation of the arm; (4) an ability to communicate, with full comprehension and no receptive aphasia, and; (5) reached a plateau in performance following conventional physiotherapy. Each patient underwent twelve 45-minute treatment sessions, spread over a period of four weeks. Treatment comprised a series of exercises aimed at increasing the range of arm movement, during which visual and auditory EMG feedback was provided from the deltoid muscle. Voluntary control of flexion of the shoulder was assessed immediately before and after treatment on a seven-point scale. The results are shown in Table 7.7.

At a general level these results confirmed that patients whose improvement appears to have reached a plateau may subsequently respond to further treatment. However, they also indicated that such improvement is not necessarily universal, nor, when it occurs, spectacular. Thus, two members of the control group derived no benefit from treatment, while in three other cases gains were minimal. That said, a number of patients with sensory loss did improve, and although overall the controls appeared to achieve a better outcome, this apparent superiority was not statistically significant. Summarising their findings, Skelly and Kenedi argued that:

> Since all patients had had a stroke at least six months before starting the experimental programme and had reached a plateau in their rehabilitation process, spontaneous recovery was likely to be minimal.

Table 7.7: Grades Gained by Subjects with Normal Sensation (Control Group) Compared with those with Impaired Sensation (Experimental Group)

Group	Initial grade	Final grade	Gain
1	4	6	2
2	1	4	3
3	0	1	1
4	1	2	1
5	0	0	0
6	4	5	1
7	4	6	2
8	1	1	0
9	1	3	2
Experimental group			
10	1	1	0
11	0	0	0
12	1	1	0
13	1	4	3
14	4	6	2
15	2	3	1
16	0	0	0
17	1	2	1
18	0	0	0
19	1	1	0
20	1	2	1

Source: 'EMG Biofeedback Therapy in the Re-Education of the Hemiplegic Shoulder in Patients with Sensory Loss', A.M. Skelly and R.M. Kenedi, *Physiotherapy* (1982), *68*(2), 34–37, Tables 1 and 2.

> Improvement noted at the end of the treatment period was therefore attributed to the biofeedback therapy.

Unfortunately, as the various studies outlined earlier demonstrated, the assumption that a patient has reached a plateau frequently proves to be unfounded. Thus, while these findings did nothing to weaken the case for including EMG feedback training in a rehabilitation programme, they fell short of proving that it uniquely affects outcome.

The final study to be described in this section also focused upon a group of patients who often prove difficult to rehabilitate. Flom, Quast, Boller, Berner and Goldberg (1976) described an uncontrolled case study in which EMG feedback training was used to treat five institutionalised geriatric patients. Flom *et al.* saw this as a particularly severe test of biofeedback, pointing out that:

> The psychophysical-clinical picture of the geriatric patient after a cerebro-vascular accident may include, in addition to some degree of paralysis, poor concentration skills, variable attention span, delayed reflexes, lack of motivation, and, not infrequently, receptive or expressive aphasia.

These problems were highlighted by the fact that two patients were dropped from the programme because they 'could not consistently maintain sufficient involvement in the treatment sessions.' However, the remaining three (all suffering from foot-drop) were able to complete a total of sixty 40 to 60-minute training sessions spread over a period of 12 weeks. During training, patients received visual and auditory EMG feedback (monitored at the anterior tibialis muscle), which signalled 'proper dorsiflexion activity.' They were also 'encouraged to practice with the electromyographic device on their own during the training sessions.' Changes in muscle strength, range of movement and gait were assessed throughout training and at a three-month follow-up. As well as quantitative data, Flom *et al.* presented individual case histories that charted the patient's progress. For example:

> *Patient No. 1.* a 73 year old man had a cerebrovascular accident on the right side seven months before the study. At the time of biofeedback training, he was unable to ambulate without the use of a quad cane and a short leg brace. He had Wernicke's aphasia, affecting expressive and receptive language ability, although the expressive deficit was more pronounced. He showed some signs of impaired auditory recognition, comprehension, retention, etc., but these abnormalities did not appear to interfere with training. The patient had five sessions of biofeedback training per week for 12 weeks (60 sessions). Optimal strength of the anterior tibialis was obtained after the second week; additional increases in muscle strength tapered off after the eighth week. At the end of three months, he had shown only minimal regression toward the baseline. Range of motion improved steadily for the first six weeks and had fallen off only slightly at the three month follow-up. Gait functioning improved sufficiently that the patient could discard the short leg brace, although he still needs a single-ended cane.

Given the extent of the patient's disability this was a rewarding outcome. Moreover, there seems to be little doubt that Flom *et al.* believed that biofeedback played a significant part in bringing it about. For example, in a further case history they described how the patient (an 82-year-old woman) was 'intensely motivated in biofeedback training'. At the same time they recognised that their study was too limited to allow them to judge whether biofeedback had operated at other than this non-specific level.

Evaluation

We saw, in the introduction to this chapter, that Basmajian *et al.* (1977) regarded the rehabilitation of the stroke patient as the most dramatic application of EMG feedback in this decade. Other authors have taken a similar, if more cautious view. For example, Yates (1980) referred to the rehabilitation of physical function as, 'one of the major successes of biofeedback'. Likewise, Carroll (1984) has argued that compared with tension headache, neuromuscular disorders 'would seem a much better prospect' for the application of EMG feedback training. Moreover, this generally optimistic view amongst academics has been echoed by those who meet patients in a clinical setting. Indeed, some of the most interesting work has originated in the clinic rather than the laboratory. For example, Sherwood and Hewlett (1984) described how micro-computers can be used to feed back EMG activity so that:

> (1) . . . the patients can clearly distinguish between the two different sorts of muscle activity . . ., (2) . . . a desired movement can be given a more accurate feedback . . ., and (3) treatment which can often be tedious or boring is made more interesting . . .

Clearly then this application of biofeedback has already gained a relatively wide degree of acceptance amongst clinicians and researchers alike. What remains to be answered is whether this acceptance is justified.

Judged solely in terms of outcome, there is no doubt that the studies described here are clinically relevant. To be sure, some patients derived no benefit from treatment and others achieved only minimal gains. However, this was only to be expected. In most instances a considerable time had elapsed since the original CVA, while two of the studies deliberately focussed upon categories of patients whose symptoms are known to be particularly resistant to treatment. At the very least, therefore, the findings described here should warn us against assuming too readily that a patient has reached a point where further treatment would be to no avail. As Gonnella, Kalish and Hale (1978) have pointed out:

> The results violate some of the present assumptions about recovery capacity and recovery time, and hence the practice of the limited time allowed for rehabilitation. For example, often a patient is told *not* to expect any recovery if it has not occurred within one year following insult.

However, when we attempt to specify the part played by biofeedback in achieving these results, the picture is much less clear.

Superficially, at least, the first three studies reviewed here all appeared to show that EMG feedback does add significantly to the effects of conventional physical therapy. Yet as we have seen, all three were open to criticism in terms of design or data presentation. Moreover, even if these specific criticisms were to be totally disregarded, the case for biofeedback as a specific method of treating stroke patients would remain unproven. Although Basmajian *et al.* (1977), Burnside *et al.* (1979) and Binder *et al.* (1981) all employed comparison groups, none included a placebo-control condition. The reason for this omission is unclear, though I suspect it was due in part to the problem of defining what constitutes an appropriate placebo. As was pointed out in Chapter 3, in carrying out a drug trial it is a relatively simple matter to produce a pharmacologically inert capsule that is otherwise identical to the one being tested. It is much less easy to produce a psychologically inert form of biofeedback. We saw, when discussing the treatment of tension headache, how a number of workers had attempted to overcome this problem by employing false feedback. However, in so far as the patient is likely to be confused by such feedback, it can hardly be said to be neutral, and is, therefore, of questionable scientific validity. Moreover, in the case of stroke patients I believe it to be ethically questionable too. Most stroke patients are only too aware of their residual deficits and frequently experience severe frustration and anxiety as they struggle to overcome them. It could only add to their distress if their attempts at muscle control were to be further disrupted by an experimenter deliberately misleading them with inappropriate feedback. Judgements about what is ethical are, of course, subjective, and it may be for quite different reasons that to date only one study has been reported in which false feedback was employed as a placebo control. In the event the outcome left the picture more, rather than less confused.

Lee, Hill, Johnston and Smiehorowski (1976) studied 18 hemiplegic patients, all of whom exhibited reduced strength in the deltoid muscle.

On each of three successive days all patients performed 20 isometric contractions of the affected muscle, each lasting five seconds, with a rest interval of ten seconds. Peak EMG activity for each of the 20 contractions was measured while the patient received: (1) no feedback, (2) true EMG feedback or (3) false feedback (consisting of activity brought about by the experimenter contracting *his* muscles). Each patient acted as his own control, the order in which the three treatments were administered being randomly determined. The outcome is summarised in Figure 7.1.

Figure 7.1: Overall Summary of Linear Regression Lines for all 18 Subjects Without Grouping. TMF, true myofeedback condition; PMF, placebo myofeedback condition; NMF, no myofeedback condition

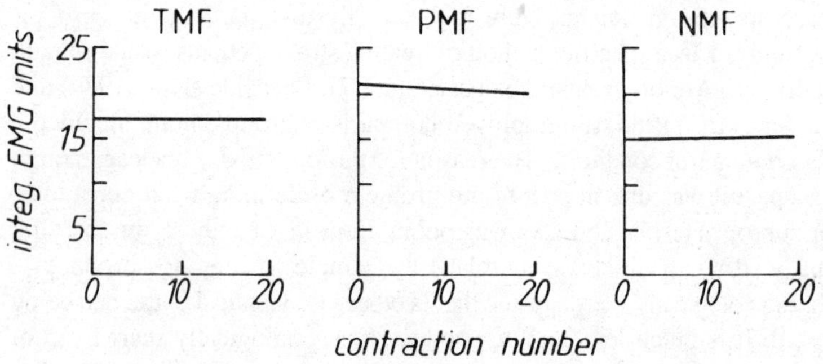

Source: 'Myofeedback for Muscle Retraining in Hemiplegic Patients', K-H. Lee, E. Hill, R. Johnston and T. Smiehorowski, *Archives of Physical Medicine and Rehabilitation* (1976), *57*, 588–91, Figure 5.

Any attempt to evaluate these findings has to take into account the fact that for each subject the duration of biofeedback training was less than two minutes. As Carroll (1984) has pointed out, this is hardly sufficient to provide a test of clinical efficacy. Nevertheless, the lack of improvement in the true feedback condition could be said to represent a failure to replicate the findings of Andrews (p. 146). However, even this conclusion needs to be qualified. As well as analysing their data in the manner shown in Figure 7.1, Lee *et al.* also grouped their subjects according to age and level of motivation. This analysis revealed that during the feedback conditions the older and less well-motivated subjects did in fact improve their EMG output across trials. It is difficult to know what to make of this finding. Certainly it is at odds with clinical observations and suggests that some uncontrolled factors may have contaminated the outcome.

By now it is clear that the clinical trials described so far lacked the sophistication necessary to show unequivocally that biofeedback operates at other than a non-specific level in the rehabilitation of stroke patients. It is frustrating to have to reach such a conclusion, for at an intuitive level it appears likely that EMG feedback training would bring something unique to the rehabilitation programme. Certainly in severe cases it is often the only means whereby the sufferer can be made aware that his attempts to regain voluntary control of a seemingly 'dead' limb are beginning to bear fruit. Moreover, this frustration is not diminished by the recognition that in principle this ought to be one of the more straightforward applications of biofeedback to research. There is rarely any question about the aetiology of the disability, the supply of patients is all too abundant, and EMG feedback training is simple and need not delay or interfere with conventional methods of treatment. Unfortunately, this is for the future. In the meantime what is the place of biofeedback in the rehabilitation of the stroke patient?

As the comments by Yates (p. 146), Flom *et al.* (p. 156) and the work of Sherwood and Hewlett (p. 156) illustrate, the effects of EMG feedback on morale and motivation can be considerable. In my opinion its use as an adjunct to conventional therapy is justified on these grounds alone, quite apart from any specific effects it may be shown to possess. For it bears repeating that, despite their shortcomings, the clinical trials described here all reported worthwhile gains by patients in whom no further improvement seemed likely.

Although the whole of this chapter has been devoted to the rehabilitation of stroke victims, there are many other examples of muscle dysfunction that, in principle, appear to be candidates for this method of treatment. Some of these are described in the next two chapters. As we shall see, these disorders differ in many respects. However, they have one feature in common; in every case the patient would benefit if the activity of certain groups of malfunctioning muscles could be brought under voluntary control. I have chosen to describe these applications under two headings; focal dystonias and sphincter disorders (plus a brief section devoted to miscellaneous conditions). However, it must be recognised that this distinction is arbitrary and is not meant to imply a particular theoretical orientation towards either treatment or aetiology.

8 FOCAL DYSTONIA

The term dystonia is often applied to a number of distinct neurological disorders, all of which are characterised by involuntary postures or movements. However, as Fahn and Eldridge (1976) have pointed out, because the aetiology of the syndrome remains obscure, the use of the term dystonia is best restricted to categorising symptoms. These are described as 'sustained, involuntary twisting movements, which may affect muscle groups of varying size in the limbs, trunk, neck or face'. Moreover, as Fahn and Eldridge further observed, within this general description there is room for considerable variability. Thus, while the involuntary movements are usually slow, they may also be repetitive, jerky or even tic-like. Similarly, while in some instances they affect the whole body, in others they may be segmented or, as in the conditions described here, focal, involving only localised muscle groups. Although the aetiology of the focal dystonias has yet to be determined, current opinion appears to favour a neurological interpretation (see the symposium introduced by Klassen, 1984, for a clinically oriented review.) However, a number of authors have continued to draw attention to the part played by psychological factors in the aetiology of these bizarre conditions. Consequently I have been guided by this consideration when deciding which conditions to include in the following review. Certainly if the only criteria for inclusion were frequency of occurrence and threat posed to the patient, then neither spasmodic torticollis nor writer's cramp would merit the coverage that they are accorded here. However, for whatever reasons, these two conditions have been subjected to considerable research, the outcome of which can, I believe, be generalised to other less-widely investigated dystonic states.

Spasmodic Torticollis

Spasmodic torticollis (wryneck) is a relatively rare condition that occurs most often in middle aged women. It is characterised by involuntary activity of the sternocleidomastoid, trapezius and splenius capitis muscles, which produces abnormal rotation of the head and neck. Muscle spasm may be tonic, in which case the head is deviated to one side in a fixed position or clonic, when the head is pushed to one side several times per minute. In common with other dystonic movements, symptoms are normally absent during sleep and increase in severity throughout the patient's waking hours. Not surprisingly, sufferers frequently become more and more withdrawn and isolated as the severity of their symptoms increases. In the words of Sorensen and Hamby (1966);

> Few conditions are as distressing to the patient and his family as spasmodic torticollis. These people, once happy and gregarious, often plunge into depression and withdraw from previous friends and social situations. Some victims change or quit their jobs. Others with latent emotional maladjustments develop overt psychological problems. Happy is the patient who can gain relief from his malady — completely or partially.

Unfortunately, relief from the malady appears to be the exception rather than the rule. Spontaneous remission is rare and response to a wide range of treatments is variable and unpredictable. Drug therapy has proved especially disappointing. While anticholinergics, dopaminergics, neuroleptics or benzodiazepines all have their adherents, evidence of their efficacy is at best conflicting. Indeed, as Klassen (1984) has pointed out, drugs that have diametrically opposed effects on neurotransmitter systems may result in similar degrees of improvement or worsening. Likewise, the same drug can produce widely differing outcomes. For example, Ahmad and Meeran (1979) presented two case reports which, they argued, demonstrated the efficacy of diazepam in the management of the disorder. Subsequently, however, Francis (1983) described how discontinuation of diazepam (initially prescribed to treat anxiety neurosis) led to a progressive decrease in attacks, so that the previously incapacitated patient was able to resume work. Little wonder then that in 1979 an editorial in *The British Medical Journal* concluded that: 'The various medical remedies have in common only their uselessness'. Moreover, the conclusion as to the efficacy of surgical procedures was only marginally more encouraging:

> Bilateral stereotactic surgery of the thalamus has produced occasional successes, but the results of most such operations have been disappointing. Anterior cervical rhizotomy, with division of the appropriate spinal accessory nerve, produced satisfactory results in some cases, but again there were late relapses. Indeed, despite all the recent attempts to clarify its causation and to find suitable treatment, established torticollis still poses intractable problems.

The BMJ might also have warned its readers that even when neurosurgery leads to a favourable outcome, success is not achieved without cost. Of 71 patients described by Sorensen and Hamby (1966), one died post-operatively, four 'obtained very little improvement or were made worse' and seven 'acquired prominent objectionable side effects and complications such as weakness and limitation of motion of the head and neck or considerable difficulty with swallowing'.

Perhaps the main reason why progress in the treatment of spasmodic torticollis has been so limited is because, in common with other focal dystonias, the nature of the underlying mechanisms remains obscure. As was pointed out earlier, attempts to account for the condition have adopted either a neurological or a psychological perspective. The former approach has been vigorously propounded by Sorensen and Hamby (1966), who, while acknowledging that 'there are, no doubt, some psychologically deranged persons whose symptomatology could mimic torticollis', went on to argue that:

> The opinion of most who see and treat this condition is that it is due to some organic change within the nervous system. A major limitation to therapy is, of course, lack of knowledge of the known site of the lesion. When such a discovery is made, more effective treatment may be anticipated. Continued evaluation of these patients and detailed postmortem examination of the involved brains and spinal cords may yet reveal pertinent information.

Up to now, however, this optimistic outlook has not been fulfilled. A detailed post-mortem examination by Tarlov (1970) of a patient with a six-year history of spasmodic torticollis failed to reveal any relevant changes in the brain.

If attempts to explain spasmodic torticollis in neurological terms have fallen some way short of total success, then a purely psychological approach has fared no better. For example, Cockburn (1971) found that compared with matched controls, sufferers from torticollis exhibited no greater degree of psychological, personality or social disturbance prior to the onset of symptoms. It is, of course, perfectly possible that a movement disorder may have more than one cause. This view was adopted by Hyslop (1949) and subsequently restated by Tibbetts (1971) who, on the basis of clinical observations, suggested a division into typical and atypical torticollis. The former was viewed as having an organic aetiology while the latter was believed to be of psychogenic origin. We shall return to this distinction when discussing the aetiology of writer's cramp. In the present context, however, it should not be regarded as anything more than an interesting working hypothesis.

Biofeedback and Spasmodic Torticollis

Although the aetiology of torticollis remains a subject of debate, there is no disagreement that the symptoms are associated with changes in the activity and structure of the neck muscles. Consequently, there is a certain logic in treating the typical postural changes with EMG feedback training. In fact, thanks largely to the work of two research groups, this particular application of biofeedback has been one of the most thoroughly investigated of all. Indeed, Yates (1980) has gone so far as to claim that the work of Korein and Brudny and their associates 'represents one of the most extensive and important large-scale contributions to the use of biofeedback in abnormalities of function'. Yates underlined his enthusiasm for the work of this group by suggesting that it merits 'very careful study by anyone working in *any* remedial area involving biofeedback'. This research is examined in due course. We begin, however, by considering the manner in which Charles Cleeland and his associates have employed EMG feedback to treat spasmodic torticollis.

The technique employed by Cleeland is unusual in that EMG activity is put to two uses. As well as providing the appropriate feedback, it also serves to trigger a switch that delivers a small electric shock to the patient's finger when tension in the neck muscles exceeds a certain limit. As the reader may be aware, response contingent aversive stimuli have been widely used by clinical psychologists to treat many so-called 'deviant' behaviours. In the present case, however, the term aversion therapy is barely justified. As Cleeland (1983) has pointed out, the current used is set at a level below that which patients find painful and most of them are reluctant to have it discontinued. An early application of this technique was described by Cleeland (1973). Ten patients (nine with spasmodic torticollis, one with retrocollis) were treated as inpatients for a period of two to three weeks. Surface electrodes (placed near the border and just above the clavicular attachment of both the left and right sternocleidomastoid muscles) fulfilled the dual role outlined above. Feedback consisted of an auditory tone that varied in pitch as a function of EMG activity. Spasm contingent shock (which was introduced after seven sessions of EMG feedback training) was delivered via two plate electrodes attached to the first and second fingers. Each session lasted approximately 45 minutes and all patients underwent one or two sessions each day. As treatment progressed, less EMG activity was required to initiate feedback and/or shock. Response to treatment was measured on a three-point scale;

(1) marked (+ +), (2) moderate (+), (3) minimal or no improvement (0). The results are summarised in Table 8.1.

Commenting on his data, Cleeland (1973) concluded that:

> The potential therapeutic benefit of the procedure described is limited by the time demands on both patient and clinician and by the specialised equipment required for the contingencies described, but the procedure may prove of benefit to some patients refractory to other treatment methods. The most significant improvement was shown by patients who were younger and for whom torticollis was a symptom of relatively short duration, although no older patients with torticollis of short duration (less than six months) were included in the study. Some of the patients in this report may well have responded to the more recently reported medical treatments available, although three of the patients were refractory to haloperidol, amantadine hydrochloride, or combinations of these two agents. One of these three patients showed marked improvement with shock-feedback; two were classified as unimproved.

More recently, Cleeland (1983) has published results relating to 52 cases treated in a similar (though somewhat more elaborate) manner to that outlined above. These showed that by the end of training 16 patients had undergone marked improvement, in 28 cases improvement was moderate, while the remaining 8 patients obtained no benefit. Follow-up data for 37 patients (after a mean period of 30.5 months) showed the numbers falling into the above categories to be 8, 18 and 11, respectively.

Similar outcomes to those just described were reported by Korein and Brudny in the other major series to be described here. Their technique differed from that of Cleeland in that the shock component was excluded and feedback training took two forms. As well as being trained to decrease spasm in the affected muscle, the patient also attempted to increase tone in its contralateral counterpart. An early application of this method was described by Brudny, Grynbaum and Korein (1974). Nine patients underwent from three to five training sessions per week for an average of ten weeks. As Table 8.2 shows, the pattern of EMG activity changed dramatically over the course of treatment. As well as changes in EMG shown in Table 8.2, all patients exhibited improved head posture and a decrease in pain. A typical 'before and after' photograph is shown in Figure 8.1.

Subsequently, Brudny, Korein, Grynbaum, Friedmann, Weinstein,

Table 8.1: Data For Nine Patients with Torticollis and One with Retrocollis

Case	Age, Sex	Symptom duration (months)	Sessions	Initial spasm frequency/5 minutes	Final spasm frequency/5 minutes	Shock effect	Initial improvement	Follow-up improvement (duration, months)
1	15, M	4	16	44	3	+	+ +	+ + (18)
2	25, F	60	6	21	6	+	+	+ (40)
3	64, M	36	23	188	168	0	0	0 (17)
4	50, F	24	10	40	1	+	+	+ (18)
5	28, M	9	8	75	46	+	+	Lost to follow-up
6*	54, F	36	8	40	0	+	+ +	+ (17)
7	18, F	2	15	11	0	+	+ +	+ + (24)
8	54, F	10	10	54	11	+	+	0 (20)
9	43, F	7	8	34	8	0	+	0 (5)
10	32, M	6	8	28	5	+	+ +	+ + (1)

* Retrocollis

Source: 'Behavioral Technics in the Modification of Spasmodic Torticollis', C.S. Cleeland, *Neurology* (1973), *23,* 1241–7, Table 1.

Table 8.2: Results of EMG Therapy

Case	Head rotation	Findings on initial examination: Units in SCM muscle, contralateral to rotation, at rest (hypertrophied)	Units in SCM muscle, ipsilateral to rotation, at rest (atrophied)	Units in SCM muscle, ipsilateral to rotation, on attempt of maximal contraction	Findings on final examination: Head position	Units in SCM muscle, contralateral to previous rotation at rest (relaxed)	Units in SCM muscle, ipsilateral to previous rotation, on attempt of maximal contraction
1	80° to R	Over 120	10	20	Neutral	6	Over 120
2	60° to L with retrocollis	Over 120	6	30	Neutral	5	Over 120
3	45° to L	Over 120	12	30	Neutral	6	Over 120
4	30° to L	60	6	45	Neutral	4	Over 120
5	90° to L	Over 120	10	12	Neutral	6	Over 120
6	30° to L	60	6	30	Neutral	5	Over 120
7	30° to R	90	8	45	Neutral	4	Over 120
8	30° to R	45	6	45	Neutral	4	Over 120
9	90° to L	Over 120	10	20	Neutral	6	90

Note: The units of deflection on the calibrated scale and the click rate were approximately proportional to the integrated EMG activity. The value was not strictly in μV.s but current apparatus is displaying information regarding the integrated EMG in μV.s seconds exactly. SCM, sternocleidomastoid

Source: 'Spasmodic Torticollis: Treatment by Feedback Display of the EMG', J. Brudny, B.B. Grynbaum and J. Korein, *Archives of Physical Medicine and Rehabilitation* (1974), *55,* 403–8, Table 2

Figure 8.1: (A) Patient Before Sensory Feedback Therapy. (B) Patient After 3 Months

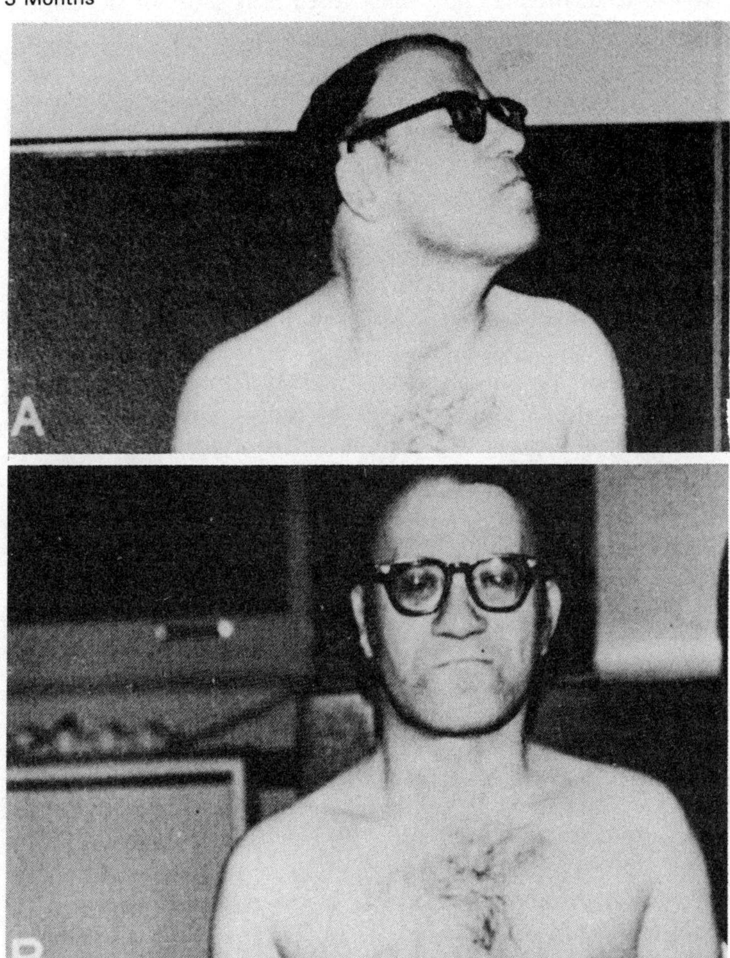

Source: 'Sensory Feedback Therapy of Spasmodic Torticollis and Dystonia: Results in Treatment of 55 Patients', J. Korein, J. Brudny, B. Grynbaum, G. Sachs-Frankel, M. Weisinger and L. Levidow, in *Advances in Neurology, 14*, ed. R. Eldridge and S. Fahn (Raven Press, 1976), Figure 3A and B, 375–402.

Sachs-Frankel and Belandres (1976) published follow-up data from a larger sample of patients. These revealed that, up to three years after treatment, signficant improvement had been maintained in 19 of 48 patients (compared with a total of 26 who showed initial improvement). Like Cleeland, Brudny *et al.* summarised their series of studies in a cautiously optimistic manner, concluding that:

> In our opinion, whenever a patient with disorders of voluntary movement resulting from CNS insult fails to respond adequately to extended conventional rehabilitation procedures, a trial of sensory feedback therapy is warranted.

More will be said of these studies later.

Although the research described above represents the most comprehensive attempts to treat spasmodic torticollis with biofeedback, other interesting, if less ambitious studies continue to be reported. For example, Jones, Massong and Buckley (1983) employed EMG feedback training to control spasm activity as the patient progressed through a range of postural changes. The results are shown in Figure 8.2.

Figure 8.2: Baseline and Treatment Counts of Number of Seconds per Minute which Showed-Muscle Spasm Activity that Exceeded Criterion Levels (Produced Observable Head Movement)

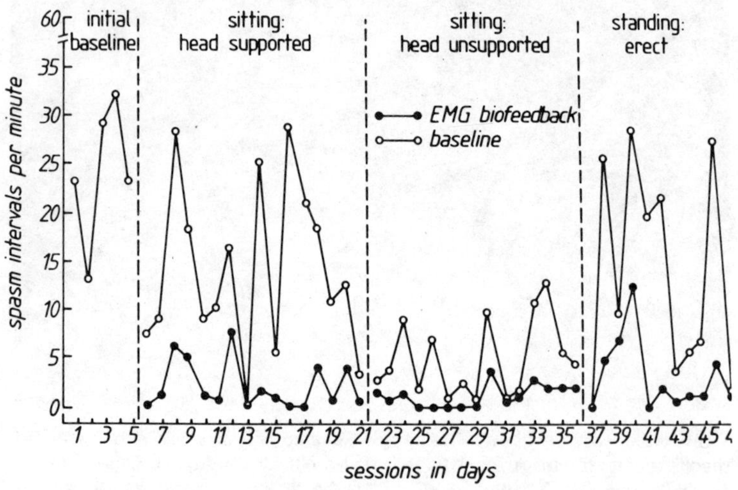

Source: 'Treatment of Spasmodic Torticollis Through Spasm Control and Muscle Reeducation: A Case Study', G.E. Jones, S.R. Massong and M.F. Buckley, *Behavior Therapy* (1983), *14,* 178–84, Figure 1.

Reduction in spasms (which had been maintained one year after treatment) was accompanied by improved head control, increased stamina and self-esteem, and reduced pain. Equally interesting is a study described by Harrison, Garrett, Henderson and Adams (1985). Despite being confined to a single patient this report merits description by virtue of the fact that the information fed back defined changes in head position, rather than fluctuations in muscle tension.

The subject was a 38-year-old woman whose condition was characterised by forward and lateral tilting of the head. Her symptoms were aggravated when visual cues were eliminated by requiring her to wear black glasses. Moreover, when denied visual feedback in this manner, she appeared unable to describe her posture accurately. Thus, when the therapist placed the patient's head in an upright position 'she reported that her head was leaning to the right and reported an increased sensation of muscle tension'. On the assumption that head tilt was in part due to 'proprioceptive/kinesthetic difficulties', a system was devised whereby postural changes could be fed back to the patient as they occurred. Briefly, this comprised two small mercury switches that responded to vertical or lateral deviations of the head. Following a baseline session during which the patient was asked to sit comfortably while maintaining normal posture, feedback training was undertaken. This involved providing auditory feedback first when the head tilted forward and later when it deviated laterally. The trial ended with what the authors described as three reversal sessions in which feedback was withdrawn. The results are shown in Figure 8.3.

Evaluation

In introducing this section it was stated that research into this particular application of EMG feedback training had yielded findings the relevance of which went beyond the treatment of this relatively rare condition. These will be discussed in due course. First, however, we need to address the more immediate question of what part biofeedback has to play in the treatment of spasmodic torticollis.

In evaluating the various outcomes described here it is necessary to sound the now-familiar warning that none of the studies utilised the control groups necessary if unequivocal statements are to be made about the efficacy of biofeedback. However, there are at least three grounds for believing that the various outcomes were not solely attributable to an uncontrolled placebo response. First, in many cases the relief obtained was long-lasting. Second, a sizeable proportion of patients who benefited had undergone numerous other forms of treatment, without success. Finally, the fact that spasmodic torticollis rarely remits spontaneously indicates that it is relatively unresponsive to non-specific

Figure 8.3: Effects of Feedback on Lateral and Forward Head Tilt

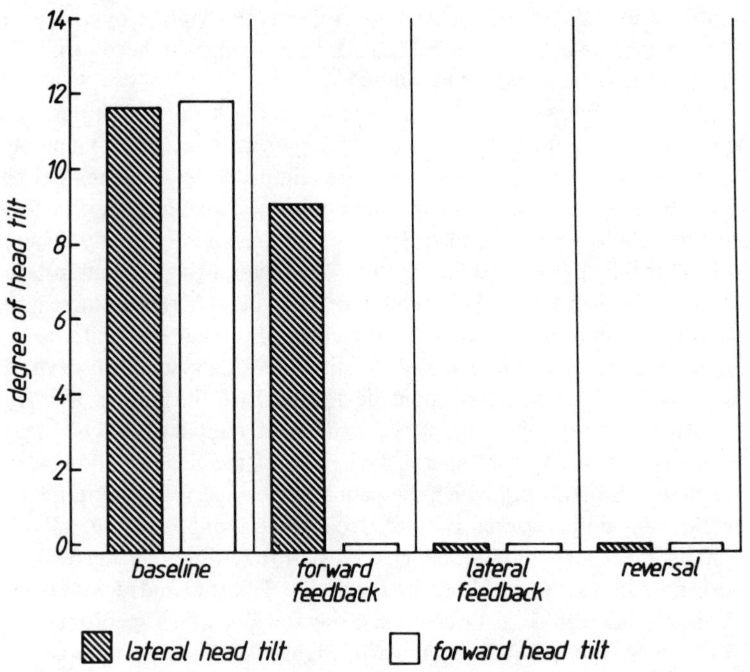

Source: 'Visual and Auditory Feedback for Head Tilt and Torsion in a Spasmodic Torticollis Patient', D.W. Harrison, F.C. Garrett, D. Henderson and H.E. Adams, *Behaviour Research Therapy* (1985), *23*(1), 87–8, Figure 1.

factors. At the same time, however, it has to be recognised that other components of the various treatment programmes might have significantly affected outcome. As the following account makes clear, Cleeland (1983) has incorporated several such procedures into his programme.

> Patients are admitted to the hospital for a period of 2–3 weeks. During that time they receive two 45-minute biofeedback training sessions daily Monday through Friday. Physical therapy often cooperates with our efforts by providing individually tailored exercises aimed at increasing the range of motion of the head. After the patient begins to show some reduction of the spasm (usually after four to six sessions) exercises aimed at spasm reduction and increased range are performed in front of the mirror twice a day for approximately 15 minutes. Since

> the degree of spasm is often increased by tasks involving hand-eye coordination patients may spend time working on individualized projects in occupational therapy (such as the hand loom or macrame) which call for maximal control of the spasm and head position. This type of activity is not begun until the patient begins to obtain substantial head control.

As well as being wary of overstating the unique contribution made by EMG feedback to the final outcome, the 30 to 40 per cent long-term success rates achieved in the two major studies described here must also be qualified. In both instances it appears that patients underwent considerable screening before being accepted for treatment. For example, Korein and Brudny (1976) excluded from their programme anyone whose symptoms were associated with organic disease, including carcinoma or cardiac conditions. Similarly, participants had to be well motivated and not suffering from severe psychiatric disturbance. It must be recognised, therefore, that the techniques described here will at best benefit only a minority of sufferers. A discussion of the extent to which this should rule out treating spasmodic torticollis with biofeedback will be reserved until the end of this section, when other applications have been described. However, before moving on to consider these applications, this is an appropriate point to consider a more general issue raised by the research described here.

In attempting to account for their relatively modest long-term success rate, Korein and Brudny (1976) noted that:

> The difficulty was in learning to incorporate the SCM (sternocleidomastoid) activity into the patterned movement and not primarily related to inability of controlling the individual muscle itself.

This observation was subsequently expanded by Yates (1980) in his scholarly analysis of the theoretical status of biofeedback. He suggested that:

> . . . although the unsuccessful patients were able to utilize feedback information to gain some degree of control over their muscle activity (in the absence of skeletal movement), they failed to learn sufficient about the components of the servosystem controlling head and neck *movement*, so that while they were able to reset some components of the system to achieve individual muscle control, they had not learned sufficient to enable them to control the entire system.

As well as accounting for the limited success of simple EMG feedback training, this conclusion raises some interesting clinical issues. For example, it suggests that the effectiveness of biofeedback might be increased if more than one category of information (including tactile, kinaesthetic and visual information) was fed back to the patient. Certainly it is not unusual to observe sufferers attempting to use environmental cues to generate their own such feedback. For example, on more than one occasion I have observed a patient seeking to maintain correct posture by constantly looking in a mirror. Similarly, Korein, Brudny, Grynbaum, Sachs-Frankel, Weisinger and Levidow (1976) described how as many as 84 per cent of their patients sought to relieve symptoms by producing some form of 'self-induced sensory feedback'. These strategies included the following: '. . . touching the hand to the chin, placing one or both hands on the back of the neck and extending to a variety of aids, such as wearing high neck collars, biting a shirt collar, or placing a rubber band about an ear.'

As Korein *et al.* pointed out, such seemingly bizarre behaviours were initially considered to be a hysterical component of the disease. However, they forcibly rejected such an interpretation and suggested instead that they represented the patient's attempt to generate the sensory feedback necessary for him to control his symptoms. It is against this background that the findings of Harrison *et al.* (p. 170) take on significance. Certainly they add substance to the suggestion that multi-modal feedback training might increase the efficacy of this form of treatment. However, this remains a question for future research. For the present, the analysis presented by Yates should warn us against undue optimism over the benefits to be derived from training patients to control just one component of the complex neuromuscular system that is involved in this form of movement disorder.

Writer's Cramp

According to Bindman and Tibbetts (1977), writer's cramp (which was first described in the medical literature as long ago as 1830, when it was attributed to the introduction of the steel-nib pen) can be described as follows:

> . . . a muscular spasm of the fingers and hand of the writing arm, often spreading to muscles of the lower and upper arm, and even to the shoulder girdle with consequent incoordination and discomfort,

leading to weakness, pain, and often tremor. The cramp occurs only when writing or during some similar activity such as typing or counting notes. The pen is grasped more and more firmly and the writing becomes more jerky and forcible, until the pen may be pushed through the paper and writing eventually becomes impossible. Distortion of the writing position occurs, with the hand supinated or over-pronated, sometimes with the pen grasped between the middle and ring fingers.

Other writers have suggested that it may be necessary to distinguish between simple writer's cramp and dystonic writer's cramp. (Marsden, 1976; Sheehy and Marsden, 1982). According to this classification, the former refers to the condition where only the act of writing is compromised (as in Figure 8.4), other manual tasks being carried out normally. The term dystonic writer's cramp is reserved for the condition in which spasm affects not only writing but a range of other manual tasks such as shaving, using certain tools or even handling a knife and fork.

Figure 8.4: Specimens of Handwriting From Three Subjects with Writers' Cramp as They Attempted to Write or Print 'King's College Hospital'. The topmost example was from a patient with writers' cramp associated with tremor; the middle and lower examples from two Subjects who found it either difficult or impossible to write

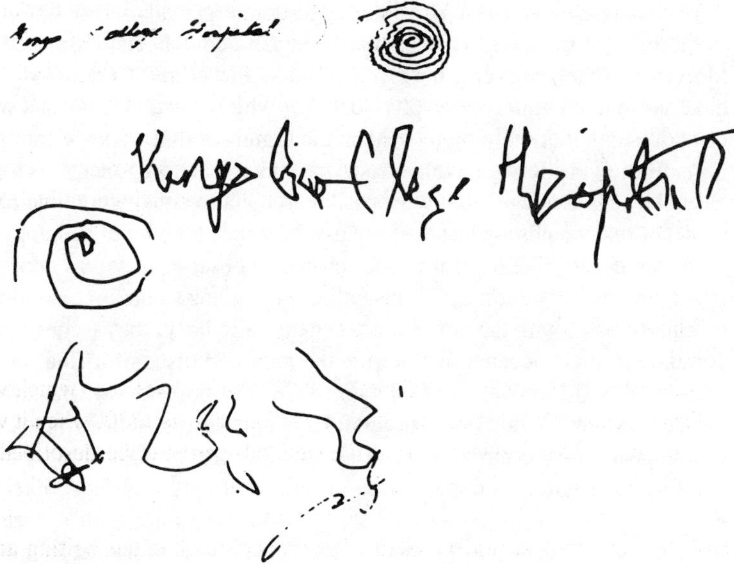

Source: 'Writers' Cramp — A Focal Dystonia', M.P. Sheehy and C.D. Marsden, *Brain* (1982), *105,* 461-80, Figure 2

In common with spasmodic torticollis, attempts to account for the onset of writer's cramp have adopted either a psychological or organic perspective. Typical of the former approach is that proposed by Crisp and Moldofsky (1965) and elaborated by Bindman and Tibbetts (1977). The latter authors presented a number of compelling case histories to support their thesis that the condition is the overt manifestation of an unresolved, unacceptable conflict that is associated with the writing situation. Typical of the patients that they described was a bank clerk who:

> . . . functioned as such very well — the routine fitted in with his obsessionality. In fact he functioned so well that he was promoted, as so often happens, to a position where his skills were less required. He became assistant manager and immediately encountered difficulty with the more subtle and personal decisions required. It was in the course of writing reports on this work that the disability began.

The reader may well recognise in this account a certain similarity with the symptoms of conversion hysteria that were described in Chapter 5. In fact Bindman and Tibbetts have argued that in some instances this condition may indeed be viewed as hysterical dysgraphia, which is close to the conversion syndrome. Given the bizarre forms that conversion hysteria may take, this is a plausible suggestion, especially when viewed in the light of the case histories that Bindman and Tibbetts described. Moreover, other workers, notably Cottraux, Juenet and Collet (1983) have presented similar descriptive data (of which more will be said in due course) that do nothing to weaken the argument that writer's cramp may, at the very least, have a strong psychological component. Yet it has to be acknowledged that it is possible to point to equally convincing evidence that weighs against a purely psychological account of aetiology.

At the descriptive level it is not unusual to observe sufferers taking positive steps to overcome their disability, even going so far as to attempt to learn to write with the non-dominant hand. Similarly, they frequently continue in their occupations despite the pain and discomfort that this may involve. Moreover, as Lishman (1978) has pointed out, in those instances where re-training is successful it is rare for substitute symptoms to reappear. Furthermore, as with spasmodic torticollis, a number of surveys have failed to demonstrate that sufferers are any more likely to have a history of psychological disturbance than the population at large. For example, Sheehy and Marsden (1982) used a standardised questionnaire (The Present State Examination, PSE) to compare the psychiatric status of 34 patients with writer's cramp (or similar occupational palsies) with that of 310 controls. This revealed no difference in the incidence of psychiatric disturbance within the two groups. The authors also reported that:

> Careful enquiry of patients and relatives into the psychiatric state of these patients at the onset of their writers' or other occupational cramp revealed a remarkably low incidence of psychiatric disability and certainly no higher than that indicated by the PSE. All but one of the 34 patients considered themselves to be in normal physical, mental and emotional health at the time.

As well as the findings outlined above, Sheehy and Marsden adduced some quite different evidence to support their thesis that writer's cramp has an organic rather than psychological aetiology. First, approximately 40 per cent of those patients who initially presented with simple writer's cramp subsequently developed features of dystonic writer's cramp. Second, they noted that other authors have observed an association between writer's cramp and certain focal dystonias, including spasmodic torticollis (Meares, 1971). Finally, they went on to report the following:

> Our own observations support the view that writers' cramp indeed can spread; what appears to be simple writers' cramp can evolve into dystonic writers' cramp in the same hand or spread to the opposite hand. What has evolved into dystonic writers' cramp may proceed then to focal dystonia of the whole limb and even to spasmodic torticollis. Indeed, in a representative sample of 49 subjects with segmented dystonia (dystonia affecting adjacent parts of the body, for example, arm and neck, arm and trunk) seen by one of us (C.D.M.), no less than 21 noted that their illness began with writers' cramp and one patient noted preceding typists' cramp.

The reader is left in no doubt as to what Sheehy and Marsden believe all this adds up to.

> We believe we have marshalled sufficient evidence to show that writers' cramp is a dystonic illness and, hence, that psychiatric factors are either accidental or secondary.

Given the detail with which Sheehy and Marsden presented their findings it is difficult not to be impressed by their argument. Yet here again the case that they offer is not without its problems. For example, as Marsden (1976a) has recognised, in the majority of cases writer's cramp does not extend to other manual actions and is even less likely to progress to clear-cut torsion dystonia (Marsden and Harrison, 1974). Moreover, we need to remind ourselves that the patients described by Bindman and Tibbetts exhibited little of the psychological stability that characterised those investigated by Sheehy and Marsden. Indeed, anyone reading the two accounts (along with the case reports presented by Cottraux, *et al.*) would be justified in thinking that they referred to quite different categories of patients. And, of course, they could well be right.

Despite their basically neurological outlook, Sheehy and Marsden were quite prepared to recognise that psychological factors may exacerbate basal ganglia diseases. Moreover, even the most die-hard neurologist would accept that cases of hysterical dysgraphia can and do occur (recall that Sorensen and Hamby (p. 162) were willing to concede the existence of 'psychologically deranged persons'). Similarly, I suspect that few would wish to argue that the part played by psychological factors need end there. Even if an organic basis was to be established (and the evidence is convincing), in some instances psychological factors may trigger an attack and in others they would undoubtedly serve to reinforce symptoms by a process of secondary gain. In other words, we may well be dealing with a condition to which the contribution of psychological factors varies along a continuum ranging from virtually none, right through to hysterical dysgraphia, which is wholly psychogenic in origin. If so, then the differences outlined above might reflect nothing more than that different researchers were studying patients from different ends of this continuum. (In this respect it may be more than mere coincidence that Marsden's work emanates from a university department of neurology, while Bindman, Tibbetts and Cottraux are all psychiatrists). There is, of course, nothing novel in this argument. Indeed, it almost exactly echoes the conclusion reached by Lishman (1978) in his account of spasmodic torticollis.

> In most large series it has seemed necessary to recognise a spectrum of causation, ranging from cases which have appeared to be purely psychogenic in origin to examples where organic influences have clearly been responsible. Uncertainty arises, however, over the position to be adopted in relation to the 'average' case where associated evidence in one direction or the other is lacking. Thus some authorities have regarded the great majority of their cases as psychogenic in origin and some virtually all their cases as organically based. Much may depend on the nature of the sample observed and also on the bias of

the psychiatrist or neurologist concerned.

It will be recalled that Lishman urged caution in accepting this account of spasmodic torticollis. However, in the case of writer's cramp it offers the only satisfactory account. It would not be surprising, therefore, if response to any form of treatment proved to be highly variable.

EMG Feedback and Writer's Cramp

An examination of the literature reveals that most authors justify the clinical application of EMG feedback by referring to Basmajian's pioneering laboratory studies in which he showed that given appropriate feedback, subjects could learn to control the activity of single motor-units (Basmajian, 1963). More recently, several workers have drawn on this finding to show that these techniques can be applied in a non-clinical setting. In particular, a number of studies have been described in which musicians were trained to control muscle tension in the hands and arms. It seems appropriate to describe one such study here. For quite apart from introducing a novel application of biofeedback, it provides a rationale for using EMG feedback training in the treatment of writer's cramp.

As Morasky, Reynolds and Clarke (1981) have pointed out, the production of string music requires very high levels of muscle control. However, it is not uncommon for muscle tension to change imperceptibly during performance in a manner that adversely affects 'the consistency, smoothness, technical facility, and richness of tone that characterize fine music'. Morasky *et al.* attempted to train nine string players (mainly violinists or cellists) to overcome this problem by providing them with EMG feedback during performance. The levels of accomplishment of the participants varied from lower level intermediate to highly advanced concert artist. Each took part in four two-hour training sessions, the inter-session intervals varying from one to seven days. Each session comprised a pre-test, a biofeedback phase and a post-test phase. In the first and third phases EMG activity was recorded (without feedback) from the left forearm extensor muscles while the subject played a series of test items. In the training (i.e. biofeedback) phase the player received feedback whenever EMG activity exceeded 90 per cent of pre-test mean levels. In order to measure any generalisation effects, activity in the left arm flexors was also monitored but not fed back. The outcome is shown in Figure 8.5.

Figure 8.5: Pre-test, Biofeedback, and Post-test Phase Mean-Integral Averaged EMG Levels from Left Forearm Extensor and Flexor Muscles of String Players Across Four Experimental Sessions

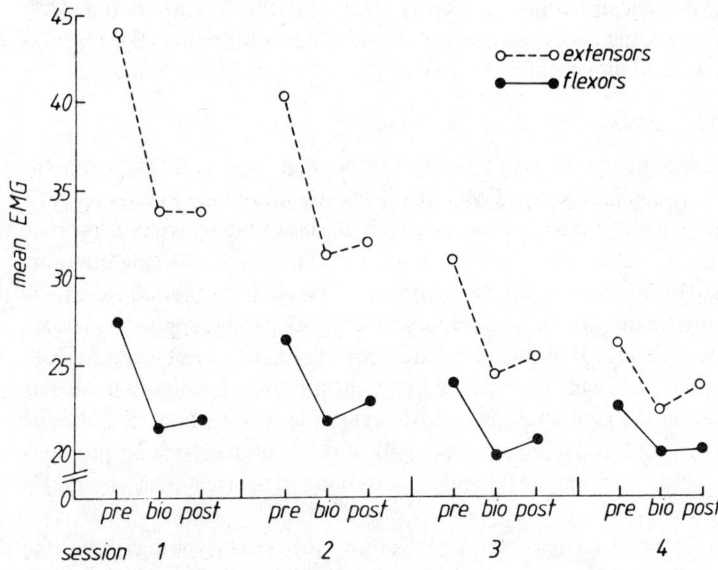

Source: 'Using Biofeedback to Reduce Left Arm Extensor EMG of String Players During Musical Performance', R.L. Morasky, C. Reynolds and G. Clarke, *Biofeedback and Self-Regulation* (1981), *6*(4), 565–72, Figure 1.

Morasky *et al.* summarised their findings as follows:

> The results indicate that EMG scores can be reduced during musical performance by string players through the use of biofeedback. Further, the decreases generalized to a no-feedback condition. However, generalization from the extensors, which received biofeedback, to flexors which were not trained, did not occur across a majority of the tasks in the no-feedback or post-test condition. This may indicate that both agonist and antagonist muscles will require biofeedback training in order to achieve coordinated reductions in EMG. The decreases in extensor EMG were not the result of 'warming up' or a practice effect.

Figure 8.5 also appears to demonstrate a learning effect across sessions. However, the authors rightly resisted this interpretation on the grounds that the inter-session differences might reflect nothing more than small differences in electrode placement.

Very similar results to those described above have since been reported by LeVine and Irvine (1984). They also used EMG feedback to train a group of advanced string players to remove inappropriate left-hand tension during performance. Discussing the favourable outcome the authors commented:

> Most players were delighted at having made rapid progress with a problem that they had previously found difficult to solve . . . Here . . . the goal was greater voluntary control over intrinsic muscles of the left hand during performance of a specific skilled task.

What are the clinical implications of this brief musical interlude? It must be emphasised that none of the participants in the two trials was suffering from the craft palsy usually described as musician's cramp. At the same time EMG feedback did enable them to achieve a hitherto unobtainable degree of voluntary control over the muscles of the hand and arm. Given that this is precisely what the sufferer from writer's cramp seeks to achieve, and that as far as we know the relevant neuromuscular system is intact, the application of EMG feedback training seems to be justified. To date, only two such applications have been described and both are of a decidedly exploratory nature.

The work of Bindman and Tibbetts (1977) has already been referred to in some detail. Although they treated a total of ten sufferers, only six of these underwent simple EMG feedback training. Curiously, this was applied initially as a form of aversion therapy, in that the volume of the auditory feedback signal was such as to be 'almost intolerably intense' when the hand was in spasm. Not surprisingly, perhaps, this was found to increase tension and make the symptoms worse. Consequently a more conventional approach was adopted. EMG activity was monitored from the flexors to the index finger and thumb on the palmar surface of the hand and fed back to the patient while he first relaxed and contracted these muscles and then attempted to write. Duration of training varied from two to seven weeks and there was a follow-up at either three or twelve months. Unfortunately no quantitative data were presented, outcome being reported on a simple four-point scale. This revealed that of the six patients treated with EMG feedback alone two were either symptom free or exhibited minimal disability. One had improved but still exhibited work disability, while the remaining three showed no change.

Similar results to those described above were obtained by Cottraux *et al.* (1983) who also used EMG feedback, either alone or in combination with systematic desensitisation, to treat 15 patients suffering from writer's cramp. Largely to demonstrate the nature of the factors that Cottraux *et al.* linked to the onset of symptoms, full details of the study are reproduced in Table 8.3.

EMG activity was monitored from the forearm and fed back to the patient while he was writing. Each session lasted 20 minutes, the number of sessions varying between subjects. Before treatment the patient copied ten lines of text without feedback and marked the script whenever he experienced spasm or was unable to write. The same measure was employed post-test and at follow-up, each script being assessed on a five-point scale by an independent evaluator (0, no change or worse; 4, normal writing). The scale took the following into account: (1) number of cramps, (2) the percentage of free hand-writing, and (3) the quality of hand-writing. No assessment was made of writing completed ouside the clinic and no quantitative data relating to changes in EMG activity were reported.

According to Table 8.3, four patients (1, 12, 14, 15) received only feedback training and of these, three (12, 14, 15) were judged 'markedly improved', while the other (1) was able to write normally immediately after treatment and at nine months follow-up. Cottraux *et al.* concluded their report as follows:

> The multimodal uncontrolled approach we used precludes any definite conclusions about the effectiveness of EMG feedback, but in eleven cases its role appeared to be important. In four cases it seemed effective as the only therapeutic technique . . .

An evaluation of just how important and effective is EMG feedback is postponed until the final two conditions to be discussed in this section have been briefly considered.

Blepharospasm

Like spasmodic torticollis and writer's cramp, blepharospasm is characterised by involuntary muscle contraction, the difference being that it is the eyes rather than the neck or hands that are affected. Although primarily involving the muscles controlling eye closure, in severe cases spasm may spread to the associated muscles of the forehead and mouth. Not only is the condition socially embarrassing, in severe cases the

Table 8.3: Details of Fifteen Patients with Writer's Cramp

Subjects	Age, sex	Duration (years)	Circumstances of onset	Treatment	Sessions	Improvement evaluation (0–4) Post-test	Follow-up
1	30, F	7	Childbirth Mistake at work	EMG FB	12	4	4(9 months)
2	23, F	4	At work Family conflict Vocational problem	EMG FB SD	25	2	2(2 months)
3	23, M	3	Family conflict Examination	EMG FB Relaxation, SD Assertive training	36	3	3(3 months)
4	34, F	1	Wish to have a second child and to stop working Conflict with husband	EMG FB Relaxation SD	11 (drop out)	2 (Last session)	—
5	33, M	1	Overwork	SD — EMG FB	5 (drop out)	0 (Last session)	—
6	26, M	3	Taking courses Physical illness antecedent	Assertive training Relaxation — EMG FB	18	2	3(2 months)
7	50, M	9	Vocational problem	SD — EMG FB	15	3	3(6 months)
8	45, M	6	Loss of job	Refusal	—	—	—
9	38, F	4–5	Sudden onset at work	Relaxation — EMG FB	3 (drop out)	2 (Last session)	—
10	39, M	5	At work — Examination	SD	3 (drop out)	2 (Last session)	—
11	50, M	1	Sudden onset at work Wants an early retirement	Refusal	—	—	—
12	37, M	3	Examination	EMG FB	16	3	3(7 months)
13	41, M	3	At work Conflict with employer	SD Assertive training	16	3	3(4 months)
14	29, M	1	At work Jobs seems satisfactory	EMG FB	17	3	3(5 months)
15	45, M	3	Overwork	EMG FB	14	3	3(1 month)

SD; systematic desensitization; EMG FB; EMG feedback
Source: 'The Treatment of Writer's Cramp with Multimodal Behaviour Therapy and Biofeedback: A Study of 15 Cases', J.A. Cottraux, C. Juenet and L. Collet, *British Journal of Psychiatry* (1983), *142*, 180–3, Table 1

frequency of spasms may be such as to render the patient functionally blind (Marsden, 1976a). Again, like spasmodic torticollis and writer's cramp, the aetiology of blepharospasm is complex. While in some cases it may be secondary to known pathology, in others no such cause is discernable. Described as essential blepharospasm, the latter condition has proved particularly resistant to a wide range of medical and surgical treatments. Similarly, methods based upon psychotherapeutic principles have at best produced variable outcomes. For example, beneficial effects of psychotherapy and relaxation training were reported by Reckless (1972) and Sharpe (1974) respectively. However a series of 26 individuals studied by Marsden (1976a) as part of a larger population of patients yielded no such outcomes. He concluded that:

> By and large, none of these dyskinesias responds to sedation, antidepressants, hypnosis, psychotherapy, behavioural therapy, desensitization techniques etc. Many of the patients described here had run the gauntlet of such therapy, all to no avail as far as a cure was concerned.

By now we should not be surprised to find that Marsden favours an organic account of aetiology. Certainly there are good grounds for doing so for while acute attacks may accompany severe depression or anxiety (Lishman, 1978) most chronic sufferers do not appear to be emotionally disturbed (Bender, 1969). It is also interesting to observe that like tardive dyskinesia (see following section) blepharospasm can occur as a side effect of phenothiazine medication and may be the presenting feature of Parkinson's disease. Again, this all points to an extrapyramidal involvement, and has led Lishman (1978) to conclude that:

> It would seem most unlikely, however, that the chronic continuing syndrome . . . owes much to psychogenesis, sensitive though it may be to psychological influences once it has become established.

EMG Feedback and Blepharospasm

Peck (1977) offered an early description of this application of EMG feedback when he treated a 50-year-old woman who had a six-year history of chronic blepharospasm. The symptoms were described as a massive contraction of the muscles around the eyes, which severely disrupted the patient's social, professional and domestic life. The aetiology of the condition was obscure, though Peck suggested that it may have been secondary to a general allergic reaction. Prior to undergoing EMG feedback training the patient had undergone opthalmic, neurological and psychiatric investigations, to no effect. Treatment was carried out in the following three phases: (1) Two sessions in which baseline EMG activity (monitored at the left frontalis and orbicularis muscles) and spasm frequency were established, (2) Two placebo sessions in which the patient listened to white noise played through headphones, having been told that this would reduce the frequency and intensity of spasms; (3) Seventeen 20-minute feedback sessions in which auditory EMG feedback was used to teach her to reduce tension in the two muscles. Changes in EMG activity and muscle spasm across trials are shown in Figure 8.6.

Figure 8.6: Reduction in EMG Level and Spasm Frequency for Baseline, Placebo and Feedback Sessions

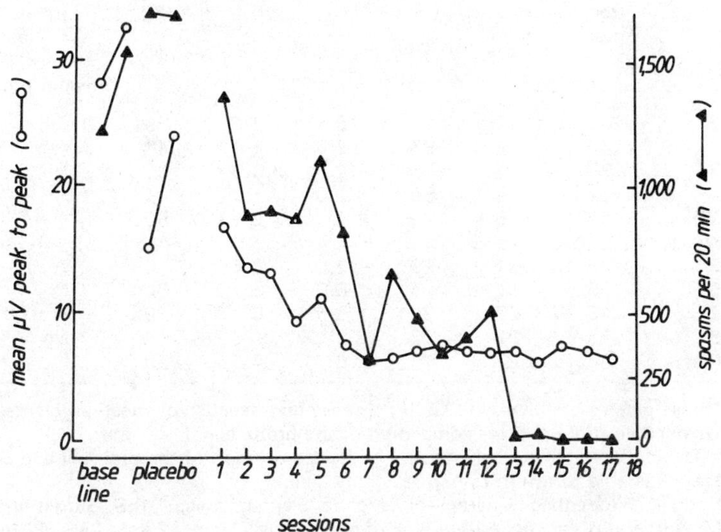

Source: 'The Use of EMG Feedback in the Treatment of a Severe Case of Blepharospasm', D.F. Peck, *Biofeedback and Self-Regulation* (1977), *2*(3), 273–77, Figure 1

As well as the data shown in Figure 8.6, Peck reported that during training the original spasm was first reduced to a pronounced wink and finally an ordinary blink. Four months after the end of treatment this improvement had been maintained.

A somewhat larger scale trial than that just described was reported by Surwit and Rotberg (1984), who employed a combination of EMG feedback and relaxation training to treat eight patients. As well as the increased number of participants, this trial differed from the earlier case study conducted by Peck in that all eight cases were positively diagnosed as essential (rather than secondary) blepharospasm. Treatment was carried out within a period of one week and consisted of the following: (1) Instruction in progressive relaxation, which the patient practised at home with the aid of a pre-recorded cassette tape, and (2) five 30-minute sessions of EMG feedback training. The outcome of the trial is shown in Table 8.4.

Table 8.4: Treatment Outcome for Eight Patients with Blepharospasm Following EMG Feedback Training

Patient	Blink rate Pre-treatment	Post-treatment	Change (%)	Resting electromyograph Pre-(μV)	Post-(μV)	Change (%)	Able to return to former activities (work, driving, etc.)
1	31	12	61	18	2.5	86	Yes
2	56	8	85	2.5	1.4	44	Yes
3	25	8	68	4.5	0.9	80	No*
4	12	4	66	2.0	1.7	15	Yes
Mean	27	8	70	7	2	56	
5	26	21	19	2.5	2.5	0	Yes
6	39	37	5	8.0	3	62	No
7	40	27	32	5.5	5	9	Yes†
8	25	22	12	8	4.5	44	No
Mean	33	27	17	6	4.0	29	

* This patient had liver and kidney disease and because of these problems was unable to work after completion of the protocol.
† This patient was treated surgically after completion of the protocol and then was able to return to her daily activities.
Source: 'Biofeedback Therapy of Essential Blepharospasm', R.S. Surwit and M. Rotberg, *American Journal of Ophthalmology* (1984), *98,* 28–31, Table 2. Published with permission from the American Journal of Opthalmology. Copyright by the Opthalmic Publishing Company.

Overall these are encouraging, if modest results. While no patient exhibited total remission of symptoms, four of them (1, 2, 3, and 4) obtained substantial relief, which was maintained at a six-month follow-up. Surwit and Rotberg were justified, therefore, in adopting a cautiously optimistic attitude to this particular application of biofeedback. At the same time they recognised the exploratory uncontrolled nature of their study, pointing out that 'More work needs to be done to elaborate fully its appropriate role in the management of patients with this uncommon, but disabling condition.' To date this work has not been carried out.

Tardive Dyskinesia

Most psychiatrists accept that the introduction of the phenothiazines marked a major advance in the treatment of schizophrenia. However, the benefit that these drugs provide is not obtained without cost. High on the list of side effects is tardive dyskinesia, described in *The Lancet* (1979) as 'a syndrome, or several syndromes, of involuntary movement arising in psychiatric patients taking neuroleptic drugs.' The article goes on to point out:

> Most of the patients are chronic schizophrenics and the condition begins insiduously with exaggerated and persistent chewing movements or variations such as sucking and smacking movements, tongue protrusion, grimacing, and grunting. This is the cephalic or bucco-linguo-masticatory part of the syndrome, and it may be accompanied by more widespread choreiform movements of the neck, shoulders and arms, and occasionally the legs and trunk.

There is some evidence that the extent of the symptoms might be age related, with older patients suffering only focal involvement and early onset characterised by more generalised dystonic involvement. Precisely how tardive dyskinesia should be classified remains debatable. Undoubtedly the condition has features in common with spasmodic torticollis, writer's cramp and other focal dystonias. For example, symptoms may disappear during sleep and are made worse by high levels of anxiety or psychological stress. Moreover, like these conditions tardive dyskinesia shows a widely variable response to drug therapy. While some sufferers derive benefit from benzodiazepines, these compounds may also precipitate or increase symptoms (Rosenbaum and de la Fuente, 1979). The relevance of these observations will become apparent when we come to an overall evaluation of the role of biofeedback in the treatment of dystonic conditions.

EMG Feedback and Tardive Dyskinesia

Although the abnormal movements associated with tardive dyskinesia may be widespread, EMG feedback training has been confined to treating the orolingual component. Moreover, it has to be said at the outset that as with blepharospasm, research into this particular application of biofeedback in no way resembles the detailed investigations of spasmodic torticollis outlined earlier. Rather, the literature consists entirely of small-scale uncontrolled trials or single-subject case reports. One such study was described by Albanese and Gaarder (1977), who trained two male sufferers to reduce EMG activity from the right masseter muscle. Details of the trial (extracted from the two case reports) are shown in Table 8.5.

Clearly it is impossible to draw any definitive conclusions from such a small-scale investigation. Undoubtedly both patients improved with treatment. However, to what extent this was directly attributable to EMG feedback remains uncertain. As Albanese and Gaarder pointed out, it is not unknown for the symptoms of tardive dyskinesia to abate once neuroleptic therapy is discontinued (though in other instances the condition worsens). Moreover, it is far from clear why EMG feedback confined to the right masseter muscle should have eliminated the abnormal hand and foot movements exhibited by case 1 (Table 8.5). This generalised reduction in symptoms suggests that at least part of the favourable outcome may have been the result of non-specific factors, as does the observation that 'a general reduction of tension was experienced by both patients and both gave reports of increased well being'. Overall, then, Albanese and Gaarder were wise to emphasise the need for further research when they concluded:

> . . . the improvement was first noted within training sessions and increased progressively with training, later extending to periods outside the training sessions. Also in each instance there had been no noticeable improvement before treatment began. We believe this observation warrants further investigation of the treatment approach, and we hope that this report will stimulate others to try similar methods.

Unfortunately, as was observed earlier, no large-scale trials of this particular application of biofeedback have subsequently been reported. However, a case report by Sherman (1979) merits discussion in that it suggests that the outcomes described by Albanese and Gaarder were not wholly non-specific.

The patient treated by Sherman was a 44-year-old man with a long history of drug and alcohol abuse, 'as well as prolonged use of chlorpromazine'. There was a five-year history of tardive dyskinesia, which had persisted for six months after the withdrawal of chlorpromazine. Initially, treatment consisted of a combination of progressive relaxation exercises and frontalis EMG feedback training. In the event, it was the outcome of this phase of treatment that proved especially interesting for while there was a reduction in tension headache and general anxiety the symptoms of tardive dyskinesia remained unaffected. These only abated when EMG feedback was switched from the frontalis to the masseter muscle. This phase of treatment was accompanied by a gradual decrease in jaw movements, so that after four training sessions all symptoms shown in the laboratory were eliminated. Subsequently this improvement carried over to the patient's everyday environment, and he was found to be free from dyskinetic symptoms at a 15-month follow-up. In so far as the first phase of treatment could be regarded as a placebo control condition, it seems reasonable to assume that in this instance the latter outcome was more than a placebo response.

Before leaving this particular application of EMG feedback training, one other widely quoted case report by Farrar (1976) should be mentioned. This involved a patient suffering from orofacial dyskinesia, a neurological disorder that Albanese and Gaarder have suggested may represent the same syndrome as tardive dyskinesia. EMG feedback training (from the triangularis and quadratus labii inferioris muscles) was used to treat a persistent tremor in the region of the mouth, lips and tongue. As well as undergoing training in the laboratory, the patient used a portable unit to practise muscle control at home on a daily basis. At the end of three weeks there was a marked reduction in dyskinetic symptoms and a general improvement in the patient's level of social interaction.

Given that none of the three studies described here provided detailed quantitative data, it would be foolhardy to suggest that they represented major advances in biofeedback research or application. At the same time the findings that emerged were consistent with those of the much larger scale studies of Cleeland and of Brudny and Korein described earlier.

Evaluation and Concluding Remarks

Although research into the behavioural control of focal dystonias has been of a relatively high calibre, it remains difficult to specify the precise role of biofeedback in their treatment. Undoubtedly one of the main reasons for this is the variable contribution that psychological factors appear to make both in precipitating and maintaining these bizarre disorders. However, the recognition that such factors may operate in this manner allows us to point to two categories of patients who would not benefit from this form of treatment. As was stressed in Chapter 5,

Table 8.5: Details of Two Sufferers From Tardive Dyskinesia Treated with EMG Feedback

Case	Age	Psychiatric history	Medication	Dyskinetic symptoms	Feedback training	Outcome	Follow-up
1	39	Paranoid psychosis following divorce	Trifluoperazine, benztropine mesylate, fluphenazine decanoate	Contortion of mouth, chewing movements, foot tapping, choreiform finger movement.	10 45-minute sessions: 1–8 weekly, 9th 2-week and 10th 3-week intervals	Total remission of all dyskinetic symptoms	Outcome maintained at 3 months
2	51	Psychotic depressive illness	Anti-depressant medication (unspecified), fluphenazine decanoate	Chewing movements, rhythmic tongue protrusion	9 sessions as above, discontinued when patient moved from area	Some residual movement of tongue within closed mouth	None

Source: Extracted from, 'Biofeedback Treatment of Tardive Dyskinesia: Two Case Reports', H. Albanese and K. Gaarder, *American Journal of Psychiatry* (1977), *134*(10), 1149–50.

biofeedback has no part to play in dealing with cases in which there is a strong element of conversion hysteria. Quite simply, it would make no more sense to treat a case of hysterical dysgraphia with EMG feedback training than it would to prescribe more powerful spectacles for a patient suffering from hysterical blindness. Likewise, it is an inappropriate method of treating organic symptoms that have become associated with a strong element of secondary gain. Were all focal dystonias psychologically initiated or maintained this would be the end of the story. However, as we have seen, this appears not to be so. Indeed, Korein and Brudny specifically excluded psychiatrically disturbed individuals from their investigations, yet were still able to assemble one of the largest groups to be studied so far. In the present context this was a fortunate decision, for their research (along with that of Cleeland and his associates) represents the most comprehensive evaluation of this application of biofeedback. It is reassuring, therefore, to know that the results were unlikely to have been contaminated by uncontrolled psychological factors. This is especially so if, as was suggested earlier, conclusions derived from the study of spasmodic torticollis might also be tentatively applied to other, less widely researched dystonic states.

The assumption that what can be said about the response of spasmodic torticollis to biofeedback applies to other dystonic states can be defended on a number of grounds. We have already seen that Sheehy and Marsden (1982) have described how simple writer's cramp may progress to a more wide-ranging condition, which they labelled dystonic writer's cramp (p. 173). Likewise they have also reported that patients with a specific focal dystonia may subsequently develop 'a more florid movement disorder'. To be sure, progression of this nature is far from inevitable. Indeed, it is the exception rather than the rule. Nevertheless, it occurs frequently enough to suggest that these diverse symptoms might all reflect a common underlying pathology. Sheehy and Marsden (1982) located this defect in the basal ganglia, while Lishman (1978) has pointed to the possible involvement of the extrapyramidal system. This view is reinforced by what we know of the relation between tardive dyskinesia (and, less often, other movement disorders) and the phenothiazine drugs. For as Kruk and Pycock (1983) have pointed out:

> It is believed that they . . . (neuroleptic induced dyskinesias) . . . are caused by an imbalance of cholinergic and dopaminergic activity in extrapyramidal brain regions following the administration of the neuroleptic drug.

It has to be accepted that all of this falls some way short of unequivocal proof that the movement dystonias described here share a common aetiology; even less that they are all due to lesions in the extrapyramidal brain regions. Moreover, we are moving even further into the realms of speculation by assuming that these various conditions will show a uniform response to biofeedback. That said, the outcome of the various studies reviewed here suggests that this might well be the case. Certainly, until it is proved otherwise, it seems reasonable to base much of the remainder of this general evaluation on the sophisticated research of Korein and Brudny.

The initial response to their detailed findings can only be one of mild disappointment. Given that the patients investigated by Korein and Brudny were carefully screened, it would have been reasonable to expect high success rates amongst those who were judged suitable for treatment. However, as we have seen, this did not prove to be the case. Moreover, as yet no-one has succeeded in predicting which patients will derive benefit from treatment. Cleeland (1983) has suggested that cases of recent onset carried the best prognosis. However, Korein and Brudny (1976) found this not to be the case. Similarly, improvement was unrelated to any of a wide range of other factors including sex, handedness or type of torticollis. It must be concluded therefore, that a clinician resorting to this method of treatment must be prepared for more failures than successes. Against this gloomy background it is hardly surprising that a number of authors have been unable to express more than lukewarm enthusiasm for this application of biofeedback. More surprising, perhaps, is that Yates (1980) should number amongst them. Yet, despite his generally favourable attitude towards the work of Korein and Brudny, he concluded that: '. . . so far, no firm evidence of a convincing kind has been forthcoming to suggest that biofeedback training is signficantly superior in its remedial effects to alternative (and less costly) methods'.

I take a different view. So far, in deciding whether or not biofeedback has a role in the treatment of a given condition, the following three criteria have been applied; (1) The extent to which the condition warrants active intervention, (2) The cost of the particular mode of biofeedback, (3) The nature of the alternatives. There is no disagreement among clinicians that conditions such as spasmodic torticollis and blepharospasm are sufficiently incapacitating to warrant treatment. Moreover, the techniques described here are relatively simple and do not require the patient to be admitted to hospital. Therefore, the decision whether or not to adopt this approach to treatment depends largely upon the nature of the alternatives. Undoubtedly drug therapy is simpler and cheaper. However, as we have seen, more often than not it proves to be ineffective and in some instances exacerbates the condition. Likewise, surgery does not appear to have fulfilled its early promise and in any case is associated with quite severe side effects. Lest anyone thinks I have overemphasised these, I offer the following account by McCord, Coles, Shore, Spector and Putnam (1984) of a standard surgical procedure (facial nerve avulsion) designed to treat blepharospasm.

> . . . the skin incision was placed just anterior to the ear in a parotidectomy like incision. This was more cosmetically acceptable to our patients and also allowed the exposure of the main trunk of the facial nerve, which could be stimulated to ensure that the buccal branch could be avulsed if necessary. All patients were operated on under general anesthesia, and a nerve stimulator was available to identify the branches of the nerve within the parotid gland. Stimulation of the main trunk of the facial nerve was performed following avulsion of branches to the eyelids, to ensure that all branches to the eyelids had been avulsed. All patients were treated with antibiotics and also had a Penrose drain inserted for two days through the surgical incision postoperatively.

More importantly, the patient's problems are unlikely to end there. As McCord *et al.* further pointed out:

> Even with successful facial nerve avulsion, there is an obvious ''trade-off'' for relief of spasm by the production of paralysis of the eyelids with drooping of the brow, dermatochalasis, lagophthalmos, and some corneal exposure. Other undesirable side effects are ectropion of the eyelid and lip paralysis. The most frustrating aspect of Reynold's procedure is recurrence of the eyelid and facial spasms with aberrant regeneration. After using Reynold's procedure, many surgeons find themselves operating on the same patient with multiple secondary procedures and then reoperating with second and third facial nerve avulsions in the recurrent cases.

Admittedly, the long-term efficacy of EMG feedback training has still to be unequivocally demonstrated in a large-scale controlled trial. Nevertheless, given such an alternative, the case for using the simple, non-invasive techniques outlined here as a first-line treatment of these distressing conditions seems overwhelming.

9 SPHINCTER DISORDERS AND MISCELLANEOUS CONDITIONS

Incontinence

All too often it is assumed that incontinence only affects the very young and the elderly. Undoubtedly incontinence is a condition that poses particular problems in old age. Indeed, in 1983 Ehrman pointed out that the condition was second only to physical disability as the cause of admission to long-term care. According to Ehrman, 55 per cent of all nursing home residents are incontinent of urine and 25 per cent are faecally incontinent. However, while these figures support the popular view, it would be a mistake to suppose that incontinence is confined to infants and elderly, institutionalised individuals. Faecal incontinence has many causes, including diabetes, multiple sclerosis, scleroderma, myelomeningocele, cerebrovascular accidents, spinal cord injuries, and direct muscle injury from surgical procedures such as haemorrhoidectomy or fissurectomy (Schuster, 1983). Likewise, urinary incontinence can result from congenital and neurological conditions, acute infection or anatomical changes following surgery or childbirth. Add to this list those cases that appear to be of psychogenic origin, and it becomes apparent that virtually anyone might fall victim to what is by any standard a psychologically and socially devastating condition.

Faecal Incontinence

Normally, as faeces enter the rectum the internal sphincter (which is under autonomic control) relaxes and almost immediately the external sphincter contracts, thus preventing involuntary defaecation. However, contraction of the external sphincter need not be prolonged, for following a period of adaptation, the internal sphincter returns to the contracted state. Once the rectum is full, defaecation is achieved by voluntarily relaxing the external sphincter to coincide with relaxation of the internal sphincter. Thus, although this sequence of events is relatively straightforward, it depends upon a sequence of reflex changes that must be perfectly synchronised if incontinence is to be avoided.

Despite the brevity of the above account, it demonstrates quite clearly the important part played by the external sphincter in maintaining continence. Specifically, failure of this sphincter to contract appropriately would lead to involuntary defaecation. That incontinence can and does occur in this manner was demonstrated by Alva, Mendeloff and Schuster (1967). They compared the anal reflexes of the twelve incontinent patients described in Table 9.1 with those of 25 control subjects.

Table 9.1: Clinical Details of 12 Incontinent Patients

Injury	No. of patients
Spinal cord lesions	
Spinal cord tumor post resection	3
Traumatic spinal cord transection	2
Anal sphincter injuries	
Hemorrhoidectomy	4
Laceration during childbirth	1
Myopathy	
Dermatomyositis	1
Ocular myopathy	1

Source: 'Reflex and Electromyographic Abnormalities Associated with Fecal Incontinence', J. Alva, A.I. Mendeloff and M.M. Schuster, *Gastroenterology* (1967), *53*(1), 101–6, Table 1.

The monitoring device shown in Figure 9.1 was placed in the subject's anal canal in such a manner that when the two lower balloons were inflated with air the upper one was surrounded by the internal sphincter and the lower one by the subcutaneous bundle of the external sphincter. In addition, a needle electrode was inserted into the external sphincter, thus enabling changes in EMG to be monitored. In order to stimulate anal reflexes the rectal balloon was rapidly distended with 50 ml of air. Pressure changes were then recorded directly from the two sphincter balloons, along with changes in EMG at the external sphincter.

The results were straightforward and unambiguous. All normal subjects exhibited relaxation of the internal sphincter and contraction of the external sphincter in response to increased intra-rectal pressure. This was in sharp contrast to the patients. In all but one case, there was no contraction of the external sphincter following relaxation of the internal sphincter. The authors summarised their findings as follows:

> This combined technique demonstrates that, in the normal resting state, the internal sphincter is strongly contracted and the external sphincter minimally contracted. Patients were studied with fecal incontinence on the basis of neurological impairment, myopathy, and anal muscle injury. Normal internal sphincter reflexes were present, but external sphincter reflexes were absent in incontinence regardless of underlying

Figure 9.1: Schematic Representation of Recording Technique

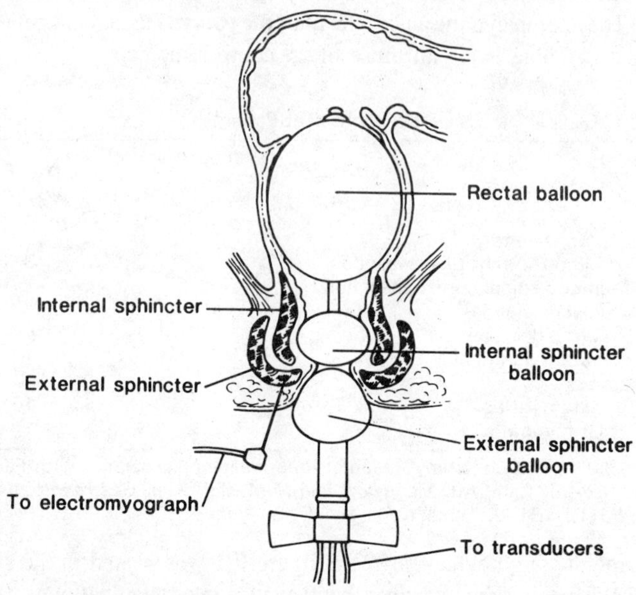

Source: Based upon 'Reflex and Electromyographic Abnormalities Associated with Fecal Incontinence', J. Alva, A.I. Mendeloff and M.M. Schuster, *Gastroenterology* (1967), *53* (1), 101–6, Figure 1.

cause, indicating that, of the two muscle components, the external sphincter plays the major role in the preservation of continence.

Biofeedback and Faecal Incontinence. Given these findings and bearing in mind that the external sphincter consists of striated muscle, it is not surprising that a number of workers should have seen a role for biofeedback in the control of incontinence. Amongst these were Engel, Nikoomanesh and Schuster (1974), who described a study in which they treated seven patients, each of whom had a long history of faecal incontinence (Table 9.2).

The method of treatment was based upon the monitoring technique described above. The same apparatus was used to increase intra-rectal pressure, thus initiating internal sphincter relaxation. During the early phase of training the outputs of the three monitoring devices were made instantly available to the subject. At the same time:

He was reminded of the differences between his responses and normal

Table 9.2: Details of Seven Incontinent Patients Treated with Biofeedback

Case	Age (years), sex	Incontinence Frequency	Incontinence Duration	Cause	Follow-up period (years)
1	54, M	Daily	4	Laminectomy	5
2	40, F	Daily	5	Proctectomy for tumor	5
3	44, F	Daily	8	Unknown	1½
4	54, F	Daily	5	Hemorrhoidectomy	1
5	44, M	Daily	5	Diabetic neuropathy	1½
6	43, F	Daily	3	Fissurectomy; radiation proctitis; vesicorectocele repair.	*
7	6, F	Episodically†	Lifelong	Myelomeningocele	½

Note: * Patient withdrew from study.
† Patient also unable to have regular bowel movements.
Source: 'Operant Conditioning of Rectosphincteric Responses in the Treatment of Fecal Incontinence', B.T. Engel, P. Nikoomanesh and M.M. Schuster, *New England Journal of Medicine* (1974), *290,* 646–9, Table 1.

responses. He was encouraged to try to modify his responses to make them appear more normal. He was praised whenever he produced a normal-appearing response, and he was told whenever the response he produced was poor. This verbal reinforcement was gradually diminished as it became clear that the patient knew what was expected of him, and as it became clear that the patient was able to affect his sphincteric responses. Each patient was able to sense the rectal distention, and each patient knew that this stimulus was the cue to initiate sphincteric control.

The later phase of the session was used to refine the sphincteric responses by matching the amplitude of conditioned and normal responses and synchronising external sphincter contraction with internal sphincter relaxation. Towards the end of this phase, immediate feedback was gradually withdrawn, though delayed feedback was provided by giving the patient access to recordings after a series of trials. Each session lasted about two hours and contained approximately 50 training trials. There was a maximum of four training sessions, which occurred at three-weekly intervals. Throughout this period each patient was required to record his ability to remain continent, and similar recordings were maintained after the cessation of treatment. Thereafter interviews took place every three months until control had been stable for six months, whereupon they were conducted annually.

Readings taken in the laboratory indicated that before training the external sphincter did not contract in response to relaxation of the internal sphincter. However, with feedback this response was acquired (Figure 9.2). Figure 9.2 is especially interesting in that initially the patient over-responded in the absence of feedback. The authors reported that while this tendency to overcontrol was seen in other patients, it diminished as training progressed. One other finding worthy of mention relates to case 7. In this instance not only was the external sphincter response lacking before training, so too was that of its internal counterpart. The authors described how:

> During the first training session, therefore, we concentrated on teaching her to relax this sphincter, which she was able to do by the end of the session . . . During the next training session we concentrated on training her to contract her external sphincter, which she also learned to do . . . After the completion of training she not only was continent but also was able to have normal bowel movements regularly.

Thus it seems that this method of treatment need not be confined to individuals whose incontinence results solely from loss of external sphincter control. (This finding is also interesting at a theoretical level in that it appeared to demonstrate learned control of a muscle that is under autonomic control.) Undoubtedly this study provided clear evidence that, under laboratory conditions, biofeedback enabled a small group of long-term sufferers to achieve the control necessary to overcome their disability. From a clinical point of view, however, three questions remained to be answered. Did these effects carry over to real life, were they long-lasting, and if so were they observable in a significant number of patients? Happily, in this case generalisation did occur. Over follow-up periods ranging from six months to five years, four patients (cases 1, 2, 3 and 7) remained completely continent, while case 4 reported ' "rare" episodes of staining, but no occasions of gross incontinence'. Futhermore, in a recent review, Schuster (1983) reported similar outcomes in all but two of approximately 100 patients treated in the manner described here. In these cases follow-up periods varied from four to eight years, leading Schuster to speculate that improvement is at least long-lasting, and possibly permanent.

So far all the research described here emanated from one group. However, a clinical trial conducted by Olness, McParland and Piper

Figure 9.2: Sphincteric Responses to Rectal Distention (↓) in a Representative Patient Showing the Response to (A) 25-Ml Distention before Training, (B) Responses to 20-Ml Distention during Early Training and (C) Responses to 20-Ml Distention with and without (*O*) Feedback

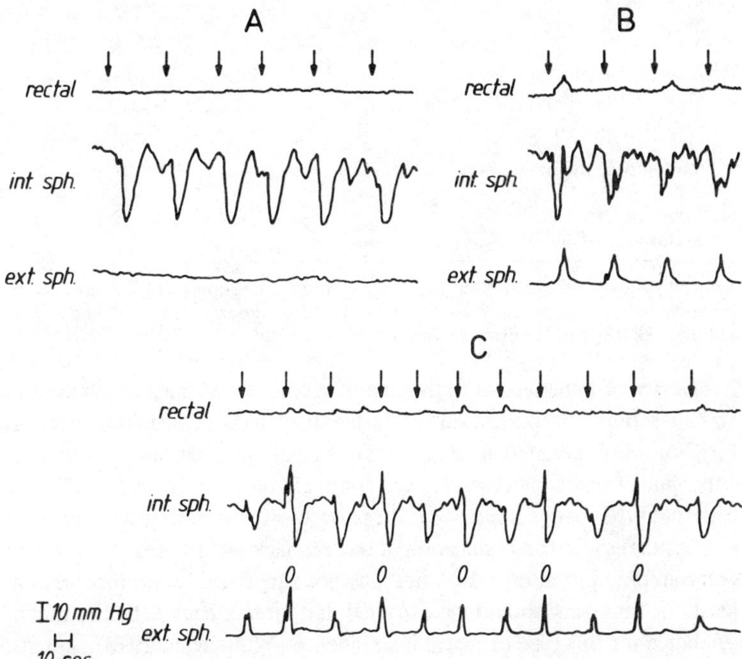

Source: 'Operant Conditioning of Rectosphincteric Responses in the Treatment of Fecal Incontinence', B.T. Engel, P. Nikoomanesh and M.M. Schuster, *The New England Journal of Medicine,* (1974), *290,* 646-9

(1980) produced a similar outcome to that described above. Briefly, they treated a group of 50 children and adolescents by using the method described by Engel *et al.* Two classes of patients took part: those whose incontinence was believed to be associated with imperforate anus repairs in infancy, and a less-closely defined group 'who had fecal incontinence associated with functional constipation refractory to usual medical management'. The outcome is shown in Table 9.3.

Summarising their findings, the authors pointed out that not only was the success rate high, it was maintained over follow-up periods ranging from six months to three years.

Table 9.3: Outcome Data for 50 Incontinent Children Treated with Biofeedback

	Functional constipation	Imperforate anus
Regular bowel movements, no soiling	24	6
Regular bowel movements, minor soiling	14	1
Regular bowel movments, major soiling	1	1
No improvement	1	2
Total number of patients	40	10

Source: 'Biofeedback: A New Modality in the Management of Children with Fecal Soiling', K. Olness, F.A. McParland and J. Piper, *Journal of Pediatrics* (1980), *96* (3, pt. 1), 505–9, Table 1.

Evaluation. On the face of it, this appears to be one of the most successful and unambiguous applications of biofeedback to have been described so far. For while detailed accounts of all the patients that Schuster and his colleagues treated successfully are not available, where such data were presented they were impressive. In particular, it is both gratifying (and all too rare) to find an application of biofeedback where theory, treatment and outcome are at one. It is perhaps not surprising, therefore, that at least one authority should have argued that biofeedback is the treatment of choice for this type of faecal incontinence (Whitehead, 1978). Against this background it might appear almost churlish to sound at least a muted note of caution. Nevertheless, it needs pointing out that the outcome described by Engel *et al.* (1974) and more recently by Olness *et al.* (1980) were the results of uncontrolled studies.

Indeed, as Whitehead (1978) recognised, not one controlled outcome study has ever been reported. Why this should be so is unclear, though the need for complex equipment and a high degree of technical expertise on the part of the therapist must have been a contributory factor. It is encouraging, therefore, that recently Constantinides and Cywes (1983) have described a simple device, based on the principles illustrated in Figure 9.1, that can be used by the patient at home. However, even if this technical advance leads to an increased interest in this particular form of biofeedback, it would be a mistake to assume that it could be universally applied.

Although some cases of faecal incontinence are attributable to lack of sphincter control, many others are not. For example, Schuster (1974), describing a group of patients suffering from psychogenic megacolon, wrote the following: 'Previous diagnostic studies in our laboratory on patients with psychogenic overflow incontinence had shown that internal and external sphincter reflexes are normal in this disorder.' Obviously the rationale for treating this type of patient by the method outlined here is much less secure. Indeed, Engel *et al.* (1974) specifically excluded them from their study, and it appears that they were wise to do so. For while no quantitative data were presented, Schuster (1983) reported that patients with severe neuroses fared less well than those whose incontinence had an organic basis. By now this conclusion has a familiar ring and it should warn us not to expect spectacular success rates when similar methods are used to treat urinary incontinence.

Urinary Incontinence

The normal adult usually feels the urge to micturate when the volume of urine in the bladder exceeds about 300 ml. Like defaecation, the process depends on a delicate neuromuscular feedback system involving both somatic and autonomic control. The sequence begins when a fall in urethral resistance is immediately followed by reflex contraction of the detrusor muscle. The neural mechanism underlying these events is complex, and has been described by Gosling, Dixon and Humpherson (1983) as follows:

> . . . the external urethral sphincter is of particular importance in the mechanisms which maintain urinary continence. Immediately prior to the onset of micturation, the active tonus of the sphincter is reduced by central inhibition of its motor neurons located in the second, third and fourth sacral spinal segments. This inhibition is mediated by descending spinal pathways originating in higher centres of the central nervous system. Concomitantly, other descending pathways activate (either directly or via sacral interneurons) the preganglionic parasympathetic motor outflow of the urinary bladder. This central integration of the nervous control of the bladder and urethra is essential for normal micturation; it is well known that discoordination of the bladder and urethral function is a frequent complication following lesions of the spinal cord.

Given such complexity, it is hardly surprising that urinary incontinence has several causes and is classified under more than one heading. Of these, stress and urge incontinence are two of the more commonly encountered, and it is the latter which has attracted most attention from behavioural scientists.

Urge Incontinence

As the name implies, this condition is characterised by urgency 'which may be so precipitate and severe that there is involuntary loss of urine'. (Smith, 1981) According to Smith, urge incontinence is a not infrequent consequence of acute cystitis, and is also a symptom of upper motor-neuron lesions. However, he also points to the role of emotional factors, noting that the condition often occurs in tense, anxious women, even in the absence of infection. Other authors go further than this and place psychological factors firmly at the forefront of the condition. For example, Frewen (1978) claimed that in 80 per cent of patients presenting at gynaecological out-patient clinics with urge incontinence, no organic, infective or structural change can be detected. Previously (1972) he had argued that:

> Urge incontinence is a psychosomatic disorder in which emotional factors play a predominant role. Associated with these emotional factors there is *a marked disturbance of autonomic function* (my italics) producing a hyperactive and hyperirritable bladder muscle and a resultant loss of its normal physiological function. The primary stimulus is not, however, a local one, but is central in origin and is under the influence of psychosocial and environmental factors. The incontinence is indeed a stress-reactive factor and its duration and severity will depend to some extent on the initial degree of emotional disturbance, as well as the degree of sustainment of that emotion.

Given this view of urge incontinence, it is not surprising that it has been viewed as a candidate for treatments based upon psychological principles. However, before moving on to evaluate these, it needs noting that urge incontinence does not always appear to be quite so closely linked to emotional factors as this quotation implies.

We saw, when discussing essential hypertension, that the unfortunate student called to face the external examiner may well show a marked increase in blood pressure. Sadly, his torment is unlikely to end there. As Blandy (1982) pointed out: 'Nobody who has ever faced an important examination will be ignorant that facilitation from higher centres may sensitize the bladder reflex arc. It is a common and distressing feature of many anxiety states.'

However, as was argued in Chapter 1, it is one thing to show that psychological stress leads to temporary changes of this nature, it is another to show that they then become long-standing. An examination of the evidence that long-term urge incontinence develops in this manner shows it to be equivocal, being based largely upon anecdotal case reports. To be sure, in some instances these are convincing, especially when they describe patients where structural causes have been systematically ruled out. For example, Frewen (1972) has described cases where the onset of incontinence followed major psychological trauma such as the death of a husband or child. However, in other instances the role of emotional factors was far less obvious and involved 'only an unessential triviality', while in yet others 'no obvious psychological trigger' could be elucidated. Moreover, temporal relationships have proved equally variable. In some instances incontinence started abruptly after the presumptive triggering event, while in others it developed much more slowly. At a more empirical level the position is equally unclear. For example, Millard and Oldenburg (1983) used a standardised questionnaire to examine the psychological status of a group of sufferers before and after treatment. This revealed that although pre-treatment scores were in the abnormal range, they returned to normal in those cases in which the treatment proved successful. Millard and Oldenburg interpreted their findings as follows:

> Although our initial assessment showed high scores of general psychopathological findings on the SCL-90 test the return of the scores to normal values in those patients who were cured symptomatically implies that the psychological disturbance is secondary to and not the cause of the urinary problem.

However, whatever doubts they may have entertained about the role of stress in causing urge incontinence, the effect of psychological factors in determining response to treatment appears not to have been in doubt. For example: 'At least 50 per cent of our failures occurred in women who had failed to complete a full three months of training, which must raise doubts about their motivation and reflects their psychological difficulties.' More will be said about this study and the general issue of motivation in due course.

Biofeedback and Urge Incontinence. Notwithstanding the reservations expressed by Millard and Oldenburg, it is still widely accepted that psychological stress is a potent factor both in the onset and maintenance of urge incontinence. Given this position, it would seem logical to use biofeedback as part of a treatment package aimed at teaching the patient to control SNS hyperactivity in the manner described by Patel and North (p. 55). However, this is not the method that has been adopted. Rather, the emphasis has been on direct feedback techniques not dissimilar to those used to control faecal incontinence. Typical of this approach was that adopted by Cardozo, Abrams, Stanton and Feneley (1978) to treat 32 women in whom:

> Detrusor instability was diagnosed by cystometry or videocystourethrography with pressure and flow studies, if a pressure rise of greater than 15 cm of water occurred during bladder filling or provocative testing. Neurological abnormalities, outflow obstruction and organic bladder pathology were excluded by physical examination, cystometry, cystoscopy and uroflowmetry.

Feedback was achieved by placing two catheters in the bladder, one for filling and the other for measuring total bladder pressure. A third catheter was introduced into the rectum in order to measure rectal pressure, which the authors assumed to be equivalent to abdominal pressure. This value was subtracted from total bladder pressure to give the detrusor pressure, increases in which led to a rise in pitch of an auditory signal and increased deflection on a chart recorder. With the patient lying comfortably, the bladder was slowly filled with 0.9 per cent saline at body temperature. During this procedure the patient was asked to attend to the two feedback signals, to say when she had the first sensation of desire to void, and when her bladder was full. Thereafter, the bladder was emptied and filling recommenced, but at a slower rate. On this occasion the patient was instructed to try to control the rise in pitch of the auditory signal by whatever means seemed appropriate. Each training trial ended when the bladder was full and within each session the patient underwent two or three such trials. If there was no improvement after four weekly sessions, therapy was terminated. Otherwise it was continued until cystometry was normal, up to a maximum of eight sessions. Throughout training patients were instructed to void only when necessary and to keep a daily record of number of urges, urinary frequency and level of incontinence. At the end of training a further cystometrogram was performed.

Five patients failed to complete the programme; the remaining 27 underwent an average of 5.4 treatment sessions. The outcome, which was assessed both subjectively and objectively, is summarised in Tables 9.4 and 9.5.

Table 9.4: Subjective Changes for the 27 Patients Treated with Biofeedback (BF)

Symptoms	No. of patients showing symptoms Before	After
Frequency		
Diurnal	23	10
Nocturnal	18	5
Urgency		
Total	26	17
Severe	25	9
Urge incontinence		
Total	22	15
Severe	20	4
Enuresis	5	3

Source: 'Idiopathic Bladder Instability Treated by Biofeedback', L.D. Cardozo, P.D. Abrams, S.L. Stanton and R.C.L. Feneley, *British Journal of Urology* (1978), 50, 521-3, Table 2.

Table 9.5: Objective Changes for the 27 Patients Treated with Biofeedback (BF)

	Before BF	After BF
First sensation (ml)	145	214
Capacity (ml)	374	446
Pressure rise on filling (cm, H_2O)	40	34
Total maximum pressure rise (cm H_2O)	57	43
Detrusor contractions (no. of patients)	26	14
Leaks (no. of patients)	25	12

Source: 'Idiopathic Bladder Instability Treated by Biofeedback', L.D. Cardozo, P.D. Abrams, S.L. Stanton and R.C.L. Feneley, *British Journal of Urology* (1978), *50,* 521-3, Table 3.

At the time they published their original data the authors concluded that:

> Our results show 81% of a group of 27 patients with idiopathic detrusor instability have been helped by biofeedback training, and that the improvement is lasting. We feel this is sufficient for it to warrant consideration as a method of treatment for the unstable bladder.

Subsequently Cardozo and Stanton (1984) attempted a five-year follow-up of participants in this and other similar trials. This revealed that of 11 patients originally reported as cured or improved only four remained completely continent. Of the remainder, two had undergone surgery and five had relapsed. Clearly, if any conclusion can be drawn from such small figures it is that the long-term success rate of this method of treatment is considerably less than the immediate post-treatment outcome might imply. Furthermore, there are good grounds for questioning whether even these limited gains owed anything to the effects of feedback training. It will be recalled that during treatment patients were required to monitor and record their symptoms and to pass urine only when absolutely necessary. In addition, it appears that they were fully briefed about the cause and treatment of their condition. We have already seen that self-monitoring and detailed explanation by a sympathetic therapist are often sufficient in themselves to reduce the severity of stress-related symptoms. In the case of urge incontinence this certainly appears to be so. Indeed, the self-monitoring and control of voiding that Cardozo *et al.* required of their patients are central to an established method of treatment, variously referred to as bladder training or bladder drill.

Bladder Training and Urge Incontinence. Although carried out in a number of centres, interest in this technique owes much to the work of Frewen. Treatment usually takes place on an in-patient basis and, as practised by Frewen, comprises a combination of behavioural and pharmacological methods. Typical of his work is a study of 40 female sufferers (10 of whom were treated as out-patients) in whom organic or structural causes had been eliminated (Frewen, 1978). On admission, each of the 30 in-patients was issued with a typescript that explained the cause of her symptoms and how she could overcome them. She was also issued with a chart on which she recorded the times and intervals of urination, along with the volume of urine passed and degree of continence achieved. According to Frewen, the chart acted as 'a measure of her success in prolonging the intervals between voidings, and the increase in her bladder capacity day by day.' In addition, all patients were prescribed a combination of sedatives and anti-cholinergic drugs. The average length of stay in hospital was 10 days, though patients 'remained on treatment and were kept under surveillance for a period of 3 months'. During this time each patient was seen at monthly intervals, when her progress was monitored. At the end of three months cystometric investigations were repeated. Success was defined as total freedom from all abnormal urinary symptoms and normal cystometric appearances. Using these criteria,

Frewen claimed an objective cure rate of 82.5 per cent.

A number of subsequent trials have shown that the outcome reported by Frewen was not exceptional. Two of these are of particular interest in that as well as serving as valuable replication studies, they sought to identify the 'active ingredients' in bladder training. In order to assess the relative contribution of the behavioural and pharmacological components, Jarvis (1981) compared the effects of simple bladder training with those of drug therapy on 50 women whose incontinence was attributable to idiopathic detrusor instability. Bladder training was undertaken on an in-patient basis, whereas drug therapy (200 mg of flavoxate hydrochloride tds and 25 mg of imipramine tds for four weeks) was carried out in the patient's home. Patients were assessed both subjectively and objectively after four weeks and subjectively after three months. Changes in symptoms after treatment are summarised in Table 9.6.

Table 9.6: Symptoms Before and After Treatment

Symptom	Bladder drill (*n* = 25)		Drug group (*n* = 25)	
	Pre	Post	Pre	Post
Frequency	25	6	25	12
Nocturia	21	4	19	13
Urgency	25	4	25	11
Urge incontinence	25	4	25	11
Stress incontinence	19	1	17	9

Source: 'A Controlled Trial of Bladder Drill and Drug Therapy in the Management of Detrusor Instability', G.J. Jarvis, *British Journal of Urology* (1981), *53,* 565-6, Table 2.

Not only was the efficacy of bladder training confirmed, it was shown to be superior to conventional drug therapy. A similar outcome was reported by Jarvis and Millar (1980) when they compared the effects of bladder training with those of urethral dilatation reinforced by suggestion. Sixty females suffering from idiopathic detrusor instability each underwent urethral dilatation and cystoscopy under general anaesthesia before being randomly assigned to one of two groups. Controls were assured that they should now be continent and were allowed home, while the remainder underwent bladder training on an in-patient basis. All participants were reassessed at three and six months. The six-month follow-up data are shown in Table 9.7.

Table 9.7: Symptoms of Patients Before and Six Months After Treatment

Symptoms	Bladder-drill group (n = 30) Before	After	Control group (n = 30) Before	After
Diurnal frequency	30	5	30	23
Nocturnal frequency	27	3	25	20
Urgency	30	4	30	23
Urge incontinence	30	3	30	23
Stress incontinence	21	3	20	16

Source: 'Controlled Trial of Bladder Drill for Detrusor Instability', G.J. Jarvis and D.R. Millar, *British Medical Journal* (1980), *281*, 1322, Table 1.

Yet again bladder training was associated with a success rate far in excess of that achieved by controls. Commenting on their findings, the authors concluded that 'bladder drill is the treatment of choice for detrusor instability in women'. On the basis of the three studies just described this conclusion is justified. Recently, however, a follow-up survey by Holmes, Stone, Bary, Richards and Stephenson (1983) indicated a substantial relapse rate over periods ranging from one to five years. Nevertheless, Holmes *et al.* echoed the view of Jarvis and Millar by concluding that: 'Despite the high relapse rate, bladder retraining is still the best primary treatment available and has an overall 3-year response rate of about 50%, with few side effects and little cost.'

Evaluation. Attention has already been drawn to some common features that emerged from the preceding discussion and the much more detailed coverage accorded to hypertension in Chapter 4. Like essential hypertension, urge incontinence appears to be due in part to increased SNS activity. Similarly, both are known to occur under conditions of psychological stress, though in neither case has it been unequivocally demonstrated that long-lasting symptoms are psychologically determined. Given these common features, it is perhaps not surprising to find that there are some marked similarities in how the two conditions respond to behavioural therapies. For example, we saw in Chapter 4 that although the direct feedback technique has sometimes produced clinically significant reductions in blood pressure, these were probably non-specific. This also appears to be the case when direct feedback of detrusor activity is used to treat urge incontinence. Thus, while a number of patients treated by Cardozo *et al.* (1978) undoubtedly derived benefit, the available evidence suggests that the key to their success was the bladder training that they also underwent. This is not to say, however, that biofeedback played no part whatsoever in the final outcome. Returning once more to Chapter 4 and the work of Patel and North, it was argued then that the inclusion of biofeedback in a multi-modal treatment programme may well act to maintain motivation and compliance during the early stages of therapy. Interestingly, Millard and Oldenburg produced evidence that the inclusion of biofeedback might have had a similar effect upon their patients. Of the 75 who underwent bladder training, 47 received additional adjunctive therapy. In 23 cases this consisted of the direct feedback technique designed by Cardozo *et al.* Of the remaining 24, nine were prescribed drugs and 15 received both treatments. According to the authors, these additional measures were introduced 'in order to promote early improvements'. The reader is left in no doubt that these adjunctive therapies helped bring this about and that biofeedback was the most useful in doing so. Does this imply then that we should supplement bladder training with direct feedback in much the same way that Patel and North used EMG and GSR feedback as an adjunct to relaxation training? In my opinion there are good reasons for suggesting that we should not.

As Millard and Oldenburg recognised, they were almost certainly dealing with an atypical group of patients. For example:

> While the over-all results among the women are not as good as those reported by Frewen or Cardozo and her associates it is believed that this is more a reflection of our clinical material than our training technique. Many of our failures were patients who had undergone multiple previous surgical procedures and who presented to us in clinical desperation.

Obviously it is unwise to draw general inferences from a 'clinically desperate' group about the effects of treatment on compliance and motivation, especially when we consider what this particular method of biofeedback involves. It is one thing to lie quietly relaxing on a couch, breathing gently, disturbed only by the occasional clicking of a GSR monitor as it signals changes in autonomic arousal. It is quite another to lie there as saline is repeatedly introduced into the bladder through one catheter, while changes in pressure are monitored through two others. I for one find it hard to believe that such a procedure would increase the motivation of more than a tiny proportion of patients to continue treatment. Indeed, it seems not unreasonable to suggest that the promise of repeated sessions of this form of biofeedback would, if anything, motivate the patient to cancel her remaining appointments forthwith! (In fact Cardozo *et al.* reported that 16 per cent of patients failed to complete treatment, while failure to attend sessions amounted to 15 per cent.) This, of course is a subjective view and as such it is open to dispute. However, what cannot be disputed is that the direct feedback technique is complex and potentially hazardous. As Cardozo *et al.* have pointed out, as well as carrying the risk of causing infection, their method of biofeedback is extremely time-consuming, requiring up to eight hours of treatment administered by a doctor or highly trained nurse and technician. Given that it brings little to the treatment of urge incontinence that cannot be achieved by the much simpler methods of bladder training, there seems little likelihood that this application of biofeedback will become established in clinical practice.

Concluding Remarks

Although this chapter illustrates that behavioural methods have a part to play in the treatment of both faecal and urinary incontinence, it would be easy to exaggerate their importance. It is important to remember that the types of incontinence suited to behavioural management represent only a part of the total problem. To take but one example: according to Frewen (1972, 1978), urge incontinence accounts for about 30 per cent of cases of urinary incontinence referred to gynaecological out-patient clinics. Even if we accept his estimate that 80 per cent of these are of psychogenic origin, this means that the studies described here focused upon only 24 per cent of the total population of sufferers. Moreover, a close reading of these reports indicates that some of this 24 per cent would be deemed unsuitable on psychological grounds. For example, Cardozo and Stanton (1984) suggested that their programme may be appropriate for a 'highly motivated group of women with . . . a good insight into their bladder problems'. Similarly, Frewen (1978) emphasised that 'Those who live in conflict with their environment or who are unable to adapt themselves to their social circumstances will not respond favourably unless their environmental conditions are remediable.' However, not all patients possess the level of motivation and self-determination that behavioural treatments require. Moreover, of those that do, many will not have it within their power to remedy their environmental circumstances. It must be assumed, therefore, that the high success rates attributed to bladder training apply only to a carefully selected group of sufferers.

Vaginismus

Vaginismus is defined as a painful spasm of the muscles surrounding the vagina. Normally the term is reserved for the spasm that may occur on penile entry during intercourse. However, as Labby (1982) has pointed out, it can also occur when a tampon is inserted or during pelvic examination. Kroger and Freed (cited by Friedman (1962)) provided the following graphic account of the behaviour that characterises the condition:

> When these patients are examined, the mere attempt or actual touch of the labia may produce spasm and pain. The introitus may become so constricted that it entirely prohibits the entrance of the tip of the finger (or during coitus the penis). The spasm may involve the perineal muscles alone or may constrict the levator ani right up to the vaginal fornices. Accompanying the spasm there is a marked adduction of thighs, even to cramp-like spasm of the adductor muscles. Reich refers to these muscles as the 'pillars of virginity'. Invariably the lumbar spine is extended in the position of lordosis. Frequently the posture assumed is one of opisthotonos, with the head bent backward. These symptoms are not only present during coitus, but can be witnessed during the attempted examination.

Estimates of the contribution that vaginismus makes to all cases of sexual dysfunction vary widely. For example, Jeffcoate (1962) claimed that it was the most common and important cause of dispareunia. Similarly Barnes, Bowman and Cullen (1984) reported it to be the aetiological factor in 55 per cent of all referrals to a Dublin clinic, and that it accounted for 70 per cent of the therapists' work load. On the other hand, Colgan and Beautrais (1977), drawing on the work of Masters and Johnson (1970), claimed that the condition was relatively rare, accounting for only 29 out of 510 cases described. Likewise, Bancroft and Coles (1976) reported that it was identified in only 12 of 102 consecutive referrals to a sexual problems clinic in Oxford. The reason for such discrepant findings is unclear, although differences in referral practices must almost certainly be a contributing factor. However, it is also entirely possible that they represent genuine, geographically related differences in occurrence, which in turn reflect different social attitudes to sexual behaviour, for it is widely accepted that psychosocial factors contribute significantly to the aetiology and maintenance of the condition.

The Causes and Treatment of Vaginismus

Only latterly has the role of psychological factors in the cause (and hence treatment) of vaginismus come to the fore. Indeed, as Friedman (1962) has pointed out, as recently as the 1950s most gynaecological texts paid little attention to such factors. For example, he cites the following (Curtis and Huffman, 1950):

> Dyspareunia of the virgin, including 'honeymoon dyspareunia', includes the largest group of those who suffer from pain at the introitus during the sexual act. Every girl who contemplates matrimony merits consideration of whether the vaginal orifice is sufficiently roomy to permit intercourse without unjustifiable suffering. A hymenectomy is seldom of material moment in affording relief, for the hymen is usually readily torn. An orifice which is too tight because of a firm perineum is a different matter. A perineostomy may be a relatively simple operation; but frequently it should be extensive and demands exacting technic.

Contrast this approach with the following case history presented by Jeffcoate little more than a decade later (1962):

> She (a nurse) was unusually attractive yet, after 4 years of otherwise happy marriage, she remained virginal. She experienced libido and was anxious for a child yet found it impossible to allow her husband access even to the vulva. He acquiesced to her every wish. The conflict caused a functional dyspepsia and it was only when this was investigated that she was referred to me. She attended on condition that no attempt at examination was made except under general anaesthesia. After several prolonged interviews the background to the trouble was revealed. As a probationer nurse she had been in an operating theatre when a foetus was delivered by embryotomy. She was appalled at the sight of the mangled foetus being dragged from the vagina and, to make matters worse, the surgeon in his haste handed the foetus to her as the first person at hand. Thereafter, she lived in dread of childbirth although she was anxious for a child. I promised her delivery by caesarean section if she conceived and thereafter she agreed to a physical examination which revealed severe vaginismus and adductor spasm. She was taught to relax the pelvic floor and gradually vaginal dilators were inserted until she became confident enough to use them herself. It took many months for her outlook to change but she conceived within one year of her first visit and that without any examination under anaesthesia. The cure was not complete, however,

because even though she became more normal as pregnancy advanced, she insisted on the promised caesarean section.

The shift in emphasis reflected in the two preceding examples has continued to the present day. For example, Gelder *et al.* (1983) refer only briefly to physical factors and emphasise instead the part played by fear, anxiety, sexual inhibition and other psychological factors. Likewise, Craig and Milne (1978) reported that 'primary physical causes are responsible for only a small proportion of the cases of sexual dysfunction that we see . . .'. Nevertheless, they saw fit to warn that such cases are encountered:

> A young woman was referred because of failure to consummate her marriage. She had been seen by a number of practitioners and a diagnosis of frigidity had been made. After two lengthy interviews she permitted vaginal examination on the clear understanding that I was to desist if pain was caused. A considerable degree of vaginismus was present but she finally did permit the introduction of the examining finger, which revealed the presence of a congenital stricture at the junction of the lower third and upper two thirds of the vagina. Subsequent explanation and removal of the stricture resulted in cure.

Although such cases underline the need to rule out primary pathology, it is worth re-emphasising that they are relatively rare. Consequently, most present-day methods of treatment focus upon resolving the psychological conflicts assumed to underlie the condition. At one extreme this may consist of little more than sympathetic counselling, while at the other it may involve sophisticated directive sex therapy such as that devised by Masters and Johnson (1970). While a detailed description of the latter approach is beyond the scope of this discussion, the following extract (from Wright, Perreault and Mathieu, 1977) illustrates its complexity;

> Although this therapy can be broken down into a myriad of different therapeutic components at least three aspects seem to be of more importance. (1) educative counselling used to eradicate erroneous sexual myths, (2) facilitation of open verbal and nonverbal communication on sexual and sensual issues, and (3) a graded series of sexual tasks.

The graded tasks involving sexual behaviour include:

(1) nonerotic physical contact, (2) nonbreast, nongenital stroking and exploration of the body keeping in mind the need for signalling pleasure or discomfort, (3) breast and genital stroking added to the previous setting, (4) self-masturbation to orgasm, (5) mutual masturbation to orgasm, and (6) intercourse (also broken down into nonanxiety-provoking segments).

Because so many forms of treatment are subsumed under the general heading of sex therapy, statements about overall efficacy and inter-trial comparisons are virtually meaningless, especially as the criteria whereby patients are selected appear to be equally variable. That said, the study by Bancroft and Coles (1976) suggested that vaginismus was especially responsive to a modified form of the technique devised by Masters and Johnson (1970). Outcome data for 29 patients are shown in Table 9.8.

In general, the success rate shown in Table 9.8 seems not to be unusual (see Wright *et al.*, 1977 for a detailed review). Thus, the question that concerns us here is not whether psychologically based therapies are effective in the treatment of vaginismus, rather it is whether biofeedback can be numbered amongst them.

Biofeedback and Vaginismus

Given that vaginismus is characterised by contraction of striated muscles, it ought in principle to be a prime candidate for EMG feedback training. Just as this technique enabled patients treated by Schuster to learn to contract the external anal sphincter, so it should allow relaxation of the vaginal muscles to be brought under voluntary control. At least one study has been described that adds substance to this suggestion. Indeed, Colgan and Beautrais (1977) claimed that appropriate voluntary control could be learned without having recourse to EMG feedback. Briefly, they applied a technique first described by Kegel (1952) whereby the patient learned to identify and control activity of the pubococcygeus muscle. Once control had been achieved, the couple were then provided with dilators that the female attempted to insert 'while practising relaxing and maintaining voluntary dilation of the vaginal outlet'. The procedure was then repeated, but with the male inserting the dilator while his partner continued to relax and contract the pubococcygeus muscle. The authors concluded that:

> Teaching voluntary control of the vaginal muscles provides the opportunity for practising vaginal dilatation in a non-threatening situation. By practising before a mirror, the female can demonstrate to

Table 9.8: Outcome and Duration of Treatment in those with Certain Problems who Completed Treatment or Dropped Out

	Successful outcome		Worthwhile improvement		No worthwhile improvement		Dropped out	
	No (%) of patients	Mean no. of sessions	No (%) of patients	Mean no. of sessions	No (%) of patients	Mean no. of sessions	No (%) of patients	Mean no of sessions
Women								
General unresponsiveness	12 (40)	8	11 (37)	13	5 (17)	13	2 (7)	3.5
Orgasmic dysfunction	3 (27)	5.5	5 (45)	14			3 (27)	3.5
Vaginismus	6 (75)	17			1 (13)	14	1 (13)	3
Men								
Erectile impotence	5 (33)	9	2 (13)	9.5	3 (20)	5	5 (33)	3
Premature ejaculation	1 (11)	18	4 (44)	10.5	1 (11)	11	3 (33)	3.5
Ejaculatory failure	2 (40)	9	2 (40)	6			1 (20)	6
Total	29 (37)	10	24 (31)	12	10 (13)	10.5	15 (19)	3.5

Source: 'Three Years' Experience in a Sexual Problems Clinic', J. Bancroft and L. Coles, *British Medical Journal* (1976), *1,* 1575–77, Table 4.

herself that she has the ability to dilate the [vagina] sufficiently to allow vaginal penetration. This helps build up confidence and lessens anxiety during subsequent insertion of dilators.

Unfortunately Colgan and Beautrais provided no empirical evidence against which the validity of their conclusion could be judged. In particular, no attempt appears to have been made to measure whether training in muscle control added significantly to the remainder of the treatment programme. Nevertheless their method had sufficient theoretical validity to warrant further exploration. It is somewhat surprising, therefore, that several years were to elapse before the next logical step in this approach to treatment was taken by Barnes *et al.* (1984). This involved facilitating relaxation by providing the patient with EMG feedback from the vaginal muscles.

Five couples were treated, selection for entry into therapy being effectively random. In order to establish the diagnosis of vaginismus, Barnes *et al.* applied two criteria. First, both spouses agreed that all previous attempts at penetration by an erect penis had failed and second, physical examination elicited spasm of the vaginal sphincter and adduction of the thighs. Details of the five couples are shown in Table 9.9.

Table 9.9: Social Characteristics of Patients and Husbands

Case	Duration of marriage (years)	Wife's age (years)	Husband's age (years)	Education status	
				Wife	Husband
1	4½	26	28	Primary	Secondary
2	5½	34	35	Primary	Primary
3	2½	24	25	Secondary	Secondary
4	1	30	35	Secondary	Secondary
5	6½	29	30	Primary	Primary

Source: 'Biofeedback as an Adjunct to Psychotherapy in the Treatment of Vaginismus', J. Barnes, E.P. Bowman and J. Cullen, *Biofeedback and Self-Regulation* (1984), *9*(3), 281–9, Table 1.

Although no details of physical examination were provided, there can be little doubt that the authors were convinced that in every case the condition was psychogenic in origin. For example, they reported as follows: (1) all five women presented with a pathological fear of the act of intercourse; (2) three of them had been raised by a dominant mother whose implied or explicit attitude to sexuality was negative; (3) one patient described her father as an ogre figure who terrorised the whole family, leading her to associate sex with violence, and (4) another was phobic and neurotic with vaginismus being part of a tendency to avoid challenging situations. Other than that they were 'gentle and sexually undemanding', no clinically relevant information was provided about the husbands.

Treatment, which was carried out by a male-female cotherapy team (Barnes and Bowman, respectively) combined various elements of counselling and directive sex therapy with EMG feedback training. Thus, following an initial interview at which the nature of the proposed therapy was explained, the therapists explored with the couple how their experiences and attitudes might have contributed to the aetiology and maintenance of the condition. Thereafter, the husband and wife acted as models while the genital organs and their changes during intercourse were explained. Biofeedback training was introduced during the third session, when the smallest of six vaginal probes (specially adapted to monitor EMG activity) was inserted (Figure 9.3).

Figure 9.3: Modified Sims Dilator Used to Provide EMG Feedback

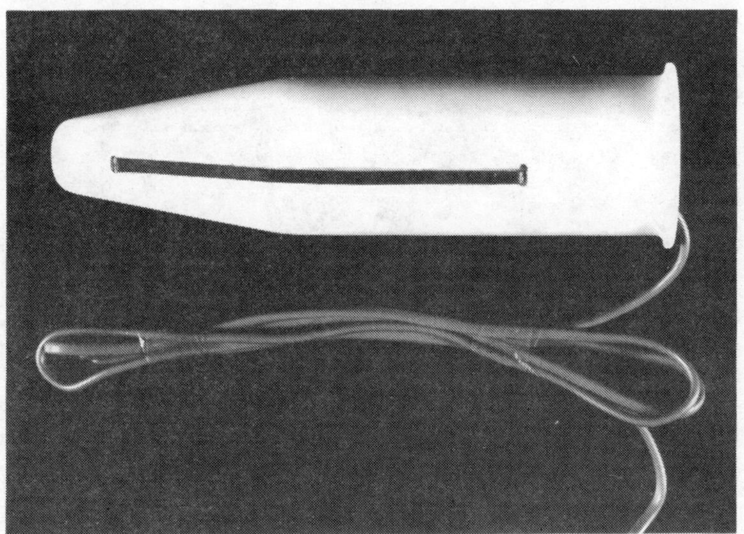

Source: 'Biofeedback as an Adjunct to Psychotherapy in the Treatment of Vaginismus', J. Barnes, E.P. Bowman and J. Cullen, *Biofeedback and Self-Regulation* (1984), *9*(3), 281-9, Figure 1.

Following an adaptation period, the woman was asked to relax and tense her vaginal muscles, the resultant EMG activity being converted to an auditory signal that was fed back to both partners. A similar procedure was adopted during subsequent sessions until the husband was able to introduce the largest probe and his wife could tense and relax without discomfort. For the several weeks during which training was being undertaken couples were asked to refrain from attempting intercourse. However, they were given 'specific mutual pleasuring tasks', which they practised at home, and were also provided with an unmodified dilator for home use.

By the end of training all five couples had achieved a successful outcome (defined as full penetration and ejaculation). Both the total number of sessions attended and the number at which feedback was provided varied across couples within a relatively narrow range (mean (range), 8.8 (6–11) and 3.8 (3–5), respectively). Specimen EMG tracings (Figure 9.4) showed clear differences in muscle activity during periods of tensing and relaxing, though no inter-session data were reported.

Figure 9.4: Specimen EMG Tracing

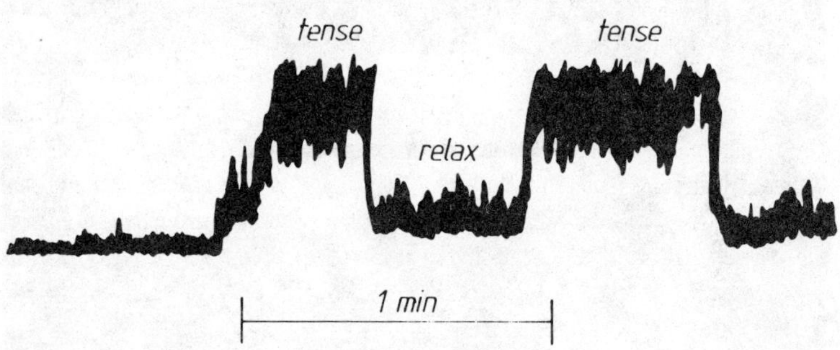

Source: 'Biofeedback as an Adjunct to Psychotherapy in the Treatment of Vaginismus', J. Barnes, E.P. Bowman and J. Cullen, *Biofeedback and Self-Regulation* (1984), *9*(3), 281–9, Figure 2.

As in the report by Colgan and Beautrais (p. 212), the failure to employ appropriate controls, meant that the specific contribution of EMG training could not be isolated. However, Barnes *et al.* reported that the number of sessions devoted to biofeedback (but not total treatment time) was almost halved in comparison to previous experience with Sims dilators. Follow-up six to nine months after the end of treatment revealed that two participants (cases 3 and 5) were pregnant and one couple (case 4) were having intercourse about twice weekly. However, the remaining two couples ceased intercourse shortly after training, though whether this was associated with a recurrence of vaginismus is unclear. (In a personal communication Dr Barnes has confirmed that a recurrence of vaginismus was not the reason for these two couples ceasing intercourse.)

Evaluation

As is highlighted by the lack of empirical data in the preceding section, this application of biofeedback is barely in its infancy. Thus, although no more than an exploratory investigation, the study conducted by Barnes *et al.* remains the most detailed to be described so far. Clearly, therefore, much remains to be done if EMG feedback training is to become established as an acceptable method of treating vaginismus. That said, the findings presented by Barnes *et al.* do raise some important issues about the treatment of sexual dysfunction.

Perhaps the most obvious conclusion to emerge from this study is that vaginismus undoubtedly responds to behavioural treatment. There can surely be no more objective demonstration of efficacy than the finding that two of the five women were pregnant within a year of undergoing treatment! However, what remains unclear is what part EMG feedback played in achieving this outcome. The interpretation offered by Barnes *et al.* was as follows:

> The auditory signal enabled husband and therapist to offer immediate reinforcement and enabled the woman to recognise that she, and not the therapist, was directly responsible for her progress through the desensitization program. No patient dropped out, and it is tentatively suggested that biofeedback was a factor in securing an early feeling of success in the participants.

This is a suggestion with which we are already familiar. It has been argued at a number of points in this book that biofeedback may play a crucial part in maintaining compliance in at least two ways. First, by making patients aware that they have the power to initiate change, and second, by speeding up the learning process. It is particularly interesting, therefore, to observe that the provision of EMG feedback was accompanied by a 50 per cent reduction in the number of sessions devoted to vaginal dilatation. On the face of it the case for EMG feedback seems to have been made by these observations alone. However, things are rarely that simple, especially when dealing with a condition as emotionally charged as vaginismus.

Although Figure 9.4 shows that patients were able to relax their vaginal muscles at will, there is no evidence that EMG feedback *per se* brought about the 50 per cent reduction in dilation exercises. Moreover, it should be remembered that the total time that this group spent in therapy was no less than when no feedback was provided. Clearly, therefore, precisely how EMG feedback affects speed of outcome has still to be answered. However, what makes this study worthy of detailed discussion is that it suggests that, in the treatment of sexual dysfunction, a speedy initial response may not always be desirable. Although none of the five cases required lengthy treatment, one couple (case 2) made particularly rapid progress and were reported to have begun intercourse by the third session. Yet at follow-up it transpired that they were no longer having intercourse and declined further therapy. Reference to Table 9.9 reveals that the woman in question was the oldest of the group and that the marriage remained unconsummated after five and a half years. These factors, along with her pathological fear of intercourse and her mother's negative attitudes to sexuality, virtually guarantee that vaginismus was but one manifestation of a complex sexually based neurosis. If so, then a treatment such as EMG feedback training, which focuses upon the physical symptoms, might at best be expected to achieve limited, short-term improvement. Thus, while there may be good theoretical grounds for arguing that EMG feedback has a part to play in treating one aspect of vaginismus, it would be a mistake to believe that in itself it offers a simple, quick remedy. Rather, as Barnes *et al.* concluded:

> It would be unwise to design a program solely to save time because these couples have to undergo major emotional change at their own pace. Biofeedback appears to be an efficient agent in learning muscle control, but it carries the risk of reversing the symptom while leaving the couple's emotional life inadequately explored. It should not diminish the holistic approach to what is a complex and disabling problem.

Concluding Remarks

This section began with the hope that research into muscle retraining might provide more information about the specific effects of biofeedback than had emerged in preceding chapters. In the event, this hope has been largely unfulfilled for while the research reviewed here suggests that biofeedback has a part to play in the treatment of many forms of muscular dysfunction, the precise mechanisms by which it operates have still to be unequivocally demonstrated. Undoubtedly, the data presented by Schuster (p. 196) strongly suggest that feedback is crucial if the actions of internal and external sphincters are to be synchronised. Likewise, in so far as learning relies upon immediate knowledge of results, EMG feedback seems uniquely placed to provide such information in the early stages of muscle rehabilitation following a severe CVA. Indeed, these two examples alone convince me that, in some instances at least, biofeedback is more than a particularly powerful means of increasing patients' motivation, compliance, and willingness to take responsibility for their own well being. At the same time it has to be accepted that the fully controlled experiments necessary to turn conviction into fact have yet to be performed. Moreover, it must be admitted that the evidence presently available suggests that non-specific effects such as those outlined above will frequently outweigh any effects that are specific to biofeedback. The implications of this assumption are discussed in the final chapter. First, though, it seems appropriate to end this section by referring briefly to two other applications of EMG feedback for while at the most general level neither add significantly to what has already been said here, they show further the potential of EMG feedback in muscle re-training.

Stuttering

There can be few benign conditions that have been more widely researched than stuttering without producing definitive outcomes. Indeed, it is barely an exaggeration to suggest that there are as many theories to account for the condition as there are people who suffer from it. Similarly, a vast range of treatments have been advocated, in some instances with almost missionary zeal. As recently as 1984 *Index Medicus* listed studies in which patients had been treated with the following methods: token reinforcement, rational-emotive therapy, desensitisation, airflow techniques, regulated breathing exercises, awareness training, contingent self-stimulation and physical exercise. It is hardly surprising, therefore, that biofeedback should have been employed in an attempt to control this unfortunate impediment.

Typical of this approach is a study described by Craig and Cleary (1982), who used EMG feedback training to treat three male stutterers aged 10, 13 and 14 years. Treatment was carried out on the following assumption:

> . . . stuttering is related to excess EMG activity, both before and

> during dysfluent utterance, in the speech musculature. Within each subject, therefore it is expected that EMG levels for stuttered words will be greater than nonstuttered words. It is thought that EMG feedback training will enable the subjects to reduce (i.e., control) the excess muscle activity associated with stuttering.

EMG activity from the levator and superior orbicularis oris muscles was fed back to the subject by means of a visual display. Before treatment, baseline data on four parameters were obtained. These comprised; EMG activity when the subject was silent and speaking; his speech rate, measured in syllables per minute (SPM); and his stuttering rate (SS), defined as per cent syllables stuttered. Thereafter, a three-phase training programme spread over 15 weeks was undertaken. Briefly, this involved the following: (1) reducing resting EMG activity, (2) reducing speaking EMG activity, and (3) transferring the skills acquired in phases 1 and 2 to the natural environment without feedback. Training was followed by a one-month maintenance phase in which subjects were required to practise formally the skills learned in training, to maintain a diary in which details of serious stutter were recorded, and to devise and implement a self-reward system for fluent speech patterns. Per cent SS and SPM were measured (in the subject's home) two and nine months after treatment. The outcome is summarised in Figure 9.5.

On the basis of these findings and those of other workers (Kalotkin, Manschreck and O'Brien, 1979), Craig and Cleary suggested that:

> Overall, these results lend support to the theory that tension of the speech musculature is related to the stuttering disorder. Results for two subjects suggest a simple relationship: i.e., the higher the speech muscle activity that a stutterer has, the greater the frequency of stuttering.

However, they were quick to point out that other workers (e.g. McLean and Cooper, 1978) found no relationship between laryngeal EMG activity and stuttering. Moreover, their own data showed this relationship, is, at best, variable. Although all three patients exhibited reduced EMG activity by the end of feedback training, in one case (subject 1) this was not accompanied by a reduction in stammering. As Figure 9.5 shows, improvement only occurred when maintenance training was introduced. Viewed against the theoretical framework proposed by Yates (p. 171), this inconsistency is hardly surprising. There can be few more complex

Figure 9.5: Severity of Stuttering (%SS) for Reading as a Function of Treatment Phase in Three Boys Treated with EMG Feedback. Odd numbers for baseline and feedback represent clinical recordings. Even numbers represent recordings taken at the subject's home. All maintenance and follow-up measures were taken at the subject's home. Measurements 1–6 are 3- to 4-day intervals, 7–12 are fortnightly intervals, 13–15 are weekly intervals, and 16, 17 are 2- and 9-month intervals after feedback

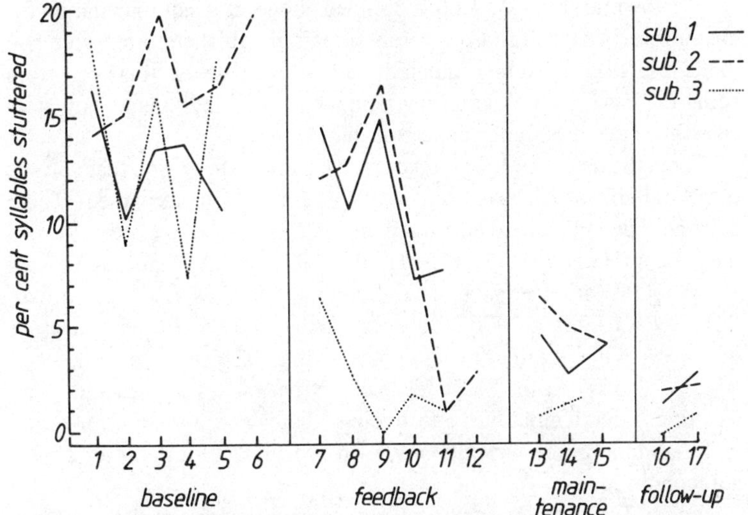

Source: 'Reduction of Stuttering by Young Male Stutterers Using EMG Feedback', A.R. Craig and P.J. Cleary, *Biofeedback and Self-Regulation* (1982), 7(3), 241–55, Figure 2.

biological feedback systems than that involved in speech production. Moreover, many stutterers experience near overwhelming anxiety when speaking in public. It would take a supreme optimist, therefore, to expect every patient to derive the same benefit from EMG biofeedback as those described here.

Cerebral Palsy

The term 'cerebral palsy' is used to denote sensory-motor defects resulting from damage to the developing brain which may have occurred either pre-natally during or after birth. Superficially, at least, the condition resembles the movement disorders described earlier, in that the sufferer lacks the ability to control voluntary movement. It is not uncommon to find the terms cerebral palsy and 'spasticity' being used as synonyms. However, as Shakespeare (1975) has pointed out, the latter term should be reserved for those cases that are characterised by over-contraction of the voluntary muscles. Although this is the most common form in which the condition occurs, a significant minority of sufferers exhibit athetosis in which there is a slow, rhythmical movement of the limbs, described by Shakespeare as 'constant writhing movements'. As well as the muscle dysfunctions outlined above, it is not uncommon for the sufferer's speech to be severely impaired. This can often give rise to the impression that he is mentally retarded. However, this is far from being the case, as the increasing number of such individuals now successfully entering higher education indicates.

Given the nature of the symptoms, it is hardly surprising that various forms of biofeedback have been used in an attempt to control them. These have included techniques in which changes in posture were fed back to the patient (Harris, Spelman and Hymer, 1974; Wooldridge and Russell, 1976) and EMG feedback from a number of sites (Finley, Niman, Standley and Ender, 1976). Both approaches have achieved a measure of success without either proving outstanding. The study to be described here also relied on EMG feedback. What makes it particularly interesting is that it employed a technology that is appropriate for use with children undergoing virtually any form of feedback training for almost any condition.

Finley, Etherton, Dickman, Karimian and Simpson (1981) designed their study on the assumption that while adults may find immediate feedback of appropriate EMG activity reinforcing in itself, children may require rewards of a more tangible nature. To examine this hypothesis, Finley *et al.* divided the patients shown in Table 9.10 into two groups.

Following three sessions in which baseline EMG measures were monitored (but not fed back), each participant attended twelve treatment sessions. For twelve patients this involved EMG feedback training, activity being monitored at the frontal-forearm flexor sites. When EMG output fell below a given threshold, a 'universal feeder' (UF) was activated to deliver a reward in the form of a toy, token, candy or money. The control group received identical training, except that they were not rewarded until after each training session. The results are shown in Figure 9.6.

Commenting on their data, Finley *et al.* concluded that:

> The principle advantage of the system is that children can learn to reduce EMG from biofeedback training without an on-line reward system, but, as shown by the supporting data, when rewards are

Table 9.10: Resumé of Cerebral-Palsied Children Trained With and Without the Universal Feeder (UF) Reward System

Patient	CP Severity level	Age (years), sex	Intelligence level	Patient able to Walk	Patient able to Talk	Medications
With UF reward system						
M.R.	Mild	7, F	Considered normal	Yes	Yes	None
J.J.	Mild	5, F	Considered normal	Yes	Yes	None
V.H.	Moderate	13, F	Mildy retarded	Yes	Yes	Mebaral, 32 mg bid
J.S.	Moderate	7, M	Above average	No	Yes	Dilantin, 120 mg/day
L.H.	Severe	22, F	Moderately retarded	No	No	Valium, 5 mg bid Probanthine*
P.R.	Moderate	10, M	IQ = 137	No	Yes	None
C.M.	Severe	4, M	Mildly retarded	No	Yes	Phenobarb, 1 tsp. bid
D.H.P.	Mild	12, M	Considered normal	Yes	Yes	None
C.M.B.	Severe	7, M	Severely retarded	No	No	Valium, 2 mg bid
J.A.	Mild	5, M	Considered normal	Yes	Yes	None
Without UF reward system						
S.E.	Severe	9, M	Severely retarded	No	No	Valium, 5 mg bid
S.W.	Moderate	4, F	Mildly retarded	No	No	None
M.M.	Mild	6, M	Considered normal	Yes	Yes	None
B.T.	Mild	12, M	Mildly retarded	Yes	Yes	None
D.H.T.	Mild	12, F	Considered normal	Yes	Yes	Slo-Phyllin, 10 mg tid. Theo-Dur, 200 mg tid. Bricanyl, 2.5 mg bid.

* Medication for drooling, which was discontinued by patient's physician mid-training because it was no longer needed.
Source: 'A Simple EMG — Reward System for Biofeedback Training of Children', W.W. Finley, M.D. Etherton, D. Dickman, D. Karimian, and R.W. Simpson, *Biofeedback and Self-Regulation* (1981), *6*(2), 169–80, Table 2.

available on line and are contingent upon criterion EMG reductions learning progresses more rapidly and the child obtains deeper muscle relaxation. Our experience with this procedure has shown that once a child understands the relationship between relaxation and 'squeezing toys out of the machine', he works very independently and requires little supervision from a technician.

As a clinical trial, this study is, of course, of limited value.

Figure 9.6: Mean Difference Scores From Baseline (BL) and 12 Training Trials for Two Groups of Cerebral-Palsied Children. The solid line represents EMG-difference scores for those who received rewards from the universal feeder on line for EMG reductions. The broken line shows EMG reductions for those who trained in a standard biofeedback situation but were given rewards at the end of each 20 to 30 minute training session

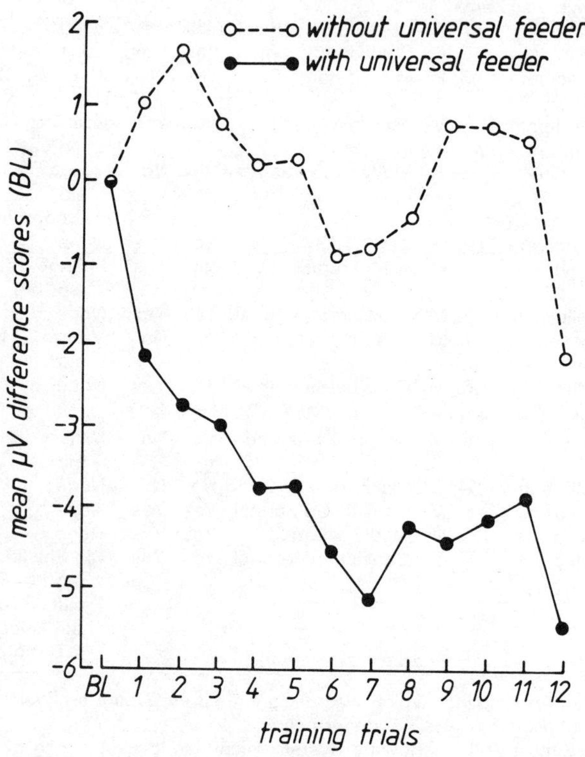

Source: 'A Simple EMG — Reward System for Biofeedback Training of Children', W.W. Finley, M.D. Etherton, D. Dickman, D. Karimian and R.W. Simpson, *Biofeedback and Self-Regulation* (1981), *6*(2), 169–80, Figure 3.

Undoubtedly both groups learned to reduce EMG activity. However, whether these reductions were accompanied by long-lasting, clinically significant improvement was not made clear. What is clear is that, under laboratory conditions, the addition of an on-line reward system significantly affected outcome. The reader may well recognise that the technique described here exactly parallels the method of operant conditioning described in Chapter 2. There an animal received food for pressing a lever; here the patient receives a toy for relaxing his muscles. The fact that the two situations are so similar immediately raises a problem. Studies using animals have shown that unless care is taken not to reward every correct response, the newly acquired behaviour quickly extinguishes outside the training environment. Finley *et al.* recognised this problem, but went on to point out that:

> Also, with the automated reinforcement procedure, the UF can be stocked with any schedule of rewards each session, thus making a variable ratio (VR) of reinforcement possible. Ultimately, the child working with increasingly intermittant VR schedules can be weaned from all physical reinforcers.

This work has much in common with that of Sherwood and Hewlett (1984) who have pioneered the use of computers in EMG feedback training with children. Whether the reward be a toy or a record score on an EMG-driven computer game, this approach offers exciting possibilities for extending this method of treating muscle dysfunction.

10 SUMMING UP AND LOOKING AHEAD

In the first two chapters of this book the development of biofeedback was traced from its origins in the psychological laboratory to the point when it was introduced into clinical practice. Since then a vast amount of research has been conducted into the efficacy and *modus operandi* of this approach to treatment. Given the common theoretical assumptions underlying the early clinical applications, it might be expected that this review would end with a detailed summary that applied equally to all forms of biofeedback. However, by now it will be readily apparent why no such summary is possible. Almost from the outset the simple principles on which biofeedback was based were found wanting. In some instances direct feedback training proved ineffective; in others favourable outcomes could only be interpreted by moving outside the narrow confines of learning theory. Accepting this lack of generalisability, most contemporary authors follow the practice adopted here of limiting detailed analyses of efficacy and underlying mechanisms to each specific application. However, that is not to say that no important general conclusions are to be drawn from the large body of research conducted in both the laboratory and the clinic over the past two decades. In fact, three such conclusions emerged during the course of this discussion. These relate to efficacy, non-specific effects and inter-subject differences.

The Question of Efficacy

Perhaps the most unambiguous conclusion to emerge here is that while biofeedback has a useful part to play in many areas of clinical practice, it is no 'wonder treatment'. Almost without exception, the favourable outcomes described in the preceding chapters were modest and applied only to a sub-group of the total population of sufferers. Certainly they bear no relation to the fanciful claims once made for this method of treatment. Recall what was promised. Biofeedback was a revolutionary new technology that would quickly put us in touch with the inner self, thus bringing health, happiness and well-being. Moreover, anyone willing to take up meditation as well could enjoy the added bonus of conquering bad habits and reversing the ageing process (p. vii). Having seen the evidence, the reader will understand my irritation when faced with such claims. Their relation to hard empirical data is so tenuous as to be virtually non-existent, and they should be dismissed for what they are — the hyperbole of the salesman who has something new to sell.

Bearing in mind the multiple aetiology of so many conditions treated with biofeedback, the above conclusion is unremarkable. Certainly it comes as no suprise to my clinical colleagues to learn that conditions as complex as essential hypertension, migraine and spasmodic torticollis respond no better to behavioural techniques than they do to conventional medical or surgical procedures. However, what does surprise many of them is my willingness to concede that the effects of biofeedback often appear to be non-specific. Their surprise is understandable for, as was pointed out earlier, as far as most doctors are concerned this is tantamount to saying that biofeedback is nothing more than a placebo. Hopefully, the reader will recognise that this is not at all what I intend to convey. Nevertheless, such a misunderstanding cannot be left unresolved, for to describe any form of treatment as a placebo is to ensure that it will quickly lose whatever credibility it may possess.

Biofeedback, Non-specific Effects and the Placebo Response

In Chapter 3 a placebo was defined as:

> any component of therapy that is deliberately or knowingly used for its nonspecific, psychologic, or psycho-physiologic effect, or that is used unknowingly for its presumed or believed specific effect on a patient, symptom, or illness, but which, unknown to patient and therapist, is without specific activity for the condition being treated.

Given the emphasis that this definition places upon non-specific psychological factors, it is not difficult to see why many doctors believe that it offers an accurate description of biofeedback. This attitude was exemplified in a letter to *The Lancet* by Pickering (1973), who, commenting on Patel's early work, wrote the following:

> . . . I believe that this type of situation fulfils most of the criteria for the ideal placebo response, as described by Shapiro . . . — namely a procedure that is 'expensive, fashionable, elaborate, detailed, time-consuming, esoteric, and dangerous.' Most bio-feedback procedures conform to all but the last of these, but Dr. Patel's is commendably simple and would, perhaps, not be classified as 'elaborate' . . . Reading the earlier literature on the treatment of hypertension I am

> impressed by the number of papers reporting significant benefits from agents such as liver extract or extract of watermelon, which have since fallen into disrepute.

Predictably, Patel (1973) did not take kindly to this interpretation of her data, dismissing it on the following grounds:

> (a) 80% of patients responded to the therapy.
> (b) Benefit has lasted as long as six months.
> (c) My procedure was anything but expensive, fashionable, elaborate, detailed, or exciting. The only thing that was liberally used was the patients' cooperation and my time. The bio-feedback instrument used was simple and inexpensive. It did not cost anything at all to the patients. It could hardly be considered fashionable and exciting to go and see a National Health Service family doctor to receive a free treatment. No promise was made regarding any benefit of the treatment.

Although the last point deserves high marks for modesty it is hardly an adequate answer to Pickering's original argument. If the inert capsules administered by Frankenhaeuser *et al.* (p. 32) could evoke a placebo response, then it is safe to assume that the programme devised by Patel and North would do likewise. And so it has proved. In every study reported here that employed the appropriate controls, we have seen evidence of a placebo effect (e.g. Budzynski *et al.*, 1973; Patel and North, 1975; Kondo and Canter, 1978). Equally, however, we have seen that compared with the effects of the treatment under investigation, it was small and transient. Thus the question at issue is not whether biofeedback evokes a placebo response, rather, it is whether improvement said to result from changes in factors such as the patient's view of his symptoms and his power to control them should be so classified.

In a thoughtful discussion of the placebo effect in biofeedback, Katkin and Goldband (1979) pointed out the following:

> Strictly speaking the concept of 'placebo' refers to the use of a pharmacologically inactive agent which is administered to a patient for a variety of reasons . . . It is not the case that a treatment is classified as a placebo because its mechanism is not understood; rather it is classified as a placebo precisely when its mechanism is well understood and there is no pharmacologically valid reason for it to succeed.

When applied to findings such as those described by Frankenhaeuser *et al.*, (1963) this account poses no problems. Given that capsules were pharmacologically inert, the changes shown in Figure 3.1 could not be other than placebo responses. Likewise, the examples cited by Pickering, though not identical to that described by Frankenhaeuser *et al.*, are no more complex. Extracts of liver and watermelon were classified as placebos because their efficacy was not maintained under tightly controlled, double-blind conditions. Here again it appears that factors such as suggestion, expectation and observer bias were responsible for favourable outcomes that were initially believed to be pharmacologically induced. However, attempts to interpret the effects of biofeedback in a similar manner soon begin to encounter problems.

The comment by Katkin and Goldband underlines a point that was amply illustrated in Chapter 3. That is, the placebo response is usually examined in a pharmacological context. Thus, in a drug trial it is regarded as a 'nuisance variable', the effects of which have to be controlled. Conversely, in a clinical setting it may be used to the doctor's advantage, as when he prescribes a 'sugar pill' in order to humour a patient whose illness is benign and self-limiting. Unfortunately, as Peek (1977) has pointed out, this concern with pharmacological factors has brought us almost to the point where any treatment that cannot be explained in the physiological-biological domain is likely to be dismissed as a placebo. Although this may be perfectly acceptable when we are evaluating drugs, it is manifestly not so in the case of treatments based upon psychological principles. While biofeedback, psychotherapy and other such treatments may eventually all come to be classified as placebos, this will not be because their effects failed to be demonstrated at a biochemical level. Rather, following Katkin and Goldband, it will be because there proved to be no *psychologically* valid reason for them to succeed, other than the changes in expectation that accompany the administration of any form of treatment. To illustrate this point, consider the role of biofeedback in the treatment of tension headache. It will be recalled that initially (not unlike extract of watermelon) EMG feedback was assumed to have a clearly defined, specific mode of action. That is, it enabled the sufferer to reduce contraction in certain groups of muscles in the head and neck. Although in some instances this appeared to be the case, we saw in Chapter 6 that the correlation between changes in EMG activity and headache relief often proves to be less than perfect. Consequently (again, not unlike the watermelon example) it became necessary to invoke psychological variables to account for the totality of the data. It is at this point that the analogy with a pharmacologically induced placebo response breaks down. As Green and Green (1983) have pointed out;

> When self regulation is activated through the use of a sugar pill, a placebo, the effect almost invariably goes away as time passes because it is attached to a sterile medical factor. But when the self-regulation effect is attached to one's own volitional effort then a skill can be developed embodying genuine self-regulation . . .

The difference between the two mechanisms identified by Green and Green was neatly demonstrated in a study described by Engstrom (1983), in which two groups, each comprising 16 chronic low-back-pain sufferers, were evaluated over a ten-week period. All 32 participants completed a subjective pain questionnaire at the commencement of the trial and again at the end of weeks 3, 7 and 10. For the first three weeks of the trial all subjects were treated with a self-administered oral placebo, at the end of which period the experimental group was told:

> You have been given placebo medication for 3 weeks, and your belief in the efficacy of the placebo has led to improvement in your pain level and other measures. You will have the opportunity to take the real medication in the future, but we would like you to first have the opportunity to learn to better understand how your beliefs influence your level of pain and to learn some coping strategies to help you to control your pain yourself. Since the placebo doses reduced your pain, and since this improvement is only attributable to your using your own internal resources, we believe that you can learn to 'internalize' your own coping skills so that you understand that you are making gains by your own skills and efforts.

No such information was given to controls, who continued taking the placebo for a further four weeks.

The results showed that during the first three weeks of the study both groups exhibited a decrease in pain. Thereafter, the level reported by the control group began to increase, so that by week 10 it had returned to its pre-trial value. This was in contrast to the experimental group, whose members showed further reductions in pain throughout the remainder of the study. Engstrom summarised his findings as follows:

> The present study took subjects from an external reinforcement system (placebos) to an internal one (self-instruction). In doing so, it used a cognitive process (explanation and instruction) to repeat a behavioural change that had already occurred (placebo effect) as a result of a cognitive event (expectation of efficacy) which the subjects

had not realized was so powerful. The rehearsals of the training sessions provided behavioural reinforcements of the cognitive experience in an interaction that represents the essence of a truly cognitive-behavioural therapy.

Unfortunately the absence of long-term follow-up data limits the conclusions to be drawn from this study. However, the findings arc in accord with the examples cited in the preceding chapters, where biofeedback enhanced the self-regulation skills to which Green and Green refer. In so far as these skills rely upon changes in the patient's psychological state, rather than in his musculature, they can be said to be non-specific. However, unlike sugar pills, their effects are often powerful and long-lasting (Andrasik and Holroyd, 1983). Certainly the systematic decline in migraine attacks shown in Figure 6.9 bears little relation to the transient placebo response exhibited by Engstrom's control group.

Undoubtedly much of the confusion surrounding the status of biofeedback arises from the use of the terms 'specific' and 'non-specific'. Perhaps for this reason a number of authors have chosen instead to refer to the two levels at which it operates as 'direct' and 'indirect'. For example, Andrasik and Holroyd (1983) concluded a three-year follow-up of tension headache sufferers treated with EMG feedback as follows:

> . . . This latter finding provides additional evidence that improvements in headache activity following EMG training are not mediated by the learned control of EMG activity and indicates that the improvements are not merely a function of transient placebo effects. These results are thus consistent with the hypothesis . . . that improvements in headache activity following biofeedback may be mediated by psychological changes *indirectly* [my italics] induced by biofeedback training.

Bakal (1979) adopts a similar approach, arguing that:

> Although biofeedback has not been proven as a powerful direct technique for gaining control over physiological functions, it might prove to be an extremely useful *indirect* technique for accomplishing this objective.

As the above quotation illustrates, Bakal appears to have no doubts that it is the indirect effects of biofeedback that are the key to its success. In those conditions where psycho-social factors are to the fore this may well be so. However, as we have seen, not every condition that responds to biofeedback falls into this category. For example, there is little need to invoke indirect effects to account for Schuster's success in treating non-psychogenic faecal incontinence. In this instance improvement appears to have been directly linked to learned control of the anal sphincters.

Although the last example illustrates that by no means all the effects of biofeedback are achieved indirectly, there can be little doubt that many of them are. This observation serves to remind us of the third general conclusion to emerge from the preceding chapters. The more a particular mode of biofeedback relies upon indirect effects to achieve a favourable outcome, the less likely it is to be universally applicable.

Who Will Benefit?

Because biofeedback is based upon psychological principles, it is perhaps not surprising that some clinical colleagues feel it appropriate to refer patients whose condition is the direct result of, or exacerbated by, some form of psychopathology. However, we have seen that symptoms that contain a significant element of hysteria or have been associated with some form of gain are no more likely to respond to biofeedback than they are to conventional medical or surgical techniques. Likewise, studies by Diamond, Medina, Diamond-Falk and DeVeno (1979) and by Blanchard *et al.* (1982) revealed a poor prognosis for clinically depressed patients. Bearing in mind the reduction in motivation and self-esteem that characterises depression, these findings are only to be expected. Rather less predictable is the existence of a further group of patients who, though exhibiting no psychopathology of any kind, nonetheless fail to benefit from this method of treatment. These are the individuals who regard all illness as the result of malign external forces that can only be dealt with by the medical profession. Even when the nature of their symptoms is explained to them they will continue to resist the suggestion that they, rather than the doctor, can control them. It is my experience that such patients rarely wish to undergo biofeedback training, and that few of those who decide to 'give it a try' possess the motivation necessary to achieve a successful outcome. Which brings us face-to-face with a major obstacle to the development of this approach to treatment.

The Problem of Motivation

As we saw in Chapter 4, the problem of motivation, as it affects compliance, is by no means confined to biofeedback. Nonetheless it has to be conceded that non-compliance can pose particularly severe problems for certain behavioural control techniques. Just how severe will, of course, depend upon the nature of the particular application. Indeed, we saw in Chapter 7 that EMG feedback may actively *increase* compliance when it is used as an adjunct to conventional forms of muscle rehabilitation training. Equally, motivation may not be an insurmountable problem when, for example, failure to comply leaves the patient with a series of incapacitating headaches. However, when, as with most cases of essential hypertension, the condition is asymptomatic and the prescribed exercises have to be carried out regularly over long periods of time, the behavioural techniques are particularly vulnerable. Just how vulnerable was thrown into stark relief by a study described by Patel, Marmot, Terry, Carruthers, Hunt and Patel (1985). They presented follow-up data from approximately 84 per cent of the subjects who participated in the trial conducted by Patel *et al.* (1981; see p. 59). These revealed that over a four-year period the *difference* in blood pressure between the two groups had been maintained (Figure 10.1).

However, as Figure 10.1 illustrates, there was a tendency for the pressures of both groups to increase across the four-year period. An increasing trend of this nature can, of course, be due to many factors. Nevertheless, a failure to maintain long-term compliance must rate high on the list of possibilities for at the four-year follow-up only 17 per cent of the treated subjects reported that they still practised relaxation on a regular basis, while less than 4 per cent had practised once a day during the week preceding the survey. In assessing the implications of these findings it needs recognising that they probably over-estimate the problem of non-compliance. It will be recalled that before entering the original trial none of the participants had been diagnosed as suffering from (let alone been treated for) essential hypertension. Consequently many would lack the motivation of the long-term hypertensive who has experienced the side-effects of pharmacological treatments. Yet despite this *caveat*, given the amount of attention that Patel and her colleagues pay to motivational factors, these data are, to say the least, disheartening. Certainly they would not augur well for this method of treatment if they proved to be the norm. However, there are certain straws in the wind which indicate that this need not be so.

The last 20 years has seen a significant change in attitudes towards

Figure 10.1: Four-Year Follow-Up Data for Patients Treated by Patel *et al.* (1981). Changes in blood pressure at each follow-up in subjects with high and normal blood pressures initially. Subjects taught relaxation. ●, controls. ○, P values test differences between treatment and control groups in mean changes in blood pressure.

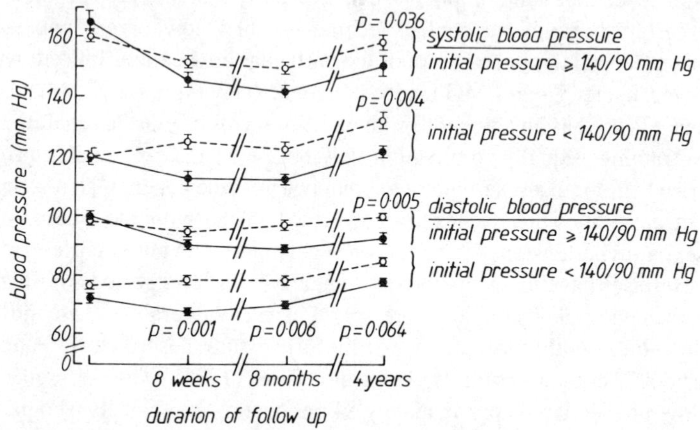

Source: 'Trial of Relaxation in Reducing Coronary Risk: Four Year Follow-Up, C. Patel, M.G. Marmot, D.J. Terry, M. Carruthers, B. Hunt and M. Patel, *British Medical Journal* (1985), *290,* 1103–1106.

health care as members of the public become increasingly willing to accept responsibility for the maintenance of their own well-being. One such example was to be found in the patient-led rejection of the over-prescribing of benzodiazepines described in Chapter 1. Similarly, changed attitudes towards smoking, diet and exercise all reflect an increasing awareness that the maintenance of good physical and mental health is far too important to be left solely to doctors and psychologists! Moreover, similar attitudes often prevail amongst individuals whose health cannot by any criterion be described as good. Thus, in my own hospital, out-patient notice boards that once announced only the date of the next League of Friends Jumble Sale are now thick with posters giving details of self-help groups for virtually every category of patient. While at present it would be foolish to read too much into these shifts in attitudes, it would be equally foolish to ignore completely the opportunity they offer for involving patients in their own treatment. Accordingly, within my own clinic I now give patients the chance to meet in order that they might discuss with each other their symptoms and the rationale for treating them by behavioural means. My impression of group meetings of this kind (admittedly in the absence of supporting data) is that as well as helping to resolve the doubts that many patients harbour towards this approach to treatment, they also appear significantly to increase the motivation and compliance of the whole group. There is, of course, nothing original in harnessing group processes to maintain compliance. It is a method that has been used to good effect for many years by organisations such as Alcoholics Anonymous, Gamblers Anonymous and Weight Watchers. In the present context, however, the use of small groups has the added benefit of helping to overcome a further obstacle to the methods described here. That is their cost.

In 1977, Patel produced a review of her work up to that point in which she addressed the question of cost as follows:

> Should this therapy be offered to all hypertensive patients? One of the arguments put forward by critics is that it is too time consuming. Admittedly, to give the training as described here would take considerable medical manpower. It could, however, easily be provided on a group basis. In a recent study (Patel and Carruthers, 1977), the relaxation training was carried out in small groups. Each patient was connected to a biofeedback instrument and the signals from it were presented to the patient by means of a specially built headphone with one earpiece only. The other ear was kept open to hear relaxation instructions given by cassette tape.
>
> A Multi-Relaxometer with ten circuits has recently become available (Alephone Ltd. Cambridge, England). Allowing 50 min per half-hour session — to include time for electrode attachment and so forth — the time involved would only be 5 min per patient per session. This is less than the average office visit to a general practitioner. Moreover, much of the training could be provided by paramedical personnel. The money saved by cutting down on drug requirements could easily pay for the medical manpower required. In view of the diminished response to experimental stress and the probable long-term reduction both in the left ventricular pressure load and in possible 'wear and tear' on the vessel walls that appear to occur with the training techniques described, time spent in such therapy would seem eminently worthwhile.

This observation is important on two grounds. First, it puts into perspective the argument that this form of treatment is too costly to be widely adopted. Second (and in my opinion more importantly), it raises the question of how costs should be measured. Undoubtedly biofeedback and relaxation training (at least initially) are expensive in terms of the time and commitment that they demand of the doctor or therapist. However, short-term costs are only one side of the equation. Benefits (both short-term and long-term) must also be taken into account and it is here that the principle advantage of the behavioural techniques emerges. As I have argued elsewhere (Marcer, 1985): '. . . when applied successfully their effects extend beyond the condition being treated, so that the patient will have taken the first steps in learning to combat a whole range of stress-linked illnesses'.

In other words, when used to treat stress-related conditions, biofeedback and relaxation training should be viewed not only as methods of controlling an existing symptom, but as prophylactic measures which may act to prevent others.

Looking Ahead

Having begun this review by outlining the early history of biofeedback, it seems appropriate to end it by looking forward to future developments. Undoubtedly there is much research that still needs to be done. It is depressing to observe how few of the studies published during the past two decades came even close to meeting the ten criteria set out at the end of Chapter 3. Consequently many of the conclusions arrived at in the preceding chapters had to be qualified to a greater or lesser extent. Fortunately there is a growing awareness of the need for more sophisticated research — especially into the behavioural control of stress-related chronic conditions. In particular there is much that still has to be learned about the indirect effects of biofeedback and other self-control techniques. Despite their exploratory nature, the small-scale studies described by Engstrom (p. 230) and Mitchell and White (p. 137) point the direction that research into this potentially potent force might take. However, more and better research will not in itself be sufficient to significantly increase the contribution that biofeedback makes to contemporary medical practice.

Although many of the studies described here were carried out by medically qualified researchers, such individuals are rare amongst medical pracitioners. Regrettably, few British doctors possess the background in psychology necessary for them to evaluate this approach to treatment, let alone introduce it into their clinical practice. To a limited extent this situation is changing as the behavioural sciences are increasingly being introduced into the undergraduate medical curriculum. However, it will be many years before the effects of this new approach to teaching make a significant clinical impact. Of much more relevance, therefore, is the changing role of clinical psychologists within the National Health Service. Traditionally, the majority of clinical psychologists have been employed in psychiatric hospitals or institutions providing long-term care for the severely mentally subnormal. However, over the past few decades it has become increasingly recognised that their contribution to medicine can extend much further than this. For example, Craig and Milne (1978) have suggested that:

> The emergent profession of clinical psychology has caused heated and controversial dispute between itself and the medical profession. Behavioural psychologists have established their own treatment facilities separate from the medical profession and have, as a result, brought criticism upon themselves from established medicine. Political and emotive dispute is not conducive to therapeutic success and objective assessment has established the necessity and values of the clinical psychologist within the therapeutic team. The time has gone when the psychologist's contribution was the measurement of intelligence, and similarly the dogmatic pronouncements of the medically qualified. Either extreme is therapeutically nihilistic. Behavioural techniques involving desensitisation, operant-conditioning and relaxation techniques have their contribution to make in the treatment of sexual dysfunction. Alternatively, the extreme view of behaviourists that orgasm is a mechanistic act excluding emotion should be regarded with caution.

Similarly, this positive commitment to a multi-disciplinary approach to treatment is reflected in the increasing number of clinical psychologists who are to be found working as part of the therapeutic team within community health centres. If (as I believe it will) this trend continues, then it seems likely that biofeedback, relaxation training and various forms of cognitive therapy (e.g. Beck, Rush, Shaw and Emery, 1979) will become much more widely used in general practice. Turning to the specific applications of biofeedback outlined in Part Two, the outlook is equally promising. Unlike psychologists, physiotherapists have a long-established role in the treatment of patients suffering from the after effects of CVAs and from other neuromuscular disorders. It is heartening, therefore, to observe that several members of this profession (e.g. Binder *et al.* 1981; Sherwood and Hewlett, 1984; Skelly and Kenedi, 1982) are actively engaged in developing what many regard as one of the most exciting applications of biofeedback.

REFERENCES

Achterberg, J., McGraw, P. and Lawlis, G.F. (1981) 'Rheumatoid Arthritis: A Study of Relaxation and Temperature Biofeedback Training as an Adjunctive Therapy', *Biofeedback and Self-Regulation, 6,* 2, 207–23

Adams, H.E., Feuerstein, M. and Fowler, J.L. (1980) 'Migraine Headache: Review of Parameters, Etiology, and Intervention', *Psychological Bulletin, 87,* 2, 217–37

Ad Hoc Committee on the Classification of Headache (1962), National Institute of Neurological Diseases and Blindness, Classification of Headache, *Neurology, 12,* 378–80

Agnew, D.C. and Merskey, H. (1976) 'Words of Chronic Pain', *Pain, 2,* 73–81

Agras, W.S., Southam, M.A. and Taylor, B.C. (1983) 'Long-Term Persistence of Relaxation-Induced Blood Pressure Lowering During the Working Day', *Journal of Consulting and Clinical Psychology, 51,* 5, 792–4

Ahmad, S. and Meeran, M.K. (1979) 'Treatment of Spasmodic Torticollis with Diazepam' [letter], *British Medical Journal, i,* 127

Albanese, H. and Gaarder, K. (1977) 'Biofeedback Treatment of Tardive Dyskinesia: Two Case Reports', *American Journal of Psychiatry, 134,* 10, 1149–50

Alderson, M.R. (1974) 'Are Clinical Trials Required', *Gerontologia Clinica, 16,* 76–87

Alva, J., Mendeloff, A.I. and Schuster, M.M. (1967) 'Reflex and Electromyographic Abnormalities Associated with Fecal Incontinence', *Gastroenterology, 53,* 1, 101–6

Anderson, T.P., Cole, T.M., Gullickson, G., Hudgens, A. and Roberts, A.H. (1977) 'Behavior Modification of Chronic Pain: A Treatment Program by a Multidisciplinary Team', *Journal of Clinical Orthopaedics, 129,* 96–100

Andrasik, F. and Holroyd, K.A. (1983) 'Specific and Nonspecific Effects in the Biofeedback Treatment of Tension Headache: 3-Year Follow-Up', *Journal of Consulting and Clinical Psychology, 51,* 4, 634–6

Andrews, J.M. (1964) 'Neuromuscular Reeducation of the Hemiplegic with the aid of the Electromyograph', *Archives of Physical Medicine and Rehabilitation, 45,* 530–2

Anthony, M., Hinterberger, H. and Lance, J.W. (1967) 'Plasma Serotonin in Migraine and Stress', *Archives of Neurology, 16,* 544–52

Bakal, D.A. (1979) *Psychology and Medicine,* Tavistock Publications, London/Springer Publishing Company, New York

——— and Kaganov, J.A. (1977) 'Muscle Contraction and Migraine Headache: Psychophysiologic Comparison', *Headache, 17,* 208–15

Bancroft, J. and Coles, L. (1976) 'Three Years' Experience in a Sexual Problems Clinic', *British Medical Journal, 1,* 1575–7

Bannan, L.T., Beevers, D.G. and Jackson, S.H.D. (1981) 'Detecting Hypertensive Patients', *British Medical Journal, 282,* 1211–13

Barnes, J., Bowman, E.P. and Cullen, J. (1984) 'Biofeedback as an Adjunct to Psychotherapy in the Treatment of Vaginismus', *Biofeedback and Self-Regulation, 9,* 3, 281–9

Basmajian, J.V. (1963) 'Control and Training of Individual Motor Units', *Science, 141,* 440–1

——— (1983) 'Introduction: Principles and Background', in J.V. Basmajian (ed.), *Biofeedback Principles and Practice for Clinicians,* Williams and Wilkins, Baltimore/London, pp. 1–4

——— Kukulka, C.G., Narayan, M.G. and Takebe, K. (1975) 'Biofeedback Treatment of Foot-Drop After Stroke Compared with Standard Rehabilitation Technique: Effects on Voluntary Control and Strength', *Archives of Physical Medicine and Rehabilitation,*

56, 231–6

——— Regenos, E.M. and Baker, M.P. (1977) 'Rehabilitating Stroke Patients with Biofeedback', *Geriatrics, 32,* 85–8

Beary, J.F. and Benson, H. (1974) 'A Simple Psychophysiologic Technique which Elicits the Hypometabolic Changes of the Relaxation Response', *Psychosomatic Medicine, 36,* 115–20

Beck, A.T., Rush, A.J., Shaw, B.F. and Emery, G. (1979) *Cognitive Therapy of Depression,* Guildford Press, New York

Bender, M.B. (1969) 'Disorders of Eye Movement', Ch. 18, in P.J. Vinken and G.W. Bruyn (eds), *Handbook of Clinical Neurology,* vol. 1, North-Holland Publishing Co., Amsterdam

Benson, H. (1975) *The Relaxation Response,* William Morrow and Co., New York

——— Kotch, J.B., Crassweller, K.D. and Greenwood, M.M. (1977) 'Historical and Clinical Considerations of the Relaxation Response', *American Scientist, 65,* 441–5

Binder, S.A., Moll, C.B. and Wolf, S.L. (1981) 'Evaluation of Electromyographic Biofeedback as an Adjunct to Therapeutic Exercise in Treating the Lower Extremities of Hemiplegic Patients', *Physical Therapy, 61,* 886–93

Bindman, E. and Tibbetts R.W. (1977) 'Writer's Cramp — A Rational Approach to Treatment?', *British Journal of Psychiatry, 131,* 143–8

Birk, L. (1973) *Biofeedback: Behavioral Medicine,* Grune and Stratton, New York

Blackwell, B., Hanenson, I., Bloomfield, S., Magenheim, H., Gartside, P., Nidich, S., Robinson, A. and Zigler, R. (1976) 'Transcendental Meditation in Hypertension Individual Response Patterns', *The Lancet, i,* 223–6

Blanchard, E.B. (1979) 'Biofeedback and the Modification of Cardiovascular Dysfunctions', in R.J. Gatchel and K.P. Price (eds), *Clinical Applications of Biofeedback: Appraisal and Status,* Pergamon Press, Oxford/New York, pp. 28–51

——— (1979a) 'The Use of Temperature Biofeedback in the Treatment of Chronic Pain Due to Causalgia', *Biofeedback and Self-Regulation, 4,* 2, 183–8

——— Andrasik, F., Neff, D.F., Teders, S.J., Pallmeyer, T.P., Arena, J.G., Jurish, S.E., Saunders, N.L. and Ahles, T.A. (1982) 'Sequential Comparisons of Relaxation Training and Biofeedback in the Treatment of Three Kinds of Chronic Headache or, The Machines May be Necessary Some of the Time', *Behaviour Research and Therapy, 20,* 469–81

——— Theobald, D.E., Williamson, D.A., Silver, B.V. and Brown, D.A. (1978) 'Temperature Biofeedback in the Treatment of Migraine Headaches', *Archives of General Psychiatry, 35,* 581–8

Blandy, J. (1982) *Lecture Notes on Urology*, Blackwell Scientific Publications, Oxford

Blau, J.N. (1982) *Migraine,* Update Publications, London

Bokan, J.A., Ries, R.K. and Katon, W.J. (1981) 'Tertiary Gain and Chronic Pain', *Pain, 10,* 331–5

Bond, M.R. (1979) *Pain Its Nature, Analysis and Treatment,* Churchill Livingstone, New York

Breuer, J. and Freud, S. (1893–5) *Studies on Hysteria,* The Standard edition of the complete psychological works, vol. 2 (1955), Hogarth Press, London

Brudny, J., Grynbaum, B.B. and Korein, J. (1974) 'Spasmodic Torticollis: Treatment by Feedback Display of the EMG', *Archives of Physical Medicine and Rehabilitation, 55,* 403–8

——— Korein, J., Grynbaum, B.B., Friedmann, L.W., Weinstein, S., Sachs-Frankel, G. and Belandres, P.V. (1976) 'EMG Feedback Therapy: Review of Treatment of 114 Patients', *Archives of Physical Medicine and Rehabilitation, 57,* 55–61

Budzynski, T.H. (1983) 'Biofeedback Strategies in Headache Treatment' in J.V. Basmajian (ed.), *Biofeedback Principles and Practice for Clinicians,* Williams and Wilkins, Baltimore/London, pp. 192–210

——— Stoyva, J.M., Adler, C.S. and Mullaney, D.J. (1973) 'EMG Biofeedback and Tension Headache: A Controlled Outcome Study', *Psychosomatic Medicine, 35,* 6, 484–96

Burnside, I.G., Tobias, H.S. and Bursill, D. (1979) 'Electromyographic Feedback in the Remobilisation of Stroke Patients', in D.J. Oborne, M.M. Gruneberg and J.R. Eiser (eds.), *Research in Psychology and Medicine*, vol. 2, Social Aspects: Attitudes, Communication, Care and Training, Academic Press, pp. 462–8

Burstyn, P., O'Donovan, B. and Charlton, I. (1981) 'Blood Pressure Variability: The Effects of Repeated Measurement', *Postgraduate Medical Journal, 57,* 488–91

Buss, A.H. and Durkee, A. (1957) 'An Inventory for Assessing Different Kinds of Hostility', *Journal of Consulting Psychology, 21,* 343

Cardozo, L.D., Abrams, P.D., Stanton, S.L. and Feneley, R.C.L. (1978) 'Idiopathic Bladder Instability Treated by Biofeedback', *British Journal of Urology, 50,* 521–3

——— and Stanton, S.L. (1984) 'Biofeedback: A 5-Year Review', *British Journal of Urology, 56,* 220

Carrobles, J.A.I., Cardona, A. and Santacrue, J. (1981) 'Shaping and Generalisation Procedures in the EMG-Biofeedback Treatment of Tension Headache', *British Journal of Clinical Psychology, 20,* 49–56

Carroll, D. (1984) *Biofeedback in Practice,* Longman, London/New York

Catalan, J. and Gath, D.H. (1985) 'Benzodiazepines in General Practice: Time for a Decision', *British Medical Journal, 290,* 1374–6

Charvat, J., Dell, P. and Folkow, B. (1964) 'Mental Factors and Cardiovascular Disease', *Cardiologica, 44,* 121–41

Chesney, M.A. and Shelton, J.L. (1976) 'A Comparison of Muscle Relaxation and Electromyogram Biofeedback Treatments for Muscle Contraction Headache', *Journal of Behavior Therapy and Experimental Psychiatry, 7,* 221–5

Cleeland, C.S. (1973) 'Behavioral Technics in the Modification of Spasmodic Torticollis', *Neurology, 23,* 1241–7

——— (1983) 'Biofeedback and Other Behavioral Techniques in the Treatment of Disorders of Voluntary Movement', in J.V. Basmajian (ed.), *Biofeedback Principles and Practice for Clinicians,* Williams and Wilkins, Baltimore/London, pp. 135–47

Cobb, S. and Rose, R.M. (1973) 'Hypertension, Peptic Ulcer, and Diabetes in Air Traffic Controllers', *Journal of the American Medical Association, 224,* 4, 489–92

Cockburn, J.J. (1971) 'Spasmodic Torticollis: A Psychogenic Condition?', *Journal of Psychosomatic Research, 15,* 471–7

Colgan, A.H. and Beautrais, P.G. (1977) 'Vaginal Muscle Control in Vaginismus' [letter], *New Zealand Medical Journal, 86,* p. 300.

Constantinides, C.G. and Cywes, S. (1983) 'Fecal Incontinence: A Simple Pneumatic Device for Home Biofeedback Training', *Journal of Pediatric Surgery, 18,* 3, 276–7

Coope, J.R. (1981) 'Management of Hypertension in General Practice', *British Medical Journal,* 282, 1380–2

Cottraux, J.A., Juenet, C. and Collet, L. (1983) 'The Treatment of Writer's Cramp with Multimodal Behaviour Therapy and Biofeedback: A Study of 15 Cases', *British Journal of Psychiatry, 142,* 180–3

Cox, D.J., Freundlich, A. and Meyer, R.G. (1975) 'Differential Effectiveness of Electromyograph Feedback, Verbal Relaxation Instructions, and Medication Placebo with Tension Headaches', *Journal of Consulting and Clinical Psychology, 43,* 6, 892–8

Craig, A.R. and Cleary, P.J. (1982) 'Reduction of Stuttering by Young Male Stutterers Using EMG Feedback', *Biofeedback and Self-Regulation, 7,* 3, 241–55

Craig, G.A. and Milne, H.B. (1978) 'Sexual Dysfunction', in R.R. Macdonald (ed.) *Scientific Basis of Obstetrics and Gynaecology,* Churchill Livingstone, pp. 525–51

Crisp, A.H. and Moldofsky, H. (1965) 'A Psychosomatic Study of Writer's Cramp', *British Journal of Psychiatry, 111,* 841–58

Cruz-Coke, R., Donoso, H. and Barrera, R. (1973) 'Genetic Ecology of Hypertension', *Clinical Science, 45,* Suppl. 1, 55–65

Curtis, A.H. and Huffman, J.W. (1950) *A Textbook of Gynecology* (6th edn), W.B. Saunders Co., Philadelphia/London

Dahlström, L., Carlsson, S.G., Gale, E.N. and Jansson, T.G. (1984) 'Clinical and Electromyographic Effects of Biofeedback Training in Mandibular Dysfunction', *Biofeedback and Self-Regulation, 9,* 1, 37–47

de Bono, D.P. and Julian, D.G. (1984) 'Disease of the Cardiovascular System', in J. Macleod (ed.), *Davidson's Principles and Practice of Medicine,* (14th edn) Churchill Livingstone, Edinburgh, pp. 122–201

Diamond, S., Medina, J., Diamond-Falk, J. and DeVeno, T. (1979) 'The Value of Biofeedback in the Treatment of Chronic Headache: A Five-Year Retrospective Study', *Headache, 19,* 90–6

Dietvorst, T.F. and Osborne, D. (1978) 'Biofeedback-Assisted Relaxation Training for Primary Dysmenorrhea: A Case Study', *Biofeedback and Self-Regulation, 3,* 3, 301–5

Ehrman, J.S. (1983) 'Use of Biofeedback to Treat Incontinence' [Letter], *Journal of the American Geriatrics Society, 31,* 3, 182–4

Elder, S. T., Longacre, Jr., A, Welsh, D.M. and McAfee, R.D. (1977) 'Apparatus and Procedure for Training Subjects to Condition Blood Pressure', *Psychophysiology, 14,* 68–72

Engel, B.T. and Baile, W.F. (1983) 'Behavioral Applications in the Treatment of Patients with Cardiovascular Disorders', in J.V. Basmajian (ed.), *Biofeedback Principles and Practice for Clinicians,* Williams and Wilkins, Baltimore/London, pp. 228–38

——— and Bleecker, E.R. (1974) 'Application of Operant Conditioning Techniques to the Control of the Cardiac Arrhythmias', in P.A. Obrist *et al.* (eds), *Cardiovascular Psychophysiology: Current Issues in Response Mechanisms, Biofeedback and Methodology,* Aldine, Chicago, pp. 456–76

——— Nikoomanesh, P. and Schuster, M.M. (1974) 'Operant Conditioning of Rectosphincteric Responses in the Treatment of Fecal Incontinence', *New England Journal of Medicine, 290,* 646–9

Engstrom, D. (1983) 'Cognitive Behavioral Therapy Methods in Chronic Pain Treatment', in J.J. Bonica, U. Lindblom and A. Iggo (eds.), *Advances in Pain Research and Therapy,* vol. 5, Raven Press, New York, pp. 829–38

Epstein, L.H. and Abel, G.G. (1977) 'An Analysis of Biofeedback Training Effects for Tension Headache Patients', *Behavior Therapy, 8,* 37–47

——— Abel, G.G., Collins, F., Parker, L. and Cinciripini, P.M. (1978) 'The Relationship Between Frontalis Muscle Activity and Self-Reports of Headache Pain', *Behaviour Research and Therapy, 16,* 153–60

Eysenck, H.J. and Eysenck, S.B.G. (1964) *Manual of the Eysenck Personality Inventory,* Hodder and Stoughton, Sevenoaks

Fahn, S. and Eldridge, R. (1976) 'Definition of Dystonia and Classification of the Dystonic States', in R. Eldridge and S. Fahn (eds.), *Advances in Neurology, 14,* Raven Press, New York, pp. 1–5

Fanchamps, A. (1974) 'The Role of Humoral Mediators in Migraine Headache', *Canadian Journal of Neurological Sciences, 1,* 189–95

Farrar, W.B. (1976) 'Using Electromyographic Biofeedback in Treating Orofacial Dyskinesia', *Journal of Prosthetic Dentistry, 35,* 384–7

Fenwick, P. (1983) 'Can We Still Recommend Meditation?', *British Medical Journal, 287,* 1401

Finley, W.W., Etherton, M.D., Dickman, D., Karimian, D. and Simpson, R.W. (1981) 'A Simple EMG-Reward System for Biofeedback Training of Children', *Biofeedback and Self-Regulation, 6,* 2, 169–80

——— Niman, C.A., Standley, J.G. and Ender, P. (1976) 'Frontal EMG-Biofeedback Training of Athetoid Cerebral Palsy Patients: A Report of Six Cases, *Biofeedback and Self-Regulation, 1,* 169–82

Fish, D., Mayer, N. and Herman, R. (1976) 'Biofeedback' [Letter], *Archives of Physical Medicine and Rehabilitation, 57,* 152

Flom, R.P., Quast, J.E., Boller, J.D., Berner, M. and Goldberg, J. (1976) 'Biofeedback

Training to Overcome Poststroke Foot-Drop', *Geriatrics, 31*, 47–52

Folkow, B. and Rubinstein, E.H. (1966) 'Cardiovascular Effects of Acute and Chronic Stimulations of the Hypothalamic Defence Area in the Rat', *Acta Physiologica Scandinavica, 68,* 48–57

Fordyce, W.E. (1978) 'Learning Processes in Pain', in R.A. Sternbach (ed.), *The Psychology of Pain,* Raven Press, New York, pp. 49–72

——— (1983) 'Behavioral Conditioning Concepts in Chronic Pain' in J.J. Bonica, U. Lindblom and A. Iggo (eds.), *Advances in Pain Research and Therapy,* Vol. 5, Raven Press, New York, pp. 781–8

Francis, D.A. (1983) 'Benzodiazepines and Spasmodic Torticollis' [Letter], *Archives of Neurology, 40,* 325

Frankel, B.L., Patel, D.J., Horwitz, D., Friedewald, W.T. and Gaarder, K.R. (1978) 'Treatment of Hypertension with Biofeedback and Relaxation Techniques', *Psychosomatic Medicine, 40,* 4, 276–93

Frankenhaeuser, M., Jaerpe, G., Svan, H. and Wrangsjoe, B. (1963) 'Psychophysiological Reactions to Two Different Placebo Treatments', *Scandinavian Journal of Psychology, 4,* 245–50

Freedman, R.R., Lynn, S.J., Ianni, P. and Hale, P.A. (1981) 'Biofeedback Treatment of Raynaud's Disease and Phenomenon', *Biofeedback and Self-Regulation, 6,* 3, 355–65

Frewen, W.K. (1972) 'Urgency Incontinence', *The Journal of Obstetrics and Gynaecology of the British Commonwealth, 79,* 77–9

——— (1978) 'An Objective Assessment of the Unstable Bladder of Psychosomatic Origin', *British Journal of Urology, 50,* 246–9

Friedberg, C.K. (1966) *Diseases of the Heart* (3rd edn), W.B. Saunders, London

Friedman, L.J. (1962) *Virgin Wives: A Study of Unconsummated Marriages,* Tavistock Publications, Charles C. Thomas, Springfield, Illinois

Gatchel, R.J. and Price, K.P. (1979) 'Biofeedback: An Introduction and Historical Overview' in R.J. Gatchel and K.P. Price (eds), *Clinical Applications of Biofeedback: Appraisal and Status,* Pergamon Press, Oxford, pp. 1–11

Gelder, M., Gath, D. and Mayou, R. (1983) *Oxford Textbook of Psychiatry,* Oxford University Press

Gonella, C., Kalish, R. and Hale, G. (1978) 'A Commentary on Electromyographic Feedback in Physical Therapy', *Physical Therapy, 58,* 1, 11–14

Gordon, B. (1981) *I'm Dancing as Fast as I Can,* Bantam, Toronto/New York/London

Gosling, J.A., Dixon, J.S. and Humpherson, J.R. (1983) *Functional Anatomy of the Urinary Tract,* Churchill Livingstone, Edinburgh/London/New York

Green, E.E. and Green, A.M. (1983) 'General and Specific Applications of Thermal Biofeedback', in J.V. Basmajian (ed.), *Biofeedback Principles and Practice for Clinicians,* Williams and Wilkins, Baltimore/London, pp. 211–71

Gross, F. and Dietz, R. (1979) 'The Significance of Volume and Cardiac Output in the Pathogenesis of Hypertension', *Clinical Science, 57,* 59s–67s

Hafner, R.J. (1982) 'Psychological Treatment of Essential Hypertension: A Controlled Comparison of Meditation and Meditation plus Biofeedback', *Biofeedback and Self-Regulation, 7,* 3, 305–16

Hannington-Kiff, J.G. (1984) 'Antisympathetic Drugs in Limbs' in P.D. Wall and R. Melzack (eds), *Textbook of Pain,* Churchill Livingstone, Edinburgh/London/Melbourne/New York, pp. 566–73

Harris, F.A., Spelman, F.A. and Hymer, J.W. (1974) 'Electronic Sensory Aids as Treatment for Cerebral-Palsied Children. Inapproprioception: Part 2', *Physical Therapy, 54,* 354–65

Harrison, D.W., Garrett, J.C., Henderson, D. and Adams, H.E. (1985) 'Visual and Auditory Feedback for Head Tilt and Torsion in a Spasmodic Torticollis Patient', *Behaviour Research and Therapy, 23,* 1, 87–8

Haynes, S.N., Cuevas, J. and Gannon, L.R. (1982) 'The Psychophysiological Etiology of Muscle-Contraction Headache', *Headache, 22,* 122–32

——— Griffin, P., Mooney, D. and Parise, M. (1975) 'Electromyographic Biofeedback and Relaxation Instructions in the Treatment of Muscle Contraction Headaches', *Behavior Therapy, 6,* 672–8

Heaton-Ward, W.A. (1962) 'Inference and Suggestion in a Clinical Trial (Niamid in Mongolism)', *Journal of Mental Science, 108,* 865–70

Henryk-Gutt, R. and Linford Rees, W. (1973) 'Psychological Aspects of Migraine', *Journal of Psychosomatic Research, 17,* 141–53

Holmes, D.M., Stone, A.R., Bary, P.R., Richards, C.J. and Stephenson, T.P. (1983) 'Bladder-Training - 3 Years On', *British Journal of Urology, 55,* 660–4

House, J.S., Wells, J.A., Landerman, L.R., McMichael, A.J. and Kaplan, B.H. (1979) 'Occupational Stress and Health Among Factory Workers', *Journal of Health and Social Behavior, 20,* 139–60

Hutchings, D.F. and Reinking, R.H. (1976) 'Tension Headaches: What Form of Therapy is Most Effective?', *Biofeedback and Self-Regulation, 1,* 2, 183–90

Hyslop, G.H. (1949) 'Torticollis of Central Origin', *Medical Clinics of North America, 25,* 747–54

Jacobson, E. (1938) *Progressive Relaxation,* University of Chicago Press, Chicago

——— (1970) *Modern Treatment of Tense Patients,* Charles C. Thomas, Springfield, Illinois

Janssen, K. (1983) 'Treatment of Sinus Tachycardia with Heart-Rate Feedback', *Journal of Behavioral Medicine, 6,* 1, 109–14

Jarvis, G.J. (1981) 'A Controlled Trial of Bladder Drill and Drug Therapy in The Management of Detrusor Instability', *British Journal of Urology, 53,* 565–6

——— and Millar, D.R. (1980) 'Controlled Trial of Bladder Drill for Detrusor Instability', *British Medical Journal, 281,* 1322–3

Jeffcoate, T.N.A. (1962) *Principles of Gynaecology* (2nd edn), Butterworths, London

Jones, G.E. and Evans, P.A. (1980) 'Treatment of Tietze's Syndrome Pain through Paced Respiration', *Biofeedback and Self-Regulation, 5,* 2, 295–304

——— Massong, S.R. and Buckley, M.F. (1983) 'Treatment of Spasmodic Torticollis Through Spasm Control and Muscle Reeducation: A Case Study', *Behavior Therapy, 14,* 178–84

Jordan, A.C. (1979) *A Synopsis of Cardiology,* John Wright and Sons, Bristol

Julian, D.G. and Matthews, M.B. (1981) 'Diseases of the Cardiovascular System' in J. MacLeod (ed.), *Davidson's Principles and Practice of Medicine* (13th edn), Churchill Livingstone, Edinburgh, pp. 145–218

Kalotkin, M., Manschreck, T. and O'Brien, D. (1979) 'Electromyographic Tension Levels in Stutterers and Normal Speakers', *Perceptual and Motor Skills, 49,* 109–10

Katkin, E.S. and Goldband, S. (1979) 'The Placebo Effect and Biofeedback' in R.J. Gatchel and K.P. Price (eds), *Clinical Applications of Biofeedback: Appraisal and Status,* Pergamon Press, Oxford, pp. 173–86

Keefe, F.J. (1978) Biofeedback vs. Instructional Control of Skin Temperature', *Journal of Behavioral Medicine, 1,* 383–90

——— Surwit, R.S. and Pilon, R.N. (1980) 'Biofeedback, Autogenic Training, and Progressive Relaxation in the Treatment of Raynaud's Disease: A Comparative Study', *Journal of Applied Behavior Analysis, 13,* 3–11

Kegel, A.H. (1952) 'Sexual Functions of the Pubococcygeus Muscle', *Western Journal of Surgery, Obstetrics and Gynecology, 60,* 521

Kessler, K.A. (1978) 'Tricyclic Antidepressants: Mode of Action and Clinical Use', in M.A. Lipton, A. DiMascio and K.F. Killam (eds), *Psychopharmacology: A Generation of Progress,* Raven Press, New York, pp. 1289–1302

Kewman, D. and Roberts, A.H. (1980) 'Skin Temperature Biofeedback and Migraine Headaches A Double-Blind Study', *Biofeedback and Self-Regulation, 5,* 3, 327–45

Klassen, A.C. (1984) 'Torticollis A Three-Article Symposium; Introduction', *Postgraduate Medicine, 75,* 7, 124–5

Kondo, C. and Canter, A. (1977) 'True and False Electromyographic Feedback: Effect on Tension Headache, *Journal of Abnormal Psychology, 86,* 93–5

Korein, J. and Brudny, J. (1976) 'Integrated EMG Feedback in the Management of Spasmodic Torticollis and Focal Dystonia: A Prospective Study of 80 Patients' in M.D. Yahr (ed.), *The Basal Ganglia,* Raven Press, New York, pp. 385–424

——— Brudny, J., Grynbaum, B., Sachs-Frankel, G., Weisinger, M. and Levidow, L. (1976) 'Sensory Feedback Therapy of Spasmodic Torticollis and Dystonia: Results in Treatment of 55 Patients' in R. Eldridge and S. Fahn (eds.), *Advances in Neurology,* vol. 14, Raven Press, New York, pp. 375–402

Kristt, D.A. and Engel, B.T. (1975) 'Learned Control of Blood Pressure in Patients with High Blood Pressure', *Circulation, 51,* 370–8

Kruk, Z.L. and Pycock, C.J. (1983) *Neurotransmitters and Drugs* (2nd edn), Croom Helm, London

Labby, D.H. (1982) in Benson, R.C. (ed.), *Current Obstetric and Gynecological Diagnosis and Treatment* (4th edn), Lange Medical Publications, Los Altos, California, pp. 486–501

Lacey, R. and Woodward, S. (1985) *Survey on Tranquillisers,* British Broadcasting Corporation in Association with MIND, London

Lance, J.W., Anthony, M. and Gonski, A. (1967) 'Serotonin, the Carotid Body, and Cranial Vessels in Migraine', *Archives of Neurology, 16,* 553–8

Lang, P.J. (1970) 'Autonomic Control or Learning to Play the Internal Organs', *Psychology Today,* October

Lazarus, R.S. (1976) *Patterns of Adjustment,* McGraw-Hill, New York

Lee, K-H, Hill, E., Johnston, R. and Smiehorowski, T. (1976) 'Myofeedback for Muscle Retraining in Hemiplegic Patients', *Archives of Physical Medicine and Rehabilitation, 57,* 588–91

Ley, P. (1974) 'Communication in the Clinical Setting', *British Journal of Orthodontics, 1,* 4, 173–7

LeVine, W.R. and Irvine, J.K. (1984) 'In Vivo EMG Biofeedback in Violin and Viola Pedagogy', *Biofeedback and Self-Regulation, 9,* 2, 161–8

Lewis, T. (1949) *Vascular Disorders of the Limbs: Described for Practitioners and Students,* Macmillan, London

Lipkin, M., McDevitt, E., Schwartz, M. and Duryee, A. (1945) 'On the Effects of Suggestion in the Treatment of Vasospastic Disorders of the Extremities', *Psychosomatic Medicine, 7,* 152–9

Lishman, W.A. (1978) *Organic Psychiatry The Psychological Consequences of Cerebral Disorder,* Blackwell Scientific Publications, Oxford/London/Edinburgh/Melbourne

Luthe, W. (1963) 'Autogenic Training: Method, Research and Application in Medicine', *American Journal of Psychotherapy, 17,* 174–95

Macleod, J. (ed.) (1981, 1984) *Davidson's Principles and Practice of Medicine* 13th and 14th edns, Churchill Livingstone, Edinburgh

McCord, C.D., Coles, W.H., Shore, J.W., Spector, R. and Putnam, J.R. (1984) 'Treatment of Essential Blepharospasm 1. Comparison of Facial Nerve Avulsion and Eyebrow-Eyelid Muscle Stripping Procedure', *Archives of Ophthalmology, 102,* 266–8

McGrady, A.V., Yonker, R., Tan, S.Y., Fine, T.H. and Woerner, M. (1981) 'The Effect of Biofeedback-Assisted Relaxation Training on Blood Pressure and Selected Biochemical Parameters in Patients with Essential Hypertension', *Biofeedback and Self-Regulation, 6,* 3, 343–53

McLean, A.E. and Cooper, E.B. (1978) 'Electromyographic Indication of Laryngeal-Area Activity During Stuttering Expectancy', *Journal of Fluency Disorders, 3,* 205–19

Marcer, D. (1985) 'Biofeedback and Meditation' in G.T. Lewith (ed.), *Alternative Therapies,* William Heinemann Medical Books, London, pp. 109–49

Marsden, C.D. (1976) 'Dystonia: The Spectrum of the Disease' in M.D. Yahr (ed.), *The Basal Ganglia,* Raven Press, New York, pp. 351–67

——— (1976a) 'The Problem of Adult-Onset Idiopathic Torsion Dystonia and Other Isolated Dyskinesias in Adult Life (Including Blepharospasm, Oromandibular Dystonia, Dystonic Writer's Cramp, and Torticollis, or Axial Dystonia)' in R. Eldridge and S. Fahn (eds), *Advances in Neurology,* vol. 14, Raven Press, New York, pp. 259–76

——— and Harrison, M.J.G. (1974) 'Idiopathic Torsion Dystonia (Dystonia Musculorum Deformans): A Review of Forty-Two Patients', *Brain, 97,* 793–810

Masters, W.H. and Johnson, V.E. (1970) *Human Sexual Inadequacy,* Little, Brown, Boston

Mathew, R.J., Ho, B.T., Kralik, P., Taylor, D. and Claghorn, J.L. (1980) 'Catecholamines and Migraine: Evidence Based on Biofeedback Induced Changes', *Headache, 20,* 247–52

Meares, R. (1971) 'An Association of Spasmodic Torticollis and Writer's Cramp', *British Journal of Psychiatry, 119,* 441–2

Melzack, R. (1973) *The Puzzle of Pain,* Penguin Books, Harmondsworth

——— and Torgerson, W.S. (1971) 'On the Language of Pain', *Anesthesiology, 34,* 1, 50–9

——— and Wall, P. (1982) *The Challenge of Pain,* Penguin Books, Harmondsworth

Miall, W.E. and Oldham, P.D. (1963) 'The Hereditary Factor in Arterial Blood Pressure', *British Medical Journal, 1,* 75–80

Millard, R.J. and Oldenburg, B.F. (1983) 'The Symptomatic, Urodynamic and Psychodynamic Results of Bladder Re-Education Programs', *Journal of Urology, 130,* 715–19

Miller, N.E. (1972) 'Learning of Visceral and Glandular Responses: Postscript' in D. Singh, and C.T. Morgan (eds), *Current Status of Physiological Psychology: Readings* Brooks/Cole, Monterey, California, pp. 245–50

——— (1978) 'Biofeedback and Visceral Learning' in M.R. Rosenzweig and L.W. Porter (eds), *Annual Review of Psychology,* Annual Reviews, Palo Alto, California, pp. 373–403

Minnesota Multiphasic Personality Inventory (1962) Clinical Psychology Monograph no. 15, *Journal of Clinical Psychology*

Mitchell, K.R., Piatkowska, O.E. and White, R.G. (1974) *The Prevention and Self-Managment of Anxiety: Part One,* Psychological Behavior Associates Press, Sydney, Australia

——— and White, R.G. (1974) *The Prevention and Self-Management of Anxiety: Part Two,* Psychological Behavior Associates Press, Sydney, Australia

——— and White, R.G. (1977) 'Behavioral Self-Management: An Application to the Problem of Migraine Headaches', *Behavior Therapy, 8,* 213–21

Mittleman, B. and Wolff, H.G. (1939) 'Affective States and Skin Temperature: Experimental Study of Subjects with "Cold Hands" and Raynaud's Disease', *Psychosomatic Medicine, 1* (April), 271–92

Moffett, A.M., Swash, M. and Scott, D.F. (1974) 'Effect of Chocolate in Migraine: A Double-Blind Study', *Journal of Neurology, Neurosurgery and Psychiatry, 37,* 445–8

Morasky, R.L., Reynolds, C. and Clarke, G. (1981) 'Using Biofeedback to Reduce Left Arm Extensor EMG of String Players During Musical Performance', *Biofeedback and Self-Regulation, 6,* 4, 565–72

Nouwen, A, and Solinger, J.W. (1979) 'The Effectiveness of EMG Biofeedback Training in Low Back Pain', *Biofeedback and Self-Regulation, 4,* 2, 103–11

O'Brien, M.D. (1971) 'The Relationship Between Aura Symptoms and Cerebral Blood Flow Changes in the Prodrome of Migraine' in D.J. Dalessio, T. Dalsgaard-Nielson and I. Diamond (eds), *Proceedings of the International Headache Symposium,* Sandoz Pharmaceuticals, Basel, Switzerland

Olness, K., McParland, F.A. and Piper, J. (1980) 'Biofeedback: A New Modality in the Management of Children with Fecal Soiling', *Journal of Pediatrics, 96,* no. 3, part 1, 505–9

Olton, D.S. and Noonberg, A.R. (1980) *Biofeedback: Clinical Applications in Behavioral Medicine,* Prentice-Hall, Englewood Cliffs, New Jersey

Patel, C.H. (1973) 'Yoga and Bio-Feedback in Hypertension' [Letter], *Lancet, 2,* 1440–1

——— (1973a) 'Yoga and Bio-Feedback in the Management of Hypertension', *Lancet, 2,* 1053–5

——— (1975) 'Yoga and Biofeedback in the Management of "Stress" in Hypertensive Patients', *Clinical Science and Molecular Medicine, 48,*(Suppl.), 171–4

——— (1975a) '12 Month Follow Up of Yoga and Biofeedback in the Management of Hypertension', *Lancet, 1,* 62–5

——— (1976) 'Reduction of Serum Cholesterol and Blood Pressure in Hypertensive Patients by Behaviour Modification', *Journal of the Royal College of General Practitioners: British Journal of General Practice, 26,* 211–15

——— (1977) 'Biofeedback-Aided Relaxation and Meditation in the Management of Hypertension', *Biofeedback and Self-Regulation, 2,* 1, 1–41

——— and Carruthers, M. (1977) 'Coronary Risk Factor Reduction Through Biofeedback-Aided Relaxation and Meditation', *Journal of the Royal College of General Practitioners, 27,* 401–5

——— Marmot, M.G. and Terry, D.J. (1981) 'Controlled Trial of Biofeedback-Aided Behavioural Methods in Reducing Mild Hypertension', *British Medical Journal, 282,* 2005–8

——— Marmot, M.G., Terry, D.J. Carruthers, M., Hunt, B. and Patel, M, (1985) 'Trial of Relaxation in Reducing Coronary Risk: Four Year Follow-Up', *British Medical Journal, 290,* 1103–6

——— and North, W.R.S. (1975) 'Randomised Controlled Trial of Yoga and Bio-Feedback in Management of Hypertension', *Lancet, 2,* 93–5

Peck, D.F. (1977) 'The Use of EMG Feedback in the Treatment of a Severe Case of Blepharospasm', *Biofeedback and Self-Regulation, 2,* 3, 273–7

Peek, C.J. (1977) 'A Critical Look at the Theory of Placebo', *Biofeedback and Self-Regulation, 2,* 4, 327–35

Petursson, H. and Lader, M.H. (1981) 'Withdrawal From Long-Term Benzodiazepine Treatment', *British Medical Journal, 283,* 643–5

Philips, C. (1976) 'Headache and Personality', *Journal of Psychosomatic Research, 20,* 535–42

Pickering, T. (1973) 'Yoga and Bio-Feedback in Hypertension' [Letter], *Lancet, 2,* 1440

Pollack, A.A., Case, D.B., Weber, M.A. and Laragh, J.H. (1977) 'Limitations of Transcendental Meditation in the Treatment of Essential Hypertension', *Lancet, 1,* 71–3

Power, K.G., Jerrom, D.W.A., Simpson, R.J. and Mitchell, M. (1985) 'Controlled Study of Withdrawal Symptoms and Rebound Anxiety after Six Week Course of Diazepam for Generalised Anxiety', *British Medical Journal, 290,* 1246–8

Raynaud, A.G.M. (1862) *De l'asphyxie locale et de la gangrene symetique des extremities,* Rigoux, Paris

Reckless, J.B. (1972) 'Hysterical Blepharospasm Treated by Psychotherapy and Conditioning Procedures in a Group Setting', *Psychosomatics, 13,* 263–4

Reeves, J.L. (1976) 'EMG-Biofeedback Reduction of Tension Headache: A Cognitive Skills-Training Approach', *Biofeedback and Self-Regulation, 1,* 217–25

Reinking, R.H. and Hutchings, D. (1981) 'Follow-Up to: "Tension Headaches: What Form of Therapy is Most Effective?" ', *Biofeedback and Self-Regulation, 6,* 1, 57–62

Rimm, D.C. and Masters, J.C. (1979) *Behavior Therapy,* Academic Press, New York, pp. 35–61

Robbins, S.L. (1962) *Textbook of Pathology with Clinical Application,* W.B. Saunders, Philadelphia/London

Roberts, A.H. (1983) 'Contingency Management Methods in the Treatment of Chronic Pain' in J.J. Bonica, U. Lindblom and A. Iggo (eds), *Advances in Pain Research and Therapy,* vol. 5, Raven Press, New York, pp. 789–94

——— and Reinhardt, L. (1980) 'The Behavioral Management of Chronic Pain: Long-Term Follow-Up with Comparison Groups', *Pain, 8,* 151–62

Rosenbaum, A.H. and de la Fuente, J.R. (1979) 'Benzodiazepines and Tardive Dyskinesia' [Letter], *Lancet, ii,* 900

Ross, J.S. and Wilson, K.J.W. (1972) *Foundations of Anatomy and Physiology,* Churchill

Livingstone, Edinburgh/London
Rugh, J.D. (1979) 'Instrumentation in Biofeedback' in R.J. Gatchel and K.P. Price (eds), *Clinical Applications of Biofeedback: Appraisal and Status,* Pergamon Press, Oxford, 187–203
Sappington, J.T., Fiorito, E.M. and Brehony, K.A. (1979) 'Biofeedback as Therapy in Raynaud's Disease', *Biofeedback and Self-Regulation, 4,* 2, 155–69
Sargent, J.D., Walters, E.D. and Green, E.E. (1973) 'Psychosomatic Self-Regulation of Migraine Headache', in L. Birk (ed.), *Biofeedback: Behavioral Medicine,* Grune and Stratton, New York, pp. 55–68
Shultz, J.H. (1932) *Das Autogene Training: Konzentrative Selbstentspannung,* Georg Thieme Verlag, Stuttgart
——— and Luthe, W. (1969) *Autogenic Therapy,* Grune and Stratton, New York
Schuman, M. (1982) 'Biofeedback in the Management of Chronic Pain' in J. Barber and C. Adrian (eds), *Psychological Approaches to the Management of Pain,* Brunner/Mazel, New York, 150–67
Schuster, M.M. (1974) 'Operant Conditioning in Gastrointestinal Dysfunctions', *Hospital Practice, 9,* 135–43
——— (1983) 'Biofeedback Control of Gastrointestinal Motility', in J.V. Basmajian (ed.), *Biofeedback Principles and Practice for Clinicians,* Williams and Wilkins, Baltimore/London, pp. 275–81
Scott, R.W., Blanchard, E.B., Edmunson, E.D. and Young, L.D. (1973) 'A Shaping Procedure for Heart-Rate Control in Chronic Tachycardia', *Perceptual and Motor Skills, 37,* 327–38
Sedlacek, K. (1983) 'Biofeedback Treatment of Primary Raynaud's Disease' in J.V. Basmajian (ed.), *Biofeedback Principles and Practice for Clinicians,* Williams and Wilkins, Baltimore/London, pp. 311–15
Seer, P. (1979) 'Psychological Control of Essential Hypertension: Review of the Literature and Methodological Critique', *Psychological Bulletin, 86,* 5, 1015–43
Selby, G. and Lance. J.W. (1960) 'Observations on 500 Cases of Migraine and Allied Vascular Headache', *Journal of Neurology, Neurosurgery and Psychiatry, 23,* 230–2
Shakespeare, R. (1975) *The Psychology of Handicap,* Methuen, London
Shapiro, A.K. (1976) 'Psychotherapy' in R.G. Grenell and S. Gabay (eds), *Biological Foundations of Psychiatry,* Raven Press, New York
Shapiro, D.H. (1982) 'Overview: Clinical and Physiological Comparison of Meditation with Other Self-Control Strategies', *American Journal of Psychiatry, 139,* 3, 267–74
Shapiro, D. and Surwit, R.S. (1976) 'Learned Control of Physiological Function and Disease' in H. Leitenberg (ed.), *Handbook of Behavior Modification and Behavior Therapy,* Prentice-Hall, Englewood Cliffs, New Jersey
Sharpe, R. (1974) 'Behaviour Therapy in a Case of Blepharospasm', *British Journal of Psychiatry, 124,* 603–4
Sheehy, M.P. and Marsden, C.D. (1982) 'Writer's Cramp — A Focal Dystonia', *Brain, 105,* 461–80
Sherman, R.A. (1979) 'Successful Treatment of One Case of Tardive Dyskinesia with Electromyographic Feedback from the Masseter Muscle', *Biofeedback and Self-Regulation 4,* 4, 367–70
——— Gall, N. and Gormly, J. (1979) 'Treatment of Phantom Limb Pain with Muscular Relaxation Training to Disrupt the Pain-Anxiety-Tension Cycle', *Pain, 6,* 47–55
Sherwood, S. and Hewlett, H. (1984) 'The Use of Microcomputers in Physiotherapy For Children', *Physiotherapy, 70,* 8, 297–9
Silver, B.V., Blanchard, E.B., Williamson, D.A., Theobald, D.E. and Brown, D.A. (1979) 'Temperature Biofeedback and Relaxation Training in the Treatment of Migraine Headaches One-Year Follow-Up', *Biofeedback and Self-Regulation, 4,* 4, 359–66
Simpson, J.A. (1984) 'Disease of the Nervous System' in J. MacLeod (ed.) *Davidson's Principles and Practice of Medicine (14th edn),* Churchill Livingstone, Edinburgh,

pp. 591–669

Skelly, A.M. and Kenedi, R.M. (1982) 'EMG Biofeedback Therapy in the Re-Education of the Hemiplegic Shoulder in Patients with Sensory Loss', *Physiotherapy, 68,* 2, 34–7

Smith, D.R. (1981) *General Urology* (10th edn), Lange Medical Publications, Los Altos, California

Sorensen, B.F. and Hamby, W.B. (1966) 'Spasmodic Torticollis Results in 71 Surgically Treated Patients', *Neurology, 16,* 867–78

Steptoe, A. (1981) *Psychological Factors in Cardiovascular Disorders,* Academic Press, London

Stoyva, J.M. (1983) 'Guidelines in Cultivating General Relaxation: Biofeedback and Autogenic Training Combined' in J.V. Basmajian (ed.), *Biofeedback Principles and Practice for Clinicians,* Williams and Wilkins, Baltimore/London, pp. 149–69

Surwit, R.S. and Fenton, C.H. (1980) 'Feedback and Instructions in the Control of Digital Skin Temperature', *Psychophysiology, 17,* 2, 129–32

——— Pilon, R. and Fenton, C.H. (1978) 'Behavioral Treatment of Raynaud's Disease', *Journal of Behavioral Medicine, 1,* 323–35

——— and Rotberg, M. (1984) 'Biofeedback Therapy of Essential Blepharospasm' *American Journal of Ophthalmology, 98,* 28–31

Sutton, E.P. and Belar, C.D. (1982) 'Tension Headache Patients Versus Controls: A Study of EMG Parameters', *Headache, 22,* 133–6

Tarlov, E. (1970) 'On the Problem of the Pathology of Spasmodic Torticollis in Man', *Journal of Neurology, Neurosurgery and Psychiatry, 33,* 457–63

Thulesius, O. (1976) 'Primary and Secondary Raynaud Phenomenon', *Acta Chirurgica Scandivanica, 465,* Suppl. 5–6

Tibbetts, R.W. (1971) 'Spasmodic Torticollis', *Journal of Psychosomatic Research, 15,* 461–9

Tunis, M.M. and Wolff, H.G. (1954) 'Studies on Headache: Cranial Artery Vasoconstriction and Muscle Contraction Headache', *Archives of Neurology and Psychiatry, 71,* 425–34

Turin, A. and Johnson, W.G. (1976) 'Biofeedback Therapy for Migraine Headaches', *Archives of General Psychiatry, 33,* 517–19

Turk, D.C. and Genest, M. (1979) 'Regulation of Pain: The Application of Cognitive and Behavioral Techniques for Prevention and Remediation' in P.C. Kendall and S.D. Hollon (eds), *Cognitive-Behavioral Interventions: Theory, Research, and Procedures,* Academic Press, New York, pp. 287–318

——— Meichenbaum, D.H. and Berman, W.H. (1979) 'Application of Biofeedback for the Regulation of Pain: A Critical Review', *Psychological Bulletin, 86,* 6, 1322–38

Turner, J.A. and Chapman, C.R. (1982) 'Psychological Interventions for Chronic Pain: A Critical Review. 1. Relaxation Training and Biofeedback', *Pain, 12,* 1–21

Tursky, B. Shapiro, D. and Schwartz, G.E. (1972) 'Automated Constant Cuff-Pressure System to Measure Average Systolic and Diastolic Blood Pressure in Man', *IEEE Transactions in Bio-Medical Engineering, 19,* 271–6

Van Boxtel, A. and van der Ven, J.R. (1978) 'Differential EMG Activity in Subjects with Muscle Contraction Headaches Related to Mental Effort', *Headache, 17,* 233–7

Vaughn, R. Pall, M.L. and Haynes, S.N. (1977) 'Frontalis EMG Response to Stress in Subjects with Frequent Muscle-Contraction Headaches', *Headache, 16,* 313–17

Verrill, P. (1984) 'Sympathetic Ganglion Lesions' in P.D. Wall and R. Melzack (eds), *Textbook of Pain,* Churchill Livingstone, Edinburgh, 581–9

Wallace, R.K., Benson, H. and Wilson, A.F. (1971) 'A Wakeful Hypometabolic Physiologic State' *American Journal of Physiology, 221,* 3, 795–9

Waters, W.E. (1982) 'The Epidemiology of Headache', *Seminars in Neurology, 2,* 1, 1–8

——— (1986) *Headache,* Croom Helm, London

——— O'Connor, P.J. (1971) 'Epidemiology of Headache and Migraine in Women', *Journal of Neurology, Neurosurgery and Psychiatry, 34,* 148–53

Weinman, J. (1981) *'An Outline of Psychology as Applied to Medicine',* John Wright and

Sons, Bristol
Weinman, M.L., Mathew, R.J. and Claghorn, J.L. (1982) 'A Study of Physician Attitude on Biofeedback', *Biofeedback and Self-Regulation, 7,* 1, 89–98
Weiss, T. and Engel, B.T. (1971) 'Operant Conditioning of Heart Rate in Patients with Premature Ventricular Contractions', *Psychosomatic Medicine, 33,* 4, 301–21
West, M. (1979) 'Meditation', *British Journal of Psychiatry, 135,* 457–67
Whitehead, W.E. (1978) 'Biofeedback in the Treatment of Gastrointestinal Disorders', *Biofeedback and Self-Regulation, 3,* 4, 375–84
Wickramasekera, I. (1972) 'Electromyographic Feedback Training and Tension Headache: Preliminary Observations', *American Journal of Clinical Hypnosis, 15,* 83–5
——— (1973) 'The Application of Verbal Instructions and EMG Feedback Training to the Management of Tension Headache — Preliminary Observations', *Headache, 13,* 74–6
Wiener, N. (1948) *Cybernetics or Control and Communication in the Animal and the Machine,* Wiley, New York
Wooldridge, C.P. and Russell, G. (1976) 'Head Position Training with the Cerebral Palsied Child: An Application of Biofeedback Techniques', *Archives of Physical Medicine and Rehabilitation, 57,* 407–14
World Federation of Neurology, Definition of Migraine (1970) in *Background to Migraine* vol. 3, Heinemann, London, pp. 181–2
Wright, J., Perreault, R. and Mathieu, M. (1977) 'The Treatment of Sexual Dysfunction,' *Archives of General Psychiatry, 34,* 881–90
Yates, A.J. (1980) *Biofeedback and the Modification of Behavior,* Plenum Press, New York/London

AUTHOR INDEX

SUBJECT INDEX